ANCIENT WORLDS

RICHARD MILES

ANCIENT

THE SEARCH FOR THE ORIGINS

WORLDS

OF WESTERN CIVILIZATION

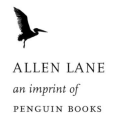

ALLEN LANE
an imprint of
PENGUIN BOOKS

ALLEN LANE

Published by the Penguin Group

Penguin Books Ltd, 80 Strand, London WC2R ORL, England

Penguin Group (USA) Inc., 375 Hudson Street, New York, New York 10014, USA

Penguin Group (Canada), 90 Eglinton Avenue East, Suite 700, Toronto, Ontario, Canada M4P 2Y3
(a division of Pearson Canada Inc.)

Penguin Ireland, 25 St Stephen's Green, Dublin 2, Ireland (a division of Penguin Books Ltd)

Penguin Group (Australia), 250 Camberwell Road, Camberwell, Victoria 3124, Australia
(a division of Pearson Australia Group Pty Ltd)

Penguin Books India Pvt Ltd, 11 Community Centre, Panchsheel Park, New Dehli – 110 017, India

Penguin Group (NZ), 67 Apollo Drive, North Shore 0632, New Zealand
(a division of Pearson New Zealand Ltd)

Penguin Books (South Africa) (Pty) Ltd, 24 Sturdee Avenue, Rosebank 2196, South Africa

Penguin Books Ltd, Registered Offices: 80 Strand, London WC2R ORL, England

www.penguin.com

First published 2010
1

Copyright © Richard Miles, 2010

The moral right of the author has been asserted

Designed and typeset by Richard Marston
Maps by Alan Gilliland
Printed and bound by Firmengruppe APPL, aprinta druck, Wemding, Germany

ISBN 978–0–713–99794–1

PAGES II–III
Children playing in the ruins of
Siwa, Egypt.

PAGES VI–VII
Church of the Holy Sepulchre,
Jerusalem.

CONTENTS

For Maisie, Jessamy and Gabriel, with all my love

INTRODUCTION

This is not a history of humankind but of civilization – its starting point the first discernible moments when humans began to cooperate, to live and work together in communities much larger and more complex than their immediate kinship groups. The story begins six thousand years ago, in the deserts of southern Iraq, where a cluster of clans became a city, and that city forged a civilization: the uniquely human phenomenon that has brought with it so much. Its rewards have included art, government, religion and law, and, perhaps most important of all, the idea of a shared humanity.

In telling this story we arrive at the furthest reaches of the historical record, but in the traces that have survived we can still feel the pulse of familiar human experiences. In the remnants of these early civilizations we can recognize the struggle to build the bonds that hold us together: hope and fear, the need to survive, and the urge to create. My career, as a historian and archaeologist of these ancient worlds, has been spent trying to reach back, through the dust of an archaeological dig or the bone-coloured ruins of a once-great city, into this remote past. And sometimes, whether it is in the eyes of an Egyptian death mask, in the words of an anonymous ancient poet, or in the story of a king simply curious to see the sea, you get a glimpse of that recognizable human spirit.

Civilization cannot be separated from the locus that created it, the city. More than 4,000 years ago, a nameless poet listed the attributes of a successful city – the place where all the aspirations of a civilization find concrete expression. The list appears in 'The Curse of Akkad', an ancient Babylonian poem, and it tells the fate of one of the earliest empires in Mesopotamia, in southern Iraq. Its details are so vivid that they could have been written yesterday:

> The warehouses were well provisioned,
> dwellings in the city were well built.

Its people would eat magnificent food,
its people would drink wonderful drinks.
Those who bathed for holidays rejoiced in the courtyards.
The people would crowd the places of celebration,
acquaintances would dine together ...
Foreigners would flock to and fro like exotic birds in the sky,
old women with good advice, and old men with good counsel,
young women with dancing spirit, young men with fighting spirit ...
All foreign lands rested content, and their people were happy.

The reality, of course, is that not everybody can be happy: every city, every civilization has its winners and losers, its haves and have-nots. This is the heavy but necessary price of civilization. But the prize was, and remains, a great one: the happy scenes expressed in this ancient poem make as much sense to us now as they did 4,000 years ago.

On my journey to the sites of these ancient civilizations, I have visited some of the world's most dangerous and troubled regions. Standing on a hotel rooftop in Baghdad, watching the sky buzz with military helicopters, you cannot help but be struck by the fragility of human civilization. That same ancient poet who described a city in its full glory also drew a sinister portrait of what happened when it all goes wrong:

Packs of dogs roamed the silent streets.
If two men walked there they would be eaten by them,
and if three men walked there they would be eaten by them.
Noses were punched, heads were smashed ...
Honest people were confused for traitors,
heroes lay dead on top of heroes,
the blood of traitors ran upon the blood of honest men ...
The old women did not restrain the cry, 'Alas for my city!'
The old men did not restrain the cry, 'Alas for its people!'
Its young women did not restrain from tearing their hair.
Its young men did not restrain from sharpening their knives.

In Iraq today you are confronted by a people who have to pick up the pieces of civilization. It is a punishingly difficult task, but not an impossible one. It is a story that has been played out again and again in this region from the time of the very first cities. When you see the worst of what humans are capable of, you also appreciate the importance of what we can do at our best: our inventiveness and our ability to communicate, and to forge a consensus based on our common humanity.

In the modern West we have lost confidence in the idea of civilization. Embarrassed by its chauvinistic and elitist connotations, we have increasingly taken refuge in less loaded terms such as culture to explain our origins. Culture, with its emphasis firmly on the organic growth of communities, tells a more palatable and soft-focused story than the tales of 'top-down' interventions and hard choices associated with civilization. Cultures are born, civilizations are made – man-made. Our discomfort with this idea has made us consign civilization to the museum display case, but in this book the idea of civilization will be rescued from its enforced retirement. Like our anonymous Babylonian poet, who so limpidly described the beauty of civilization and the terror of losing it, here I celebrate civilization and humanity's steadfast appetite to rebuild after the mighty collapse of entire empires. *Homo sapiens* has existed for about 160,000 years, civilization for about 6,000 years; it has not come easily. It is something that we have had to fight hard to achieve and even harder to maintain, and the greatest threats to it have come from our own talents for destruction.

Civilization is always a work in progress as each generation seeks to find different ways to create and maintain a viable and successful community. From the first cities in Mesopotamia, the Egyptian royal courts, the palaces of Minoan Crete and the citadels of Mycenae, the universal empires of Assyria and Babylon, the city-states of Classical Greece, the heroic kingship of Alexander, the mercantile sea power of Carthage, the Roman imperial machine and the Christian 'City of God', this book charts civilization as it has experimented with autocracy, oligarchy, kingship, democracy, empire and theocracy. What will become clear is that the march of civilization is more often a painful odyssey, revisiting the same mistakes and failed solutions time and again. Civilization marks the ultimate triumph of hope over experience.

Geography is central to the story of civilization. It was no accident that the very first cities on earth sprang up in the Euphrates and Tigris river valleys, narrow arteries of fertility and abundance that cut through vast swathes of barren nothingness. If agriculture was to be viable in this parched land then irrigation canals and ditches had to be built and maintained, all work that required the cooperation of large numbers of people. It was from this harsh reality that the first cities would eventually spring. An equally important component was the navigability of both rivers, meaning that people, goods and ideas could easily be spread.

It was from these great river ways that civilization would flow towards the Mediterranean, the next great theatre for its emergence. Again, it was no coincidence that the Mediterranean possessed the same essential combination of geographical factors. The Mediterranean might be classed as a sea but it is almost completely enclosed by heavily populated land, meaning that it served as an information superhighway *par excellence*. At the same time the Mediterranean's twisting coastlines and jutting peninsulas gave its inhabitants a powerful sense of security and separateness from the 'others'. The Mediterranean has always managed to be both one sea and a collection of many different seas: Aegean, Adriatic, Tyrrhenian and Ionian. It was out of this strange combination of interconnectivity and isolation that the city-state grew; physically isolated enough for a sense of independent identity to be fostered, whilst benefiting from the skills, ideas and goods that were borne on the sea from one community to another.

Plato, the great Athenian philosopher, described the ancient Greeks who had colonized the Mediterranean as 'frogs around a pond', but his analogy applies to all the diverse peoples who were to be found there. It is the croaks, the conversations that took place between Greeks, Romans, Etruscans, Phoenicians, Egyptians, Assyrians and Babylonians, amongst others, that are the central focus of this book. They may have croaked in different tongues, but they communicated with each other, spreading ideas and exchanging vital information about the different ways in which societies could be organized. This joined-up approach to thinking about the past is lost when we are taught history in the conventional way, where the great civilizations of the ancient world are presented as freestanding and autonomous. By reconnecting the great powers of the Near East and the Mediterranean with the wider political, economic, religious and cultural universe that they inhabited, this book will shine a light on the conversations that kept civilization alive, moving and evolving dynamically through time up to the present day.

Trade was the great engine of progress and it was the trade routes across the deserts and mountains of the Middle East and around the Mediterranean that made it possible to spread ideas throughout the region. And most of the conversations that went on were about the exchange of goods: Plato's frogs were usually croaking about prices and supply, import and export. As we will see, the growth and, in times of crisis, the very survival of civilization has often depended on the trading of goods, ideas and people, but these exchanges are almost always an exercise in pragmatism rather than some altruistic civilizing mission. If people were going to trade with you then they needed to appreciate your products. Good business meant that it was not just goods but tastes and aspirations that needed to be exchanged.

Even in the twenty-first century, the idea that Western civilization is built on the bedrock of ancient Greece and Rome has remained an extraordinarily powerful one. Our notions of love, hate, desire, beauty, justice, freedom and art are all presented as being part of an extraordinary patrimony bestowed upon us by the Classical World. It is not the intention of this book to deny the enormous debt owed to the Greeks and Romans, but rather to question the nature of that debt. The glittering achievements of the Graeco-Roman world and, by association, the body of ideas and values that we associate with the modern West, owe much to the unheralded contributions of many other ancient peoples. The genius of the Greeks and the Romans lay as much in their appropriation and adaptation of the ideas of others as it did with their own innovations. By tracing the journeys made by the great ideas that have provided the basis of Western civilization, as part of the cargo of the traders and colonists on the relentless anti-clockwise currents of the Mediterranean, this book will show that great advances – that are often attributed to the Graeco-Roman world – had a far more 'exotic' and, indeed, surprising provenance.

We might fondly imagine that it is humankind's natural state to co-habit together in communities that extend beyond clan or blood ties. The first chiefs who decided on such a course of action in southern Iraq would have made no such assumptions. There is nothing natural about cities, and their founders understood that its very survival relied on compromise, ruthlessness, sacrifice and toil. Civilization is a hard-won achievement, constantly under threat from both internal and external pressures. The story of civilization is not one of endless progression; it is a series of tales about the rise and fall of different civilizations in different places, there are moments of great enlightenment punctuated by warfare and desperation and acts of cruelty. Civilization embodies both the best and worst of what humans can do. The story I want to tell you now is not just of ancient worlds that have long passed away. It is the glorious incompleteness of the extraordinary, ongoing experiment of civilization that makes these tales from distant worlds so resonant. It is the story of us, then.

1

REVOLUTION:
THE FIRST CITIES

1
MESOPOTAMIA: FROM CLANS TO THE EARLIEST EMPIRE

The first great city known to history emerged in what is now southern Iraq. The ancient Greeks called this region Mesopotamia, the 'land between two rivers', the Tigris and the Euphrates; it had been occupied for at least a thousand years by people scratching a living in small, scattered communities of 2,000 people at the most. But then, just under 6,000 years ago, a remarkable thing happened. People left the security of their family compounds and tribal villages. They came together with other strangers to create something far more complex and difficult: a city, a civilization. The beginnings of Sumerian civilization, as we now call it, were sown when the heads of several different family groups resolved that their chances of a prosperous and secure future would be enhanced if they worked together as a more or less permanent collective. It was this decision that resulted in the creation of Uruk, the mother of all cities.

There is not much left now at the site of Uruk, which is about 250 kilometres south of Baghdad, but this initial experiment in urban living was extraordinarily successful. At its height, around 3000 BC, Uruk was home to about 40,000 to 50,000 people. The city walls were nearly eleven kilometres in circumference and enclosed an area of about six square kilometres. This was bigger than Athens would become even at the peak of the Classical period (five square kilometres). The world's first city is celebrated in the world's first work of epic literature; 'The Legend of Gilgamesh' told the story of Mesopotamia's King Gilgamesh, two-thirds god, one-third man, who was credited with the building of Uruk's famous city walls. In praising the city's scale and beauty – 'Go up, pace the walls of Uruk' – this early epic begins an ongoing tradition of the ancient world: the literary celebration of a civilization that ends up outliving the civilization itself.

The archaeological record at Uruk is complex but suggestive. Starting just under 6,000 years ago, it reveals a period of intensive building and rebuilding which went on for four or five centuries. In that period, the people of Uruk built

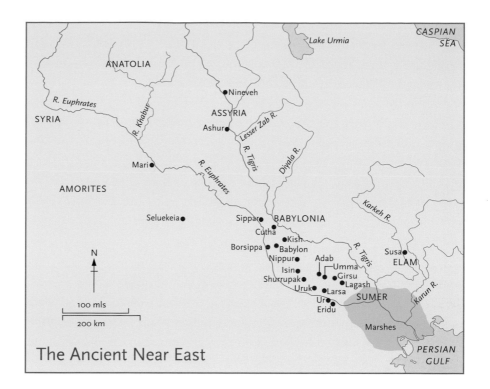

The Ancient Near East

a dozen or more large public buildings; temples, palaces, assembly halls – no one knows for sure what they were, but all of them were of different shapes and sizes. They would carefully level what had stood there before, seal the materials that had been used in a ritual fashion, and then build something entirely new on top, often trying out a new building material or a new technique, like the distinctive cone mosaics that were used to decorate walls. Behind all this restless building and rebuilding, you get the feeling that the Urukians were searching for ways to express through architecture the revolutionary new social structures that had come into being here, the shape of things to come.

Uruk is now seen as the prototype for other cities that made up the first Sumerian civilization. While most of the rest of humankind struggled to progress beyond simple agricultural techniques, the Sumerian people, all across the flat plains of southern Mesopotamia, were enjoying many of the benefits and trappings of a civilized urban life. Sophisticated religious institutions and systems had sprung up; immense religious complexes had been built in which elaborate rituals were performed to a pantheon of gods. Society was governed by the rule of law; legislation was recorded in writing. Craftsmen produced luxury objects, often with elaborate decorations and complex meanings. Merchants travelled all over the Middle East selling and bartering goods, sometimes in exchange for the raw materials needed to produce yet more goods. These were radical new ways to be human, but they were evidently successful: by the time that the first stones of that towering monument of prehistoric Britain, Stonehenge, were erected (around 2500 BC), 80 per cent of the population of Mesopotamia lived in cities of over 40 hectares in size, with populations of between 15,000 to 30,000.

The emergence of these thriving communities made up of individuals and groups with no blood ties was unprecedented in human experience. How did these extraordinary advances happen? The answer partly lies in the harshness of the environment. Civilization was forged in a place where life could be preserved only by the utmost human ingenuity and vigilance. This world, which its inhabitants simply called the *Kalam*, literally 'the Land', was a place of

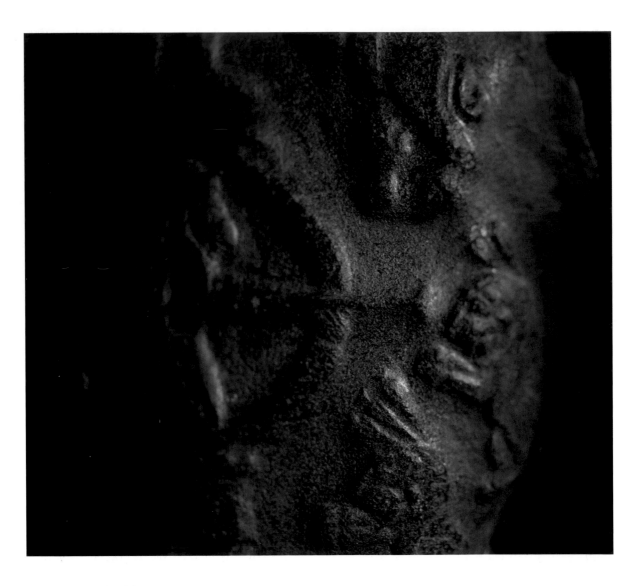

extremes, where narrow strips of fertile river valley were bounded by thousands of kilometres of sterile desert and toxic marsh. As the meagre rainfall of the region was incapable of sustaining agriculture, it was only through sophisticated irrigation that the land could be made fertile. The Tigris and the Euphrates rivers, which ran through Mesopotamia, provided the water; human ingenuity driven by necessity would provide the means to get that water to the fields.

Agriculture predates the first cities by thousands of years, but by about 5300 BC farming techniques became more intensive, maximizing food production. Simple irrigation methods, like direct inundation, and more advanced farming techniques, like mono-cropping (as opposed to crop rotation or 'slash and burn'), were developed by roughly 5000 BC. But in the formidable environment of southern Iraq, these were not enough. The only way for humans to flourish here was by combining their resources to manage the great rivers that passed through their territories so that they could break the cycle of feast or famine that dictated their existence. The Mesopotamian river valleys were vibrant arteries that cut through a barren wilderness. If their waters could be diverted and controlled then this sterile landscape could be transformed into a patchwork of fertile fields and a sedentary life of farming could be adopted. From its inception the city was inseparable from man's first serious attempts to control the physical environment around him.

We'll never know what made the people in this region take this dramatic step into the unknown. Perhaps an environmental crisis in the form of a prolonged drought or the change in the course of one of the two rivers' wandering tributaries forced people to think beyond their small-scale family units and combine with their neighbours to create an elaborate infrastructure of dams, channels and canals to manage the waters on which their survival depended. These projects demanded specialized workers and the division of labour, which in turn initiated patterns of hierarchy, specialization and mutual dependence that would become the foundations on which civilization stood.

At roughly the same time as the emergence of Uruk, another city appeared, 950 kilometres to the north at Tell Brak in present-day Syria. Tell Brak is an incredibly rich archaeological site, with structures that date back to the fifth millennium BC. Among the many finds unearthed here have been the distinctive eye amulets that were also found in great numbers in Uruk, suggesting that people from Uruk travelled north, bringing with them radical ideas about irrigation and city life. But perhaps one of the more striking artefacts to be found at Tell Brak is the bevel-rimmed bowl (BRB). When we think of the ancient world we tend, naturally, to focus on the iconic and the awe-inspiring: the Venus de Milo, the Great Sphinx. But for me the clumsy little bowl is as

important as any armless goddess or noseless mythical beast. It does not look like much. It is a rather crudely constructed vessel, made from unglazed clay, quickly and easily formed using a mould. But the BRB is remarkable because there are just so many of them – so many, in fact, that archaeologists working here simply rebury them at the end of a season's dig. And it's not just Tell Brak that is infested with BRBs: they have been found in their thousands at sites from Turkey to Syria, Iran to Iraq. They travelled with Uruk civilization, an indicator of Sumerian influence across the region, but also a great archaeological clue as to how this civilization organized itself.

What were all these modest-looking bowls used for? One theory is that they were used for distributing grain rations to workers: an ancient pay-packet, a standardized bowl of food in payment for labour. The BRB suggests that the first cities had a redistributive economy: a dominant, central power with enough wealth and authority to coerce or cajole the general population to undertake large-scale projects on its behalf, such as irrigation and intensive grain cultivation. The fruit of all this work was then taken by the central authority and small amounts were redistributed to the labourers to sustain them.

Because intensive farming is more productive than small-scale subsistence farming, it can generate a surplus of food, allowing a proportion of the harvest in a bumper year to be banked as protection against future lean years – food security, in other words. A surplus of food supplies also allows some fields to be turned over to non-food production, creating raw materials for manufacturing – textiles, for instance. This creates a need for skilled craftsmen and for merchants; it is the beginning of industry and consumerism. Agricultural surplus can also underwrite and sustain other specializations within the population – soldiers, builders, musicians, doctors, fortune tellers, prostitutes – all supported, directly or indirectly, by the food surplus.

The centre of power in the first city-civilization was located in the temples. This was theocratic government: religion rather than politics provided the ideology to mobilize the hard labour needed to build and maintain canals, the spectacular city walls and the fields of barley. Mesopotamian religion taught that all these projects were undertaken in the service of the gods, and that people themselves had been created expressly to serve the gods. Religion itself was clearly much older than the cities but it became an indispensable focus for the hopes and fears of these new communities as they struggled to understand and validate their new ways of life. Mesopotamian religion was suffused with an overwhelming sense of the fragility of civilization. All the hard work, all that had been achieved, could be swept away in a moment. It is no coincidence that the myth of the great flood originated in Mesopotamia, a land of marshes and wandering rivers where the line separating solid from liquid was uncertain. For Sumerians and Akkadians (the Akkadian Empire being the neighbouring Mesopotamian civilization to the Sumerians) water was the origin of life, but it was also the chaos to which everything could return if it was not for the protection of the many gods, among them An, the god of heaven, Ki, the goddess of the earth, and Enki, the god of fresh water. Each Sumerian city-state also had its own patron deity who protected the interests of its population and gave it its identity. And that protection had to be earned the hard way, by backbreaking labour.

With such a powerful theological argument for both piety and industry, it is not surprising that these temples, like the monasteries of Medieval Europe, became powerful economic centres, owning large tracts of agricultural land and overseeing manufacturing on an industrial scale. It is estimated that the temples in the city of Ur, for example, employed 40,000 workers, mainly in textiles.

The priests were self-appointed gatekeepers to the gods; they created and controlled the temples, the dwellings of these deities. And so the temples were the first great institutions of the city. Ever more opulent temples were built, with huge storerooms for the produce grown on the temple estates, which were administered by a staff of managers, overseers and bookkeepers. The flat Mesopotamian plains came to be dominated by ziggurats, massive terraced, pyramid-like structures on which the palaces of the gods were built. The gods and goddesses were envisaged in human form. Their statues were clothed in gorgeous robes and fine meals were offered to them.

The temples occupied a privileged position within the first cities. Even citizens not directly employed by them were expected to give up some of their labour in service of the gods. It meant that over time the temples accumulated huge surplus produce which could be exchanged for more land. This extra capacity generated yet more surplus which, in turn, could be used to diversify and support temple craftsmen and artisans – another valuable revenue stream. The revenues generated by these enterprises meant that the temple also served as a primitive kind of bank, making loans and offering mortgages, and acting as a kind of social services department, taking in the children of the poor as temple slaves. Smallholders, unable to compete with this kind of financial muscle, often went into debt and saw their farms repossessed and their autonomy lost as they were taken on as hired hands by the sacred land banks that had driven them to the wall. Mercilessly monopolistic and divinely sanctioned, the temples were dynamic engines powering the formation of the first redistributive economies.

We know a surprising amount about the way the temples and the first cities were organized thanks to the development of an important new technology: writing, one of the other foundation stones on which all civilizations rest. The script first used in Sumer and Akkad was cuneiform, the world's oldest known writing system, which had evolved from an earlier, more simple pictographic system. Basic records were first inscribed in wet clay in Uruk and other cities: lists of people and things, simple bookkeeping. But within a few hundred years writing systems had become much more sophisticated, capable of recording concepts as well as lists; soon after that there were even special schools where the art of writing was taught by an important new specialist: the scribe. In a very literal sense, this is where history begins. Before writing, we are floating on the ocean of the past; with writing, the past becomes a matter of record, the anchor drops and we can begin to say, with some degree of certainty, 'this happened'. The clay tablets that the Sumerians used for writing were tough and resistant to fire, as opposed to the delicate papyrus used by the ancient Egyptians and Greeks. Indeed far more documents have survived from Bronze Age Mesopotamia than Classical Greece largely because they were written on clay rather than papyrus. The fires that plagued the first cities and destroyed their archives often merely baked rather than destroyed the documents that they housed.

Writing was complicated, labour-intensive work, and it had to earn its keep by being, first and foremost, useful. But over time, the scribes started to take on subjects beyond the merely bureaucratic, and soon more or less everything was being written down: spells and medical cures, how-to handbooks, diplomatic treaties, myths and fables, law codes, lullabies and love songs. There were also religious texts, the so-called god lists, which attempted to rationalize the hundreds of local gods into a smaller pantheon of regional gods. It was a kind of religious reformation brought about by tidy-minded scribes.

The huge archives of documents that have survived from the first cities of the Near East detail the most minute and mundane aspects of urban life, and they demonstrate how the written word facilitated the control of the many by the few. Commands could be codified and vested with a new authority, bolstered by the permanence of the written record. Laws could be written up that either challenged or subsumed the tribal and familial customs that had long dictated the social, religious, economic and cultural norms of the Mesopotamian people. These documents show how city living may have given citizens freedom from the mercurial seasons and the struggle of subsistence farming, but it also separated them from their lands, their traditions and their customary rights. They were now totally reliant on the institutions that employed them. The paradox of urban existence was that whilst offering new security for its inhabitants, it also created new vulnerabilities. Security was bought at the cost of autonomy.

The growing social, political and economic tensions caused by the dominance of the temples were countered by another novel institution spawned by the city: the palace. A new, impressively dressed figure began to appear in the art that provides a beautiful but brutal window on to life and death in ancient Iraq. Whether he was hunting lions, fighting enemies or taking part in sacrifices and other religious ceremonies, this man was impossible to miss because he was depicted as being twice the size of all the other actors in the scenes. In Sumerian he was fittingly known as the *lugal*, literally 'the big man'. We know him as the 'king'. The palace (in Sumerian *é-gal*, literally 'the big house') became not just the residence of the royal family and the administrative nerve centre for the city, but also a huge industrial complex replete with workshops and warehouses, an important political counterweight to the temple, centred around a charismatic flesh-and-blood individual rather than a distant god. Gradually, across the third millennium BC, monarchies took charge of the commercial life of the city, with all foreign trade concessions falling under their control. The temples had to accommodate this new power in the land. Religious ceremonies promoting the

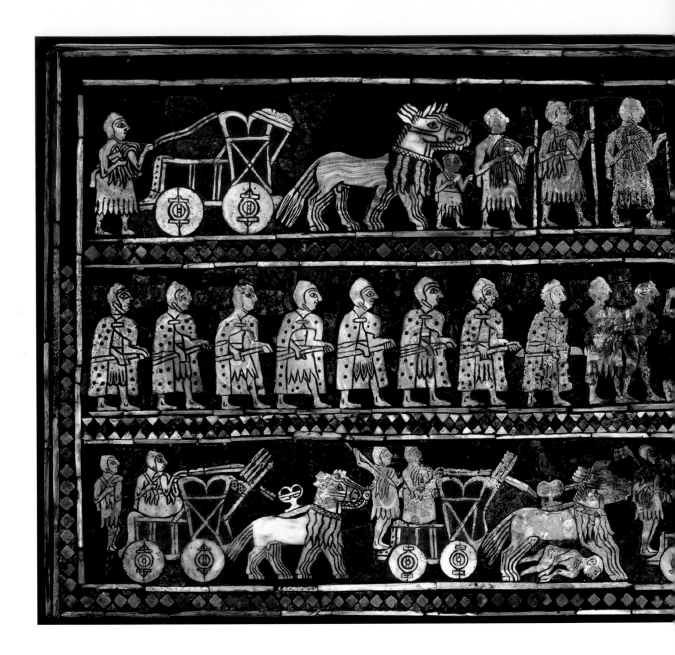

Royal Standard of Ur, 'War'
(*c.* 2600–2400 BC). Although
thought to be some kind of
standard by its excavator,
Leonard Woolley, its actual
function remains unclear.
The main panels are known
as 'War' and 'Peace'. 'War'
shows one of the earliest

representations of a Sumerian
army, with chariots pulled by
donkeys and cloaked infantry
with spears. Enemy soldiers are
depicted being trampled and
killed with axes, while others
are paraded naked and in front
of the king.

king as protector of the city and special companion of the gods were developed. Palace and temple soon learned the value of a united front that wove religious and secular concerns into a seamless whole to dazzle and cow an awe-struck population.

Anthropologists tell us that in tribal societies the power of leaders is rarely absolute. Restrained by a complex web of expectations, traditions and taboos, rulers are subject to the collective will of their communities. They can lead, but only as far as the people are prepared to follow. In the first cities, the webs of tribal life dissolved. Schooled by palace and temple in the new system of hierarchies and specializations, people quickly learned how to be followers. As for the 'big men' – and the occasional woman, too – they, like the temples, creamed off the economic benefits of being at the centre of things. Now they could afford to re-imagine and re-present themselves in new guises: priest-king, father-figure, law-giver, builder and architect, wise governor, shepherd of the people, mighty hunter. There were many ways to be a king in the ancient world, but every one carried with it an argument for a natural right to rule. Kings, and the dynasties they spawned, set out to be different from the rest, in life and death.

This was made dramatically clear in the discoveries of pioneer archaeologist Sir Leonard Woolley who, in the 1920s and 1930s, excavated the ancient Mesopotamian city of Ur and uncovered evidence of how kings and their dynasties set themselves apart from the rest of the population. The site of Ur, in what is now south-eastern Iraq, is particularly famous for the remains of a magnificent ziggurat dating from about 2100 BC. This Bronze Age structure was in ruins by late Babylonian times, although it has been restored and reconstructed by subsequent rulers, from Nabonidus, the last Babylonian king, in the sixth century BC, to Saddam Hussein in the 1980s. The site now sits far inland, a victim of the wandering waters of the Euphrates, but Bronze Age Ur was near the mouth of the river on the Persian Gulf, making it well connected for trade by river and sea. Woolley and his team studied more than 1,800 burials, dating from around 4,500 years ago. Most of them were simple affairs, a single body wrapped in a reed mat or wooden coffin resting in a small rectangular pit surrounded by a few personal possessions: weapons, jewellery, cups and plates. But sixteen of them were very different. These were mass burials involving dozens of people, male and female, and animals. Their bodies lay in ranks in an outer chamber of an elaborate tomb. And in the inner chamber was the focus of all this carefully choreographed death: a single figure surrounded by objects of the most amazing rarity and beauty. Woolley called these burials the 'death pits' but they are now known, rather more sedately, as the 'Royal tombs'. They have been mostly dated to about 2600 BC.

With treasures this spectacular, these were indisputably royal tombs, and inscriptions found there allow us to put names to some of these long-lost royals: 'Meskalamdug the King' and 'Puabi the Queen'. But what about the other bodies that had accompanied Meskalamdug and Puabi in death? In his classic book, *Ur of the Chaldees*, Woolley explained his findings with a compelling picture of a royal funeral: the dead ruler laid in the tomb's inner sanctum, the outer chamber slowly filling with wailing mourners, ladies in waiting, loyal soldiers and servants. As solemn music plays, the tomb is sealed from the outside, the mourners take poison and then, lit by the flames from the guttering oil lamps, one by one they die, presumably to be reborn on the other side of the grave ready to serve their beloved ruler once again.

It is fantastic stuff, but the truth about the death pits is possibly even more bizarre. According to some theories the bodies of the mourners were placed, one by one, in the tomb in the years after the death of the ruler, a slow reassembling of the royal household as each member passed away. Some of the mourners may even have died before the king or queen, their skeletons stashed away and then carefully dressed and placed in position when their master or mistress finally died. We simply do not know enough about the beliefs of the Mesopotamians to be sure, but one thing is clear: even in death, the charisma of royalty could exert a powerful pull. People would follow kings, in life, in death and beyond.

RIGHT
Life-size bronze statue of a nude young man. Originally found in the village of Bassetki in northern Iraq, this statue is very significant because of the inscription on its pedestal. It records a request to the gods by 'his city' that Naram-Sin of Akkad (c. 2254–2218 BC) be given divine status because 'he secured the foundations of his city in times of trouble' – the first surviving evidence for the emergence of divine kingship.

And people would, of course, also follow their king into battle. Of all the guises adopted by the kings of the first cities, the warrior-king was the most potent; the success of the first cities had partly derived from the protection they offered from the sporadic raids of the nomadic tribes who lived on the fringes of the desert – the eternal 'other' in the history of civilization. The Sumerian kings presented themselves as the defenders of their people from the violence inflicted upon them by outsiders. But that was just the start.

It was not long before these kings wanted to do more than protect their own cities. Attack became the first rule of defence, with the result that Mesopotamia was not only the first seat of civilization but also the scene of the first great wars of annihilation. War would always be the intimate of civilization, its shadow marching alongside it, dark and inseparable. The growth of monarchy in the ancient Near East brought with it an explosion in organized violence. It was under royal patronage that new military technology such as the war chariot, capable of killing far greater numbers of people in battle, was developed.

It was a Mesopotamian king, Sargon, who added a new unit of currency to the political economy of the ancient world: empire. In the twenty-third century BC, Sargon conquered his way, city by city, through Mesopotamia until finally he could declare himself to be 'king of kings', from the Mediterranean to the Persian Gulf. According to the self-generated myths surrounding his life and exploits, Sargon worked his way up from humble beginnings, possibly the son of a gardener, to become cupbearer to Ur-Zababa, king of the city of Kish. Sargon was tasked with overseeing irrigation projects and through this gathered around him a gang of disciplined and loyal labourers who probably formed the core of his first army, helping him displace Ur-Zababa and become king and founder of the Akkadian dynasty. By the end of Sargon's long reign (thought to have lasted fifty-six years), he ruled the first centrally controlled, multi-ethnic and brutally subjugated empire, from his new capital on the Euphrates, Akkad.

But there was never to be a 'Pax Mesopotamia': the systems of empire were too weak, the geographical distances too great and the concept itself too novel to be accepted without a fight (it would fall to later empire-builders to benefit from the pioneering work of this first emperor). Sargon was constantly at war to retain the spoils of empire, and his successors inherited a violent and turbulent legacy. The reigns of both of his sons, Rimush and Manishtushu, ended in assassination, and his grandson, Naram-Sin, spent most of his forty-year reign fighting, suppressing constant revolts and adding new territories to his grandfather's empire to replace those that fell off the imperial bandwagon. Naram-Sin accumulated titles as readily as he did territory. He called himself *shar kibrat 'arbaim*, 'King of the Four Regions', and then promoted himself to *shar kishshati*, 'King of the Universe'. After that there was only one place to go: heavenwards. Naram-Sin was the first Mesopotamian king to proclaim himself a living god.

In the centuries that followed his reign, dark and troubling legends accumulated around Naram-Sin. 'The Curse of Akkad', written in the time of the self-consciously pious Babylonian kings, recounts a desperate act of sacrilege committed by him when one of the gods threatened to withdraw their favour from his city: Naram-Sin destroyed a temple to Enlil, the chief deity of the Mesopotamian pantheon. The consequences for Akkad were catastrophic. 'For the first time since the cities were founded,' says the poem, 'the fields produced no grain. The people flailed at themselves with hunger...' – a reminder of the critical link in this era between political stability and food security. Today, some archaeologists interpret 'The Curse of Akkad' as evidence of severe climate change that affected the region some time around the end of third millennium BC: a dramatic drop in rainfall that made it impossible to sustain an urban civilization and a resilient imperial state. The Akkadian Empire, under Naram-Sin's son, was defeated in about 2083 BC by invading armies from the Zagros mountains, in what is now Iran: the original 'barbarian' horde, 'sweeping in' from the wilds to extinguish an empire and inaugurate a Dark Age.

II
EGYPT: A GLITTERING ONE-OFF?

Only a few centuries after the first cities had sprung up along the valleys of the Tigris and Euphrates rivers, a comparable but independent experiment in city civilization was under way in Egypt. Ancient Egypt, with its staggering, monumental architecture, its divine god-kings and its all-pervasive preoccupation with death and what comes after, puts the hubristic pretensions of the last Akkadian kings into perspective. The matchlessness of ancient Egypt's macabre grandeur and colossal brutality certainly captures the modern imagination more than any other ancient civilization but it is Egypt's very uniqueness that, in the story of our ancient worlds, makes it such a one-off, with much to learn but little to teach.

Though land-locked on three sides, ancient Egypt was essentially a ribbon-shaped island, protected from its neighbours by mountains to the south and deserts to the east and west. Its frontier to the north was defined by the marshy delta of the Nile, the river which shaped the civilization that developed there. The annual flooding of the great river ensured that the land on either side was some of the most fertile in the world, leading the ancient Greek historian Herodotus to make the famous observation that Egypt was 'the gift of the Nile'. Yet this dark brown, nutrient-rich, Nile-fed soil often only extended a few hundred metres away from the river's banks; after that, there was just barren desert. For the Egyptians the Nile was the great provider, which bestowed on them all that they needed and more. Even the famous papyrus rolls on which they wrote their hieroglyphic script were made from the reeds that grew in the shallows of the river. The river was so central to life in ancient Egypt that for its people, north was known as 'downstream' and south as 'upstream'. The seasons of the year were simply split into 'Inundation', 'Going-Down of Inundation' and 'Drought'. Instead of the labour-intensive, high-maintenance canal systems that the Mesopotamians developed to capture and control the waters of the Tigris and the Euphrates, the Egyptians simply banked up their fields to hold the floodwaters in place for a crucial forty to sixty days at the start of 'Inundation'. After this, the mud banks were broken, the life-giving water drained off and a fertile layer of black mud was left to receive the seed. Some years there was too little water, some years too much; but there were no Bronze Age technologies that could control floods or ameliorate droughts. All the Egyptians could do was carefully monitor the fluctuations by a system of 'nilometers', and anticipate the feast or the famine that would follow (the biblical story of 'Joseph in Egypt' beautifully illustrates the political benefits of canny disaster management).

The two regions of the Upper Nile and the Lower Nile were united under one ruler around 3150 BC, and Egypt quickly emerged as a homogeneous but socially differentiated society with a temple-centred religious elite and monarchy at its apex, both of which jealously protected their wealth and power. As ever these elites used the vast resources at their disposal to commission sophisticated art, architecture and literature that both justified and bolstered their dominance, but the quality, scale and ambition of Egyptian art sets it apart from the rest of the ancient world. The brilliance of its material culture was heightened by the coherency of its message. Its particular environment, the limited amount of cultivable land, coupled with the Nile's excellence as a transport artery meant that Egypt was always more susceptible to centralized control than many of the other, more fractious kingdoms of the ancient world; the Nile suggested the natural cohesion of this uniquely blessed land, and the rulers of Egypt were quick to take the hint.

Egypt's kings (the title 'pharaoh' is strictly speaking reserved for the kings of the later Bronze Age) refined the religious and ideological model that had

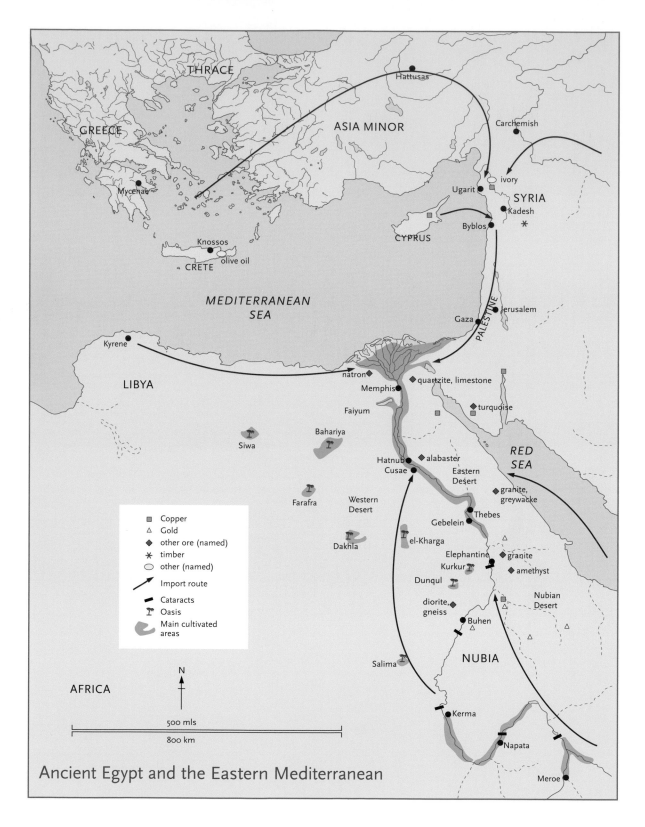

THRACE

Hattusas

ASIA MINOR

Carchemish

GREECE

Mycenae

Ugarit

ivory

SYRIA

Kadesh

Byblos

CYPRUS

Knossos

olive oil

CRETE

MEDITERRANEAN
SEA

Jerusalem

Gaza

PALESTINE

Kyrene

natron

quartzite, limestone

LIBYA

Memphis

turquoise

Faiyum

RED
SEA

Bahariya

Siwa

Hatnub

alabaster

Cusae

Eastern
Desert

Farafra

Western
Desert

granite,
greywacke

Thebes

Gebelein

Dakhla

el-Kharga

Elephantine

granite

Kurkur

amethyst

Dunqul

Nubian
Desert

diorite,
gneiss

Buhen

AFRICA

Salima

NUBIA

N

500 mls

Kerma

800 km

Napata

Meroe

Ancient Egypt and the Eastern Mediterranean

■	Copper
△	Gold
◆	other ore (named)
✳	timber
◯	other (named)
➤	Import route
▬	Cataracts
🌴	Oasis
〰	Main cultivated areas

evolved under Mesopotamian rulers. The king was carefully presented to his subjects as the incarnation of sacred power. His mandate did not merely cover the day-to-day running of the Egyptian state. He guaranteed and safeguarded the cosmic and earthly order known by the Egyptians as *Ma'at*, the correct balance/truth. To his subjects he was omnipotent. As one inscription baldly proclaims: 'If anything comes from the mouth of his Majesty it happens immediately'. These infallible rulers took image management to a completely new level; they appeared before their subjects dressed in full royal regalia of kilt, bull's tail hanging from the waist, ceremonial beard, flail and crook, and on the royal head they wore the great double crown of Egypt, with an ivory cobra rearing up on the forehead, ready to destroy any who opposed them with its venomous spittle. The massive pyramids showed that, even in death, the Egyptian king intended both to intimidate and astound.

It is easy to be beguiled by the all-consuming and triumphal nature of Egyptian imperial rhetoric. Yet behind the façades of great temples, mighty pyramids and glittering ceremonies lay a far more interesting and complex story. The first autocrats had been able to control personally the small cities they ruled over, but success and expansion brought with it a battery of new problems. No man, even if he did claim to be heaven-sent, could watch over a great empire on his own: the Egyptian kings had to rely on a retinue of potentially treacherous family members, officials and soldiers to oversee this expanded state. The instructions given by the pharaoh Amenemhat I (*c.* 1991–1962 BC) to his successor and son Sesostris stand as a poignant reminder of this vulnerability:

> Watch out for subjects who are no-marks,
> Of whose conspiracies one is oblivious.
> Do not put your trust in your brother, keep no friend,
> Allow no one close; it has no value
> When you take your rest, keep watch over yourself,
> Because no one has any lackeys on the day when disaster strikes.
> I donated to the beggar, and raised the orphan,
> I gave to the needy as I did to the well off.
> But he who shared my bounty stirred up trouble,
> He whom I trusted used it to conspire against me.

Such fears were fully justified; all Bronze Age rulers were far more likely to be killed by relatives or courtiers than by foreign enemies on the battlefield. Despite the fictional continuity created by the emphasis on dynastic rule, Egyptian royal history was full of assassinations, usurpations and regime change.

ABOVE A camel at the stepped pyramid of the pharaoh Djoser (2691–2625 BC), Saqqara, Egypt.

By pegging the success of their regimes to the scale of their foreign conquests, the Bronze Age Masters of the Universe were caught in a trap of their own making. The paradox was that by creating ever-larger kingdoms, they became increasingly dependent on subordinates to govern for them. As Egypt and its foreign dominions came to be managed by the massed ranks of royal bureaucracy, the more peripheral the king himself potentially became. When the bureaucratic class became too indispensable, they could operate effectively without the personal authority of the king. To balance this out, Egypt was the first civilization to spin a complex court structure that allowed the ruler to control his nobles by a judicious mix of rewards, threats and manipulations.

This was all beautifully enacted during the celebrations organized by Amenophis III (who reigned from about 1386 to 1349 BC) to celebrate the jubilee of his coronation. At his capital he had a new park built, replete with pavilions, palaces and a huge artificial lake. Then, in front of a great mass of his subjects, the pharaoh publicly rewarded his most senior officials. His administrators, soldiers and courtiers were presented to him in strict rank order to receive their gifts, consisting of gold trinkets and ribbons. They then all sat down to breakfast with their monarch. Here we witness the very public affirmation of a royally sanctioned hierarchy designed to reward loyal officials. Next, though, the generals, bald-headed eunuchs and other well-fed officials were instructed to get behind the oars of the royal barge moored on the lake and row their monarch across it. The public spectacle of a group of men from the highest echelons of society engaged in such a menial undertaking brilliantly reinforced the authority of the pharaoh to all who were present.

The kings had other less subtle devices at their disposal. The ranks of royal administrators were regularly purged, often for no real reason other than the need to keep subordinates on their toes. Rival government departments were encouraged to inform on one another. The pharaoh sabotaged the smooth running of his own government to secure his own position at the top. Yet, even in the assertion of total supremacy, the pharaohs had to perform a delicate balancing act. Much has been written about the strange sun worshipping king Akhenaten (who reigned from about 1353 to 1336 BC). Akhenaten ordered that only the sun god was to be worshipped by his firmly polytheistic subjects, and after his death Akhenaten was effectively expunged from the historical records by his successors. It has traditionally been argued that this was because of his unacceptable political beliefs and military inactivity. The real reason, however, probably lies in the half-forgotten city Akhetan, which he built as his new capital.

Akhetan was a splendid city with two grand palaces housing colossal stone sculptures of Akhenaten and a series of huge temples dedicated to his sun god. The pharaoh also built a whole neighbourhood of lavish homes for his officials next to the palaces, all fitted out with their own mini solar shrines. There were other strange new developments too. In the tombs of those who worked in the Royal Palace, the scenes of private life that had traditionally adorned Egyptian burial chambers suddenly disappeared and were replaced by portraits of the official waiting on or abasing themselves in front of Akhenaten and his family. The pharaoh was intruding upon the private life of his staff even in death. He had, in essence, tried to establish the world's first totalitarian regime where nowhere was off-limits for state interference. Akhenaten's subsequent obliteration from the records by his own brother and successor, Tutankhamun, shows that other godlike but perhaps more pragmatic pharaohs understood that supremacy had to be moderated.

The ambitions of Egypt's kings reached far beyond the banks of the Nile, and their perspective was unrelentingly belligerent and imperialistic. They sought to achieve supremacy not only over their own people but also over non-Egyptian lands. Each year the king would set out with his armies to extend his realm in some way. At its height the empire would stretch from southern Sudan all the way to Syria and the Lebanon. Yet although Egypt was one of the major political players in the Near East, it was not the only big beast in that particular jungle. In what is now Turkey, a people called the Hittites had built a formidable empire, and in Mesopotamia, the Assyrians and then the Babylonians held sway. Not that any self-respecting Egyptian god-king would ever admit to having equals: the standard line in countless official documents and pieces of art was that all foreigners, even those who were fellow monarchs of large and powerful empires, were there to be subjugated.

Most Egyptian royal palaces were decorated with bloodthirsty scenes depicting the monarch killing or taking captive various foes. Bound captives were painted on the pavement of the royal court at Amarna so that whenever the pharaoh walked anywhere, he was literally trampling on his enemies. The centrepiece of the great victory celebrations at the royal temples was the ceremonial execution of large numbers of prisoners of war. Such was the control that the royal media machine had over the population of Egypt that even embarrassing

setbacks were portrayed as mighty victories. Their imperial ambition sprung from the firm belief that all non-Egyptians were fundamentally inhuman and needed to be subjugated. In Pharaonic Egypt we see for the first time a process we will witness countless times in this historical odyssey: the construction of an imperialist rhetoric that sustained itself on the idea that others who were not part of their self-proclaimed community were both alien and inferior.

The longevity and conservatism of ancient Egypt make it appear almost statically timeless; thousands of years of stability and majesty. This image was partly created by the dynastic propaganda of ancient Egypt, which implied endless generations of divinely ordained succession. But just as the kings themselves were in reality vulnerable to intrigue and assassination, so the empire at times succumbed to assault from external, hostile invaders – the outsiders that Egyptian civilization regarded as so inferior.

There is a depiction of such foreigners in the tomb of Khnumhotep, a vizier during the Twelfth Dynasty. The foreigners are identified in this tomb as 'Asiatics', probably from present-day Syria, and they are doing what all foreigners had to do if they wanted to avoid violent retribution: paying tribute. But even in timeless Egypt things changed. Within a few centuries, by around 1650 BC, the descendants of these subservient Asiatics were ruling large parts of Lower Egypt from their capital at Avaris. Quite how the Hyksos, or 'shepherd kings', achieved their spectacular coup is subject to fierce debate. The Hyksos are thought to be the descendants of the Asiatics who were brought into the region as labourers

and allowed to settle there, and some historians imagine a gradual takeover of key economic, political and military positions by the Hyksos as the native dynasties lost their centralizing grip. Others argue for a sudden, dramatic conquest by Hyksos armies thanks to their mastery of a new war-making technology: horsepower.

The Hyksos were no flash in the pan – they ruled Lower Egypt for about a century, establishing their own dynasty and building a capital city at Avaris in the Nile Delta. They even made alliances through marriage with distant kingdoms, like Minoan Crete. To make matters worse for the Egyptians, the same period saw Upper Egypt under the control of Nubian kings from the kingdom of Kush, leaving the native kings ruling a rump state from Thebes. For the once mighty Egyptians, this was a harsh lesson in how the wheel of imperial history can turn, and you can hear the humiliation and fury that this state of affairs generated in the seething words of the Egyptian king Kamose the First:

What serves this strength of mine, when an Asiatic in Avaris and a Nubian in Kush and I sit united, each in possession of his slice of Egypt? … No man can settle down when despoiled by the taxes of the Asiatics. I will grapple with him that I may rip open his belly! My wish is to save Egypt and to smite the Asiatic!

In about 1555 BC Kamose's wish came true; he launched an attack on the Hyksos from his Theban base, starting a campaign that lasted nearly thirty years before culminating in the final routing of the Hyksos from the kingdom. With the Hyksos defeated, the Egyptian New Kingdom (c. 1570–1070 BC) went from strength to strength, taking Egypt to new levels of prosperity and foreign influence.

In the tomb of the Theban vizier Rekhmire, made about a century after the defeat of the Hyksos, images show the unclean foreigners back where they belong: paying tribute. There are more than 400 years and a hundred kings between the images in Rekhmire's tomb and the ones that adorn the tomb of Khnumhotep, but the idea and the ideology are essentially the same: the shepherding Asiatics, the Kushites with their ivory and giraffes, the Minoans with their distinctive conical jugs are all there to bend the knee and buy the goodwill of mighty Egypt.

But the chauvinism of Rekhmire's tomb disguises a broader, more profound truth about the ancient world: beyond the narrow confines of Egypt it was a big, wide world inhabited by many different peoples. They were known to each other and each had things that the others wanted. So instead of just viewing these images as Rekhmire would have done – as proof of Egypt's dominance

– what you can really see is the picture of an international market based on the exchange of desirable goods.

Trade, and in particular maritime trade, rather than warfare was the great engine of civilization. Egypt's physical isolation and xenophobic ideology meant that interaction with foreigners rarely went beyond subjugation. More practically, Egyptian boats were specifically designed for the Nile with wide flat bottoms that made them unsuitable for sea travel. The very chauvinism that was such a pillar of Egyptian imperial success was the root cause of the limits that were placed on the export of its political and social culture. Pharaonic Egypt, despite its incredible achievements, had little of the long-range impact that the cities of Mesopotamia had. The overwhelming uniqueness and dominance of the Nile caused Egypt to develop its own way, socially, politically and culturally. Its cultural influence and its reputation were enormous, but just as there was only one Nile so there could be only one Egypt; the blueprints for civilization that were developed here largely remained here. It was Mesopotamian rather than Egyptian art, architecture, alphabet, literature and religion that provided the bedrock of civilization in the Mediterranean world. Egypt was primarily a source of exotica, a sprinkling of the other-worldly to add lustre to the everyday.

III

CIVILIZATIONS FOR EXPORT

By the eighteenth century BC, the Near East, Anatolia and the eastern Mediterranean increasingly resembled a joined up, cosmopolitan world. We might have lost any record of the conversations between these different peoples, but the possessions they left behind reveal a world of ever broadening horizons. In one north Syrian city, Mari, obsidian from Greece, amber from the Danube, lapis lazuli from Afghanistan, tin and silver from Cyprus, purple dye and timber from the Levant, pottery and linen from Egypt, weapons from Anatolia, onions from Palestine, honey and leather boots from Crete, could all be found. It is through this urge to trade, and through that to communicate and explore, that the first great civilizations started to interact and forge a more lasting human legacy.

Commerce was without doubt the single most important agent in the creation of this Bronze Age world where different geographical and cultural circumstances contributed to the emergence of a swathe of different civilizations.

The individuals who exported so many of the cultural, economic, political and religious characteristics of the Mesopotamian cities to far-off lands were merchants more interested in turning a profit than the progress of civilization. This is powerfully brought home by an extraordinary series of documents attesting to the presence of a large group of merchants working from the ancient city of Kanesh, located in Anatolia, now part of modern-day Turkey. From about 2000 to 1600 BC, Kanesh was a distant but vital trading hub established by the kings of Assyria, which dominated northern Mesopotamia and Asia Minor. Kanesh was governed for 4,000 years from a palace on the hill by a local dynasty of Anatolian kings. There is scant remaining evidence about this monarchy, but extensive documents survive that tell us a lot about the busy lives of the foreign merchants who lived in the lower city. In the ruins of Kanesh, there are the remains of the houses, warehouses and workshops of these foreign merchants from Assur, an Assyrian city which is 1,500 kilometres, or 50 days by mule, east of the city (Assur was in Mesopotamia, located in what is now Iraq, about 280 kilometres north of Baghdad). This district was known as the *karem* (port)

of Kanesh, a permanent colony of expats who had come west to make their fortunes by running import-export businesses.

These Assyrian merchants were an essential link in a network of trade stretching from Afghanistan in the east to the Mediterranean coast and Egypt, stitching together the Bronze Age world in an ancient precursor of our own global economy. The Assyrians had access to things that people in Anatolia wanted: tin, which they bought from the Elamites further to the east (in what is now south-west Iran); textiles, some from the cities of southern Mesopotamia, others spun in Assur itself; also, more exotic raw treasures, like lapis lazuli from distant Afghanistan. In exchange for these goods, the Assyrians received silver and gold which they sent home to Assur, using it to finance the next consignment or banking it for a rainy day. The *karem* ran on a clear set of rules, financial, legal and commercial. Take taxation, for example: the palace on the hill received 5 per cent of the value of all textile sales and 3 per cent for tin. They also took a levy of 4 per cent on the silver and gold that the merchants sent back home to Assur. In return the local kings guaranteed the merchants safety on the roads and paid compensation to them in cases of theft or murder committed in their territory. Protected by these treaties, mule trains would regularly make the 1,500-kilometre journey from Assur to Kanesh. The merchants in Kanesh would then divide up their consignments from Assur for further distribution to the forty or so other Assyrian trading posts which were scattered over Anatolia and beyond, further strands in the web of Bronze Age trade.

We know a huge amount about the Assyrian merchants because thousands of their letters have survived. Most of them, as you'd expect, are concerned with money matters: contracts, loans, bills of sale, warehouse inventories, bureaucratic entanglements and legal wrangles, all recognizable business paperwork. But there are also personal letters from the merchants and from the women in their lives which tell another, very human side of this story in voices that still speak to us across the millennia. There are lonely men far from home looking for a girl from the home country to come and look after them (though evidently there were limits as to how long they were prepared to wait):

I am alone here, there is none who serves me, or dresses my table for me. Your father wrote to me about you, proposing that I should marry you . . . If you do not come I will marry a girl from Wahsusana.

There are letters from Anatolian girls from Kanesh who have married these strangers from far away, and then there are the loyal wives who have followed their footloose husbands from Assyria:

You went to Kanesh and told me 'I will stay there for 15 days' but instead of 15 days you stay a full year! From Kanesh you wrote to me, come up to Hahhum. It has been one year that I am in Hahhum and in your shipments you do not even mention my name!

Then there are the wives who stayed at home in Assur, feeling abandoned and worrying about their children growing up without a father to look after them:

Make an effort, break your obligations there … our young daughter has grown up, come home and put her under the protection of the god Assur, come and touch the foot of your god.

The wives left behind in Assur were not just relaxing in baths of asses' milk, spending their husbands' hard-earned silver; they were also an essential thread in the complex network of trade and exchange. They were the ones who oversaw the shipments of tin, and they often wove the textiles that were sent on to Kanesh. They were business partners as well as wives, and the tone of some of their letters is often assertive. These were women who knew how to stick up for themselves. One wife really put the pressure on her husband, a merchant in Kanesh:

When you left, you did not leave me any silver, not even one shekel. You emptied the house and took everything away. What is this extravagance about which you always write to me? There is nothing here to buy our food! But you think we are extravagant? I sent everything we have to you, and today I am living in an empty house! Send me the money you have received for my textiles so that I can buy some necessities!

Here another wife impatiently asks:

Since you left, Salim-ahum has already built a house double the size! When will we be able to do the same?

These wives might have been having a tough time of it, but everything is relative: if keeping up with the Salim-ahums is one of your main concerns it suggests, at the very least, that there is an expectation of better times ahead. And aspirations like that were only possible because of the sophisticated political and social mechanisms that stitched together the diverse and distant cities of the region.

Assyrians and Anatolians may have been very different in terms of their

language, culture and religion, but they were united by mutual self-interest: the need to exchange what they had for what they wanted, the soft power of trade as opposed to the hard power of war and conquest. Things did not always run smoothly, of course, as can be seen from the remains of the palace at Kanesh, destroyed by a terrible fire sometime in the nineteenth century BC. It must have been a fearsome blaze because the mud brick walls here have been vitrified – turned to glass – by the intensity of the heat. But when they were not burning each other out of house and home, the rulers of the middle and late Bronze Age displayed surprising levels of cooperation and mutual respect, cemented by trade and commerce, oiled by the exchange of costly gifts and of women too – sisters and daughters dispatched to distant courts to marry foreign kings in order to strengthen political alliances with family ties.

Long-distance trade became increasingly controlled by the palaces, merchants acted as royal ambassadors and gift exchange between rulers became an essential symbol of Bronze Age power relations. In their letters, written in the common diplomatic language of Akkadian, kings refer to each other as 'brother', 'father' and 'son'. The level of interdependence was so great that a political agent from the city of Ugarit, writing in the eighteenth century BC, concluded: 'No king is great on his own.' But of course no king calls another king 'father' unless he has to. There was a clear distinction between *sharru rabu*, 'great kings', and *sharru sehru*, 'little kings', and it was maintained at the point of a spear where necessary. A letter from one king to another lays bare the raw power politics that underpinned the warmer familial language of 'fathers' and 'sons': 'That man of Taishama,' wrote one of the 'big kings', referring to one of the 'little kings' of the region, 'he is your dog. Why then does he negotiate with the other little kings? Does my dog, the man of Sibuha, negotiate with other little kings?'

But even a dog fight needs rules, and the greatest rule givers of the ancient world were the kings of 'the lands of Hatti'. In Anatolia, what had been a patchwork of small competing city-states was united as the Hittite Empire in the eighteenth century BC: a conglomerate that self-consciously aped the diplomatic, political, religious, cultural and economic structures of the Mesopotamian kingdoms. The Hittite kingdom emerged in roughly the same geographical area as Kanesh but a few hundred years after the Assyrian merchant colony. Hittite culture may have been greatly influenced by the first cities to the south and east, but every kingdom brings its own flavours to add to the mix. With the Hittites it was storm gods, curly-toed boots, a flair for horsemanship and chariot-warfare, and a distinctive faith in the letter of the law. From family life to international politics the Hittites believed that relationships between individuals and kingdoms could be managed through legally binding agreements and treaties. The Hittites were the ancient world's most assiduous diplomats; they wanted to build an empire out of the small print. In Hattusa, the capital city of Hatti, fragments of more than seventy peace treaties have been found; they seem to have had an almost religious dread of breaking their word. When one of their kings did so, by launching a sneak attack on Egypt, plague came to Hattusa and thousands died, including the king himself. The king's son considered this divine judgment and wrote a series of 'plague prayers' accusing his father of bad faith and seeking forgiveness from the storm gods in whose name the original treaty had been signed.

It took a long time to patch up relationships with Egypt. The bad blood culminated in the battle of Qadesh in what is now Syria, in the early thirteenth century BC. It was perhaps the largest ever chariot battle, involving as many as 6,000 chariots. The battle was commemorated at the temple of the Egyptian pharaoh Ramesses the Second at Abu Simbel. It ended in a stalemate, and with the drawing up of a new peace treaty between Egypt and Hatti. It can be seen today in Egyptian hieroglyphics on the walls of a temple at Karnak and in Akkadian on a copy of the treaty discovered at Hattusa. Often described as the world's first international peace treaty, it contains all the usual pieties about eternal peace and brotherly love, sworn in the name of the sun god of Egypt and the storm god of the Hittites. Buried in there are more practical measures that a modern diplomat would recognize as the meat of any treaty worth the clay it is printed on: mutual military support in the event of an attack by a third party, for example, and the capture and rendition of 'suspects' who have fled from one kingdom to another.

The conquest of the Upper Sea, as the Mediterranean was known to the Mesopotamians, opened the lands of the West to their influence and a further opening up of the Bronze Age world. By the middle of the third millennium BC, merchant ships from northern Syria and the Levant were regularly travelling across the 'wine-dark' sea to Cyprus, Canaan, Egypt, Anatolia and Greece. At the centre of operations were the Phoenician cities in what is now Lebanon and the Syrian city of Ugarit, which rapidly came to be the Venice of the ancient Near East, an open port where merchants from an array of different places lived and traded with one another. Skilled artisans (particularly metal workers and potters) as well as diplomats moved between the different states that made up this Bronze Age world that now stretched from Mesopotamia in the east to Greece in the west.

Perhaps the best-preserved example of this cosmopolitan Bronze Age world is found on the island of Crete. Minoan Crete dominated the Aegean region from about 2000 to 1400 BC. By the nineteenth century BC, Crete possessed all the trappings of statehood, including a series of monumental palaces which acted as the centres for small-scale political units ruled by local royalty. Within the palaces provision was made for the extensive storage of produce and the manufacture of luxury goods, often made from materials imported from afar. Extensive records were kept, written in the Linear A script, a writing system that has still to be deciphered.

Minoan Crete's significance now lies in its status as the home of the first civilization in the western Mediterranean, a complex culture to match those of the Near East. Many early scholars (Minoan remains were first uncovered by archaeologists in the 1920s) were keen to see Minoan Crete as a rather self-contained, European civilization, denying a strong Near Eastern influence on its

LEFT
Statue of Ebih-il, Superintendant of Mari (*c.* 2400 BC). Ebih-il holds his hands clasped together against his chest in the traditional posture of Sumerians in prayer. A high-quality work of art – the inlaid lapis lazuli gives the eyes of the statue a particularly life-like intensity.

development. The existence of a Minoan culture promised to lay to rest doubts that Graeco-Roman civilization, which Europe's great imperial powers had so self-consciously modelled themselves on, had its origins in the decadent Orient. But this failed to explain why such an advanced civilization should suddenly appear on this eastern Mediterranean island. In fact, the one obvious factor in Minoan Crete's development was its position on important sea routes to Egypt and the Levant, which suggests that Crete was deeply influenced by the Near East. The Mesopotamian states, in particular, had long been interested in the Mediterranean region and the Minoans were heavily involved in trade in the eastern Mediterranean and the Aegean. Goods from Egypt and the Near East have frequently been found in Minoan tombs and in the ruins of their palaces. Large amounts of mass-produced Minoan pottery found its way to destinations as far away as Syria, Lebanon and Egypt. The more naturalistic style of Minoan art had a marked influence on its Egyptian, Syrian and Greek counterparts. Likewise, many of the most common motifs found in Minoan art are borrowed from the Near East.

Minoan Crete was clearly an important coordinate in the Bronze Age trade network. Yet, although these societies clearly influenced each other, the differences that continued to exist between them were often quite marked. Unusually, women held a far more prominent position in Minoan culture than they did in other Bronze Age societies, with female priests and queens portrayed on the palace frescoes as often as their male counterparts. It also appeared that, unlike in the violent Near East, warfare played a far lesser role in Minoan Crete, a conclusion drawn from the conspicuous lack of battle scenes in their artwork. Their palaces and towns appear to have had no fortifications and were not even built in defensible positions for a very long period of time. It appears that the Minoan influence on the Aegean region was the result of trade rather than conquest.

As a figure at the centre of this complex web of diplomacy, marriage, gift-giving and trade, there are few more attractive than Zimri-Lim, who for twenty years ruled as king of Mari, beginning some time around 1779 BC. Mari occupied a strategic position about halfway between the cities of Mesopotamia and the ports of the Mediterranean. The city was close to the river Euphrates, and a canal connecting it to the river was dug through the centre, creating an inland port of great economic value. For centuries Mari had been ruled by a succession of governors, whose wise, calm, Buddha-like faces make statues from the city instantly recognizable. Some time around 2000 BC, with the arrival of the Amorites, the ruling classes changed; the *shakkanakku* – the generals – took over. And after them came the kings of whom Zimri-Lim was both the most celebrated and the most unfortunate. As a young man he had had to fight for his throne following a period of exile, and ultimately he would lose it again, betrayed by his closest ally.

But history has treated him more kindly because, in the traces that he has left, we have, for the first time, the outlines of a recognizable personality. There is something endearing about Zimri-Lim. His urbanity and his enthusiasms set him apart from the rather faceless kings whom he competed against or cooperated with. From all that we know about him, it seems that Zimri-Lim was the most 'civilized' ruler in this first period of civilization. He built himself a huge, imposing palace, covering an area of 25,000 square metres. The throne room was designed like a temple; its walls were covered with frescoes painted by craftsmen imported from Minoan Crete, depicting the king as warrior, hunter and builder. The palace was a legend in its own lifetime, with extraordinary and original details, such as the statue with a channel running from the base up to a bowl held by a horned goddess. The statue was connected to a cistern placed somewhere above it, and the water, seeking its lowest level, would have magically flowed from the goddess's bowl: imagine that, a statue with cold running water! The palace even had its own ice-house so that the king's honey-sweetened wine could be served cold. No wonder Zimri-Lim's neighbouring kings were impressed.

RIGHT
The Royal Palace, Mari, Syria.

The palace archives tell the usual story of diplomacy, trade and politics, but there are also revealing personal details. Zimri-Lim was evidently something of a pleasure seeker, and could get impatient when he felt his needs were not being catered to. For example, he wrote a letter to one of his governors complaining about the quality of the truffles he had sent him. And when his sister, Liqtum, married a Syrian king he sent her a letter saying: 'In the land where you dwell there are many ostriches; why have you sent me no ostriches?' Zimri-Lim did not fill his time only with kingly indulgences. He had an army, and he used it in the great game of kings. He allied himself with Hammurabi, the king of Babylon, and together they successfully went to war against the neighbouring kingdoms of Elam and Larsa.

But Zimri-Lim fell foul of Hammurabi, and it would lead to the destruction of all that he had worked so hard to achieve. Hammurabi turned on his former ally over bitumen, a dark, sticky, tar-like substance, which, when found naturally, indicates that somewhere beneath there is probably oil. Even in the days long before the internal combustion engine, bitumen was useful stuff, used to waterproof boats and buildings. According to one fragmentary text from this period, Hammurabi asked Zimri-Lim to send him a consignment of bitumen but Zimri-Lim refused. So, in 1757 BC, Hammurabi marched on Mari

and destroyed it, and with it Zimri-Lim's beloved palace. It could be said that Zimri-Lim was the loser in the first oil war.

About ten years before Hammurabi destroyed Mari, Zimri-Lim made a journey from his capital city to the coast of the Mediterranean, a round trip of more than 1,500 kilometres by river and land. He took with him his family, his court officials, his cooks, his physicians and musicians, and his army; some 4,000 people put in motion by the whim of a great king. He visited fellow kings and royal in-laws, distributing and receiving gifts as he went. He even found time to arrange a divorce for one his daughters whose marriage to a neighbouring king had not worked out. His final destination was Ugarit, the important port-city on the Mediterranean coast. This grand tour took around five months to complete. It must have been hugely complex, expensive and disruptive, but there was no obvious reason for it, except curiosity. I think that Zimri-Lim, the king of land-locked Mari, just wanted to see the sea. Zimri-Lim knew very well that Mari was only a small part of a much bigger world, a world connected by trade, diplomacy, marriages and, when the occasion demanded, war. But it was also connected by the waters of the Mediterranean. Trade ships plied these coasts, spinning the web of commerce to places far distant from Mari and the first cities of Mesopotamia.

About twenty-five years ago, just off the coast of south-west Turkey, archaeologists made an extraordinary discovery: a shipwreck dating from the end of the fourteenth century BC, about 3,300 years ago, the high-water mark of the Bronze Age. In the quarter of a century since the discovery of the Uluburun wreck, archaeologists have recovered more than seventeen tonnes of artefacts from the sea floor, around 15,000 items all told; pieced together, they offer a detailed snapshot of Bronze Age civilization and its surprising interconnections.

What this nameless wreck tells us is that this was a joined-up world. Items have been found that came from as far afield as Syria, Greece, Cyprus, Egypt, Nubia, the Balkans, Iraq, Italy, central Asia and the Baltic. An amazing ten tonnes of copper from Cyprus were recovered, in the form of 'oxhide' ingots, the standard shape and weight used for trading this vital raw ingredient throughout the eastern Mediterranean. Mixed with tin, copper was used to make the metal alloy that gave the Bronze Age its name. But the cargo is just the start. Thanks to other items that have been recovered and some brilliant detective work by the archaeologists, it is possible to say, with a fair degree of certainty, where the ship came from. The clues start with the distinctive stone weight anchors which suggest that the ship's home port was Tel Abu Hawan, near Haifa in present-day Israel. The way the cargo was arranged on board also suggests that it was loaded as a single consignment, so Abu Hawan presumably operated as a kind of distribution centre for goods that had been gathered in, by sea and land, from all corners of the ancient world. Packed with its diverse cargo, the ship would have set off, navigating from headland to headland, north and then west from the Levantine coast to the underbelly of Turkey.

Personal effects found at the wreck site have provided further clues about the ship: who was on board, and where they were going. A sword and dagger in the Canaanite style probably belonged to the ship's captain and owner. Animal-shaped weights and writing boards belonged to merchants. Fishing nets, lines and hooks belonged to the crew, tools to allow them to supplement their dull shipboard diet. The archaeologists also found items from much further afield, which tells us that the ship was carrying passengers, and, judging from the style of their personal items, they were Greeks from the kingdom of Mycenae. There seem to have been at least two Mycenaeans on board, and a third figure from northern Greece, possibly some kind of mercenary bodyguard. The quality of the Mycenaeans' possessions suggests that these were no ordinary merchants. They were perhaps high-ranking officials or ambassadors accompanying the cargo on its journey from Tel Abu Hawan to Mycenae, part of the elaborate system of gift exchange that Bronze Age rulers of the eastern Mediterranean used to acknowledge each other's existence and status, a form of diplomacy expressed in material terms.

What the Uluburun wreck makes clear is that out there, on the fringes of the Bronze Age world, there were new kingdoms and rulers important enough to be included in the diplomatic exchanges that had gone back and forth for centuries between the more well-established players in Mesopotamia, Egypt and the Near East. It seems that civilization had finally reached the West. The lessons of the now venerable first cities were being learned and applied by people and cultures still new to the idea of civilization. Through the medium of these maritime trading routes, the idea of civilization had spread. In the next chapter we will see how these seagoing trade links kept civilization alive through a period of darkness, warfare and cultural regression.

2

THE END OF THE BRONZE AGE
AND ITS AFTERMATH

I

BRONZE AGE SYSTEMS FAILURE: CATASTROPHE AND THE SEA PEOPLES

In the twelfth century BC, the Bronze Age cities of the Near East, the eastern Mediterranean and the Aegean suffered a series of disasters on an almost unimaginable scale. In Anatolia the mighty Hittite Empire and, in Greece, the Mycenaean kingdoms were toppled. Many of the cities of Syria and the Levant were reduced to rubble. Smaller settlements in more remote locations simply disappeared. The causes of the great Bronze Age collapse and the story of the new worlds that grew up in its wake will be the subject of this chapter. It is a sobering reminder of the fragility of civilization, but also of its tenacity. For in the new age of iron that followed this ancient Dark Age, civilization would re-emerge, tempered in the flames of conflict, tougher and more resilient than ever before.

One of the city civilizations lost in the tsunami of catastrophes was Ugarit. Located in what is now Syria, on the south-eastern Mediterranean coast, Ugarit had been a thriving, cosmopolitan Bronze Age port-city from about 1450 BC. It had palaces, temples, warehouses and factories, markets and shops, streets and houses and a population of tens of thousands. Just over 3,000 years ago, sometime in the 1190s BC, it was destroyed, never to be rebuilt.

Clues about the destruction of Ugarit and the collapse of the other great civilizations of the high Bronze Age have been found in letters, written on clay tablets, which were found in the House of the Ovens at Ugarit. The tablets were discovered in the ovens, suggesting either that they were being fired for preservation or perhaps that they just fell into the ovens from the room above when the building collapsed. Whatever the reason for their survival, 'Letters from the Oven', as they are known, is a suitable title for some of the ancient world's most dramatic texts. The letters were mainly to and from Ammurapi, who has gone down in history as 'the last king of Ugarit'. They provide us with vivid, fragmentary snapshots of the destruction that was unleashed by a mysterious enemy who appeared from the sea. One fragment comes in a letter from the Hittite King Suppiluliuma to Ammurapi:

The enemy advances against us and there is no number ... Our number is ... Whatever is available, look for it and send it to me.

This is from the leader of one of the most powerful kingdoms in the region; you do not have to read between the lines to sense the panic and desperation in his plea.

Another letter, from Ammurapi to his father-in-law, the king of Alasiya (now the island of Cyprus), suggests that Ugarit responded to the pleas of Suppiluliuma and sent 'whatever is available', with disastrous results:

My father, behold, the enemy's ships came; my cities were burned, and they did evil things in my country. Does not my father know that all my troops and chariots(?) are in the Hittite country ... Thus, the country is abandoned. May my father know it: the seven ships of the enemy that came here inflicted much damage upon us.

That such chaos was unleashed by just seven ships goes to show how vulnerable these Bronze Age cities were to disasters, whether natural or man-made. King Ammurapi also, rather touchingly, takes time to reassure his mother: 'And thou my mother be not afraid and do not put worries into thy heart,' which is rather optimistic given how dire circumstances obviously were. A letter to someone called Zrdn pulls no punches:

Our food on the threshing floor is burned and also the vineyards are destroyed. Our city is destroyed and may you know it.

That was it for Ugarit, game over: a civilization in ruins. Judging by the letters from the House of the Ovens, they never really knew what had hit them.

Elsewhere, others had a clearer sense of who was behind their attacks. At Medinet Habu, near Luxor in Egypt, stands the mortuary temple of Ramesses III. Of all such temples from ancient Egypt, this is one of the most intact. The temple precinct is huge (about 200 by 300 metres) and the whole complex has nearly 7,500 square metres of decorated walls. Amongst these decorative images is an illustration of what happened after the ships that had wiped Ugarit off the map headed south to the Nile Delta. King Ramesses is there, gigantic, with his bow drawn, while the warships of the invaders cluster like dead leaves around his feet: it is a triumphant, propagandistic image of total annihilation in typical

Egyptian style but the long-term consequences of the events depicted here were rather more complicated. The Egyptians had been troubled by sea-borne raiders in the past, but in the eighth year of Ramesses' reign – some time around 1180 BC – they appeared in greater numbers than ever before. And there was something else that was new and troubling. The invaders had brought women and children with them, suggesting that this was not just another hit-and-run raid: these were whole populations on the move, displaced perhaps from their own lands in the west, and forced to fight for new and safer territories to settle in.

But who exactly *were* the audacious enemy who had destroyed Ugarit and then dared to challenge the might of Egypt? According to Egyptian accounts these were the Sea Peoples, and they were named as the Peleset, Tjeker, Shekelesh, Denyen, Habiru and Weshesh. Scholars have spilt much ink trying to identify these places, but the consensus favours mainland Italy, Sardinia, Sicily and the islands of the Aegean – the fringes of the civilized world, in other words, but intimately connected to it by the highway of the sea. It is generally thought that the Sea Peoples were not some organized band or homogeneous ethnic group but the flotsam and jetsam of a rapidly disintegrating world: pastoralists, nomads, landless peasants and disbanded mercenaries who had no stake in the narrow world of the Bronze Age palace. No one knows for sure what might have caused the mass migration of populations in this period, why these people were so determinedly on the move. Explanations have ranged from a natural disaster to a cascade of mass tribal movements that began as far away as China and spread west in a cataclysmic domino effect.

Whatever the ultimate cause, for the Egyptians it was a real and present danger: 'The foreign nations plotted together in their lands,' says one Egyptian account. 'None could stand before their arms. They laid their hands upon the land as far as the circuit of the earth, their hearts confident and trusting: "Our plans will succeed!"'

According to the version of events recorded at Medinet Habu, the armies of Ramesses routed the invaders, but for much of the rest of the civilized world the defeat of these desperately fierce, or fiercely desperate, people came too late. Over a period of some five decades, from 1200 to 1150 BC, centres of Bronze Age culture, from mainland Greece to the Near East, were snuffed out one by one. In the West: Pylos, Mycenae, Asine, Iria, Thebes, Gla, Iolkos, Midea, Tiryns and Sparta; in the East: Ugarit, Hattusa, Tarsus, Carchemish, Alalah, Qatna, Qadesh, Hazor, Lachish – one by one their names were added to the roll-call of destruction, some never to recover. The rapidity of the disaster is clear from the end of Kokkinokremos, a modest settlement on the island of Cyprus. It was abandoned so suddenly that the local bronze smith hid his copper supply and tools in a courtyard pit. Silver ingots were concealed between two stones of a bench whilst jewellery and gold sheet were placed in another pit. Their owners evidently thought they would be able to come back and reclaim them; it is surely ominous that they did not. Taken together, these fragmentary pieces of evidence from a dying world show that there was not one great invasion or event that brought the Bronze Age states crashing down, even if the final destruction of many of these city-civilizations seems to have happened with extraordinarily sudden drama.

This calamity occurred over such a relatively short time span and was so widespread that for many years archaeologists thought that it must have been the result of some cataclysmic natural disaster. It is now thought that a constellation of causes combined over a period of time to bring about the breakdown of political, economic and social order. Natural disaster may have had a place: there is evidence of a major volcanic eruption around 1000 BC, and of earthquakes in this region. There is also evidence of drought. Again and again, Assyrian letters and texts dating from the eleventh and early tenth centuries BC complain about 'scanty' rains and failures of harvest, and an Assyrian chronicle talks about 'a famine so severe' that people turned to cannibalism. Resources became so scarce, records tell of offerings to the gods being cancelled. Even in Egypt, there was famine and disorder, with tomb robbery breaking out. What seems clear is that the redistributive economies of the palace and temple fell apart as harvests failed and carefully hoarded surpluses were denuded, leaving the elites weakened and their subjects rebellious. The complex web of relationships and obligations which underwrote the Bronze Age city began to break down, making them far more vulnerable to the migratory raids of the Sea Peoples.

The priestly and military elites of the Bronze Age kingdoms ultimately provided their monarch with too shallow a power base to overcome any serious challenges. Social problems were exacerbated by a too rigidly centralized and controlled economy, which simply did not allow enough wealth to trickle down to the poorer classes. One only has to read a few of the Bronze Age tablets to realize how ponderous and stultifying the palace bureaucracy was: this was Bronze Age big brother. Such a world could survive and even flourish until it came under serious external pressure. Once raiders had made agriculture difficult and maritime trade impossible, the end for many Bronze Age palace-temple societies was nigh. The collapse of the Bronze Age was caused by a fatal combination of factors: this was a classic case of systems collapse on an epic scale.

Some of the more powerful states, such as Egypt, Assyria and Babylon, would survive, though greatly weakened. These civilizations proved to be big enough

to absorb the shocks from external threats and also to insulate themselves from internal discontents by operating a marginally more generous redistributive system. With more to lose, citizens of these states stuck with the devil they knew. This was something that the quasi-feudal Mycenaean society – the first major foothold of civilization on mainland Europe – did not manage to achieve, and it paid a heavy price.

Mycenaean civilization flourished in southern Greece between about 1600 and 1100 BC. It is thought that the Mycenaean region was first settled by about 2000 BC by farmers and herders, speaking an Indo-European language that is considered the common ancestor of all European languages. Mycenaean Greece developed under the influence of Minoan civilization, and eventually superseded it; the Mycenaeans finally conquered Crete by around 1450 BC, Minoan Crete having possibly been weakened by the devastating eruption of the volcanic island of Thera (Santorini). Mycenaean Greece developed as a patchwork of states each centred on heavily fortified citadel-palaces: Athens, Thebes and Pylos are all significant Mycenaean archaeological sites, along with Mycenae itself, about a hundred kilometres south-west of Athens. Unlike in Minoan Crete, there were no cities or even towns in the Mycenaean world: most of the population lived either in small settlements based around the palace or in scattered villages. The temples, key institutions in the Near East, carried little influence in Mycenaean Greece. There is also little sign of one central political authority;

none of the Mycenaean palatial centres appears to have been powerful enough to be dominant over all the others. The reasons for these differences are probably connected to the fact that only some of the rudiments of complex statehood that had been perfected in the Near East and Egypt reached Mycenae. The most striking difference of all, however, was the central role played by war within Mycenaean elite culture.

Mycenaean Greece was the source of later Hellenic legends about the founding of Greek civilization. Even if Homer's tales of Agamemnon, Menelaus and their great siege of Troy do not represent cast-iron historical fact they do at least seem to contain vague memories of real world events and civilizations that had once existed. Many of the gods which the Mycenaeans worshipped would become important members of the Greek divine pantheon. The Mycenaean language, which was written with the Linear B script, was an early precursor to ancient Greek. Mycenaean Greece was split into a patchwork of kingdoms ruled over by warrior kings not unlike the heroes described by Homer. The walls of

their citadels were so thick that the Greeks of the Classical Age believed that they could only have been built by the Cyclopes, the race of one-eyed giants. Each palace resembled a heavily fortified stockade, with deep wells bored into the ground to ensure fresh water during a siege. The great chiefs were buried in circular subterranean burial chambers, often with richly ornamented swords and other weapons. The frescoes with which their palaces were decorated showed a heroic warrior lifestyle of feasting, hunting and, most popular of all, war.

Mycenae was evidently heavily imbued with a warrior culture very similar to the one described by Homer. This was further backed up by evidence from the precious Linear B tablets which allude to an almost feudal society with the *Wanax* (king) at its head, assisted by an elite warrior caste, the *heqetai*. At the bottom of this socio-economic pyramid were the *doeroi*, a class of serfs who performed all the agricultural labour. As in the states of the Near East and Crete, the agricultural surplus produced by the *doeroi* was used to feed the king and his warriors as well as the professional class of priests and local administrative officials. The Linear B tablets highlight the economic stranglehold that the Mycenaean palaces held over their territories. They dominated trade, manufacturing and agriculture. The king and his nobles were the main landowners, and the palace employed large numbers of women and children in the manufacture of textiles.

The first suggestion that all was not well for the Mycenaean world comes in the thirteenth century BC with evidence for the building of new defensive

LEFT
Coiled snake made of fired clay (c. 1250–1180 BC). Found in the subterranean 'House of the Idols', which was part of the temple located on the citadel of Mycenae, these serpents were votive offerings. They might represent another link with Minoan Crete, where a snake goddess was worshipped.

fortifications and wells, suggesting increased concern about the possibility of siege. From roughly the same period, Linear B tablets recovered from the Mycenaean palace at Pylos in the Peloponnese record the existence of a new military office, the 'Watchers by the Sea', suggesting that the Sea Peoples were already making their presence felt on the western fringes of the civilized world. This was followed by a catastrophic era of around twenty years at the end of the thirteenth and beginning of the twelfth centuries BC, when all of the Mycenaean palaces were burnt to the ground, as were 90 per cent of the other known settlements. Most were never rebuilt. In short, Mycenaean Greece suffered a dramatic and sudden depopulation. The appearance of the Sea Peoples, armed with new, more cheaply available weapons made from iron, is thought to be behind this decline.

Iron predates what we call the Iron Age by millennia. But it had been a rare and costly material, more precious than bronze. The revolutionary change came from the discovery and spread of the technique of carburization of iron to make steel, and the discovery of quenching to temper the steel; really, it should be called the Steel Age. These advances in steel working first appeared around *c.* 1200 BC in the Hittite kingdoms. It is thought that the chaos and flux brought about by the subsequent destruction of the Hittite Empire by the Sea Peoples caused the dissemination of steel-working. Iron ore was more widely available than the copper and tin needed to make bronze, so the production of iron was less easily monopolized, controlled and centralized by the palace-temple elites. The weapons were also harder-edged, tougher, the perfect material for this new tougher, harder-edged world. Iron technology took weapons out of the hands of the aristocratic warrior class; the age of iron democratized weaponry with potentially revolutionary consequences. In the Mycenaean kingdoms, internal problems made it vulnerable to the repercussions of the spread of iron weaponry: an impoverished and dispossessed serf class was, it seems, ready to turn on its warrior elite when they were already vulnerable from outside attack. By the late twelfth century BC, Greece had been sent back to year zero. The first Greece was dead, and it would be a very long time before it was brought back to life.

The catastrophe of the Sea Peoples is one of those dramatic break points in our story, as when the radio goes off air. In this first Dark Age, writing disappeared from large areas and, with it, history itself. Agricultural output collapsed, populations dwindled, cities were abandoned, towns became villages. The connections between people withered and died, the world shrank. Artefacts became crude and clumsy as craftsmanship and culture took second place to survival, and that precious, complex, vulnerable organism called civilization seemed to teeter on the edge. But the Bronze Age collapse was not fatal for all; civilization was too good an idea, too useful to humankind, to be allowed to disappear, and some civilizations did manage to cling on during this first Dark Age, prospering as they grabbed the opportunities presented by the collapse of the old order. But the second time around the story of civilization will unfold in a different world – a harsher world, perhaps, as befits this new age: the age of iron.

II

THE RISE OF THE MIDDLEMAN: THE PHOENICIANS

The collapse of the Bronze Age kingdoms was like the disappearance of the dinosaurs: with the big beasts out of the running, and in some cases completely extinct, a variety of smaller, more adaptable mammal kingdoms got their moment in the sun. But who were they, the survivors of a catastrophe that had taken out so many stronger contenders? Among the inheritors were the people known to history, though not to themselves, as the Phoenicians. It was on their shoulders that the achievements of Bronze Age civilization would be carried forward into the new age of iron.

For a people who do not usually loom large in the histories of the ancient world, the list of Phoenician achievements is impressive. They pioneered ship-building and navigation techniques, the exploration and colonization of the central and western Mediterranean; all of this was crucial for the preservation and advance of civilization following the Bronze Age collapse. But their most enduring achievement was a technology that transformed the ancient world: the alphabet.

The oldest surviving example of an alphabet can be found on an inscription that runs round the top of the sarcophagus of Ahiram, the Phoenician king of Byblos some time around 1100 BC. Ominously enough it is a curse against anyone who dares to disturb the tomb, but the development of an alphabet by the Phoenicians was a blessing that we are still benefiting from today. The written alphabet was probably not a purely Phoenician invention; it seems most likely to have developed in Mesopotamia around the fifteenth century BC. But it was the Phoenicians who adapted the letters to make it simpler to use and did the most to disseminate it across the eastern Mediterranean. Earlier writing systems, such as Egyptian hieroglyphics or Akkadian cunei-form, were, broadly speaking, representational. This meant that they consisted of an array of symbols, sometimes hundreds of them, which stood for the things described. They were a kind of bureaucratic code and the skills required were usually restricted to a class of trained specialists known as scribes. An alphabet works differently; it is more like a speech-recording device. Each letter indicates the sound of a spoken word, or part of it, so if you can pronounce the alphabet correctly you can sound out a word even if you do not know what it means (this is how children read to learn phonetically). Quicker and

easier to use, the alphabet made literacy more widespread, and it also allowed literature to become more expressive and inventive, echoing the music and rhythms of speech.

The alphabet may be their most enduring legacy, but the Phoenicians were renowned among their contemporaries for their mastery of the sea. It was a relationship born of both natural affinity and geographical necessity. The port-cities of the Phoenicians were located where the modern nation of Lebanon is now. They perched on the edge of the sea, their hinterlands hemmed in by steep, cedar-covered mountain ranges, with little more than a narrow coastal strip of viable farmland to feed the local population. In fact, some Phoenician cities were barely connected to the land at all. The most famous of these states, Tyre, was actually an island just off the mainland. Surrounded by reefs on two sides, the city was well protected from attacks by land or sea. Her topographical position made the priorities of her citizens clear. Turning her back on the land, Tyre embraced the sea. There were twin harbours, one natural, the other hewn out of the rock, so that ships could always catch the necessary winds and tides to start their journeys promptly.

The Phoenicians were the first to use the Pole Star for navigation, which allowed them to reduce travel times by sailing on the open seas and by night; the star came to be known as the Phoiniké in recognition of this advance. The Phoenicians were no less revolutionary in their approach to ship-building: they developed the keel, which gave their boats much needed stability, and they were the first to coat the wooden planks of hulls with bitumen tar so that they remained watertight. Phoenician merchant ships were the envy of the world. They were called *gauloi* ('bathtubs') by the Greeks because of their huge bulbous hulls that could store tonnes of goods. With their high-walled hulls, big, rounded bows and bitumen-sealed planks, these ships were designed to take the maximum amount of cargo through the worst that the Mediterranean could throw at them. Despite their size, the ships were deceptively nimble, with a single huge square sail to catch the wind and teams of oarsmen to manoeuvre them swiftly into the right direction. It has been calculated that in good conditions they could cover up to 150 kilometres a day.

With their *gauloi* and their advanced navigations skills, the Phoenicians, from the twelfth century BC onwards, began to stitch together a web of trade that would ultimately link Asia Minor, Cyprus, Armenia, the Ionian islands, Rhodes, Syria, Judah, Israel, Arabia and the Near East. But what were they carrying in those bathtub boats? One of the region's most sought-after resources was timber from the legendary 'cedars of Lebanon'. These days the mountains of Lebanon have been more or less cleared of these spectacular trees, but back then they were a plentiful and vital supply of the tall, strong, straight, sweet-smelling timber ideal for building ships and temples. The increasing confidence and authority of the Phoenicians, and the relative decline of Egypt following the Bronze Age collapse, is reflected in the story of Wenamen, a high temple official from Thebes in Egypt who came to Byblos sometime around 1075 BC. 'The Report of Wenamen' purports to be a first-person account of his mission to acquire some of the legendary cedars of Lebanon from the Phoenician middle-men. It is a sobering tale of what happens when your international credit rating falls through the floor.

In the Bronze Age Byblos had been a subservient vassal kingdom of Egypt. Once, an Egyptian pharaoh had only to snap his royal fingers for a whole forest of cedars to be dispatched south. But, as Wenamen discovered, by the eleventh century BC, things had changed. According to his rather woeful account, his journey to Byblos had not been easy: he was robbed on the way and then he was made to hang about in the harbour at Byblos for twenty-nine days before he finally secured a grudging interview with Zakar-baal, the prince of the city. 'What your father did and what the father of your father did, you too will do,' says Wenamen grandly. To which the prince of Byblos replies: 'True, they did it, and if you pay me for doing it I will do it too. I am not your servant, and I am not the servant of him who sent you either.' So there it was: the relationship between Byblos and Egypt was now strictly business, cash on delivery. It is a powerful indication of how Egypt's power was in decline, after two centuries

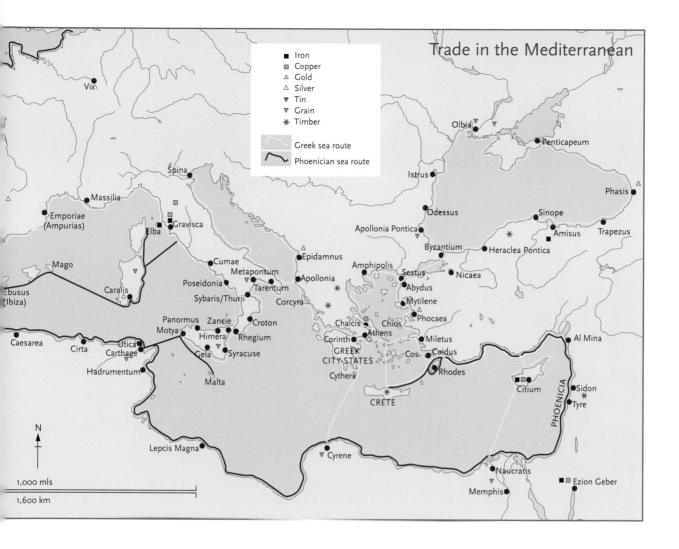

Trade in the Mediterranean

Legend:
- ■ Iron
- ▫ Copper
- △ Gold
- △ Silver
- ▽ Tin
- ▽ Grain
- ✳ Timber
- ⌇ Greek sea route
- ⌇ Phoenician sea route

Vix
Massilia
Emporiae (Ampurias)
Elba
Graviska
Spina
Mago
Caralis
Ebusus (Ibiza)
Caesarea
Cirta
Utica
Carthage
Hadrumentum
Motya
Panormus
Himera
Gela
Zancle
Rhegium
Syracuse
Malta
Cumae
Metapontum
Poseidonia
Tarentum
Sybaris/Thurii
Croton
Corcyra
Epidamnus
Apollonia
Lepcis Magna
Cyrene
Chalcis
Corinth
GREEK CITY-STATES
Cythera
CRETE
Amphipolis
Sestus
Abydus
Mytilene
Phocaea
Chios
Athens
Cos
Miletus
Cnidus
Rhodes
Olbia
Penticapeum
Istrus
Odessus
Apollonia Pontica
Byzantium
Heraclea Pontica
Nicaea
Sinope
Amisus
Trapezus
Phasis
Al Mina
Citium
Sidon
Tyre
PHOENICIA
Naucratis
Memphis
Ezion Geber

N

1,000 mls
1,600 km

of darkness and confusion wrought by the Sea Peoples and the subsequent famine and unrest. Even when Egypt stabilized, around 1100 BC, it was clear that its glory days were over: never again would a king of Byblos have to grovel before an Egyptian pharaoh.

For the trading cities of the Mediterranean coast, the Bronze Age collapse acted like the 'Big Bang' – it was a case of financial deregulation on a regional scale. Liberated from the control of kings in palaces, the traders in coastal cities like Byblos quickly organized themselves into 'firms' based around the networks of their extended families. When the kings returned, their control over trade was no longer absolute. They cooperated with the merchant princes rather than commanding them, acting as banks and underwriting their ventures. For their part, the merchants sat on advisory councils, shaping the policies of the cities,

OVERLEAF
Temple of Obelisks, Byblos, probably built in honour of the Lady of Byblos, c .1600 BC.

always with the bottom line in mind. It was an early demonstration of the dynamic power of free enterprise and market forces.

As well as cedar, the Phoenicians traded luxury goods such as jewellery, fine wines, olive oil, incense, ornately carved furniture and delicately crafted ivories. These goods would be traded for badly needed raw materials such as corn, precious stones and metals, and also slaves. The slaves would then be sold on; the raw materials would be consumed, sold on or processed into more luxury goods that could be traded. The Phoenicians also cornered the market in the production of one of the ancient world's most valued commodities – a powerful dye celebrated for its dense colour, the colour of congealed blood according to the Roman author Pliny. It was known simply as 'purple'. The dye was produced from murex, a sea mollusc, and it was extracted in a process that was notoriously difficult and foul-smelling. It is from this dye that the name Phoenicians comes: the Greeks called them after their word for purple, *phoinix*, hence the Phoenicians, the 'Purple People'.

Of all the Phoenician trading cities, Tyre was to become the most successful. If you were to travel there by sea 3,000 years ago, you would be able to tell that it was a Phoenician city you were approaching. The first clue would be geographical: a spit of land sticking out into the sea or perhaps, as in the case of Tyre, a sizeable inshore island joined to the land by a man-made causeway. These were the kind of sites the Phoenicians chose for their cities – amphibious places, half water, half land. Get in closer and you would see a double harbour which allowed ships to make it safely into port whatever direction the wind was blowing from. And if a harbour was not naturally occurring, the Phoenicians would build one. In the harbour, at anchor and docked for loading and unloading, would be the 'bathtubs' – those bluff-bowed Phoenician ships with their high-walled hulls designed to swallow enormous loads and carry them safely through the vicious chop and swell of these treacherous waters. Finally, just as you were docking, the wind would change direction and there would be the unmistakable, foul stench of the purple dye-works on the outskirts of the city, the source of so much portable and exportable wealth.

Like Byblos and Sidon, Tyre had grown fat on trade, exporting cedars and purple and importing riches from all around. In fact, Tyre had grown so fat that around 1000 BC it was becoming an important power in the region, to its neighbours the object of some fear and a lot of envy. In the Jewish bible, the prophet Ezekiel paints a vivid picture of Tyre in its glory days. In a long and highly detailed passage he names twenty or so cities in the region and the imports brought to Tyre from each: there is silver, iron, tin and lead from Tarshish, ivory, ebony and saddlecloths from Dedan (present day Saudi Arabia), spices, precious stones and gold from Sheba, wine and wool from Damascus; the list goes on and on.

> Tyre, you used to say, I am a ship perfect in beauty.
> Your frontiers are far out to sea:
> Those who built you
> Made you perfect in beauty . . .
> When you unloaded your goods
> To satisfy so many peoples
> You enriched the kings of the earth
> With your excess of wealth and goods.

Isaiah went further, accusing Tyre of 'playing the whore to all the kingdoms of the world', but the only profits the merchant-princes of Tyre were interested in were the ones you could add up at the end of the financial year.

The growth of Tyre was relatively sudden. It happened under the guidance
of father and son, Abi-baal and Hiram. King Hiram, who reigned from 980 to
947 BC, built Tyre's second, artificial, harbour, called 'The Egyptian', an acknow-
ledgement that the land of the pharaohs was still an important market that
could not be ignored. But Hiram was also aware of new markets opening up:
if the Hebrew Bible is to be taken as a reliable historical document, he sealed
a deal with King Solomon, the king of the Jews, sending materials and craftsmen to help build the first temple in Jerusalem in exchange for silver, wheat and
olive oil. It is also reported that Tyrian sailors manned Solomon's ships for an
expedition to Ophir in the Persian Gulf. Archaeological evidence, meanwhile,
points to a huge copper- and iron-smelting operation at Ezion Geber on the Gulf
of Aqabba, said to be the most advanced in the ancient world and manned by
craftsmen from Tyre.

Hiram of Tyre was also a religious innovator, putting in place new spiritual
structures as well as political and commercial ones. The Phoenician religion
was polytheistic like practically all the religions of the region. They had a high
god called El, and a multi-faceted, multi-purpose god called Baal – the Lord
– who provided a more day-to-day point of religious contact for the people.

Alongside El and Baal was an array of other gods and goddesses with powers and attributes equivalent to the full range of human experience and imagination. Hiram decided to inject a new god into this already elaborate system; a ticklish business, but one that could pay political dividends.

Introducing a new god is a good move for rulers who feel they need to adjust the balance of power between the temple, run by the priests, and the palace, run by them. As we have seen, from the time of the first cities, temples had often become powerful economic and political counterweights to the king. The priests commanded some of the most enduring and conservative loyalties of the citizens, and they could mobilize them if they felt their position was being threatened. So it took a certain amount of political courage and self-confidence for Hiram to start meddling with these matters. The relationship between secular and religious power, faith and politics, is labyrinthine and often treacherous but Hiram of Tyre seems to have negotiated the pitfalls with great skill. By building new temples and underwriting elaborate new religious ceremonies, a new god duly emerged as the ruler of the divine pantheon in Tyre. He was called Melqart, which means 'king of the city'. At the great annual Melqart feast, held every spring, all foreigners were obliged to leave Tyre, before a giant effigy of the god was launched on to the sea and set on fire, and the king and his chief wife, playing the part of Melqart and his consort Astarte, were ritually married. The political message was clear and simple: what is good for Melqart is good for Tyre, and also good for the ruler of Tyre. Gods, of course, live longer than men, even if they do not always live up to their billing as immortal. Melqart certainly outlived Hiram: distant colonies of Tyre were still sending 10 per cent of their wealth as tribute to the Melqart temple in Tyre centuries after the 'King of the City' first made his divine debut.

The Phoenicians were not the only ones to benefit from the elbow-room created by the collapse of the great Bronze Age kingdoms. Travel inland from the thriving port-cities of the coast and you would enter the land of one of the most intriguing peoples in the ancient world: the Jews, whose amazing spiritual and political story is told in one of the world's greatest literary monuments, the Hebrew Bible. For some, the Bible is not just a divinely inspired text, it is a historically reliable account of what actually happened all those centuries ago. Others, myself among them, take a different view: we see the Bible as a religious-political manifesto in which the lines separating historic fact and pious hopes have been blurred. It is fantastically rich and compelling material but needs to be handled with care. According to the Bible, 3,000 years ago Jerusalem was the capital of the kingdom of Israel, founded by King David and carved from divinely ordained conquests in 'the land of Canaan'. David's son,

Solomon, was powerful enough to make an ally of the king of Tyre, and it was Hiram who sent the materials and craftsmen with which Solomon built the first temple, a sanctified moment in the history of the Jews. Some archaeologists now question just how powerful and unified Solomon's kingdom really was. For them, the Biblical account, written long after the events it describes, is a vision of a Golden Age that never really existed.

But sceptics and true believers both agree that, after Solomon, there were two distinct Jewish kingdoms in this region: Israel in the north and Judah in the south. And over the coming centuries North and South would in turn suffer the fate of all the small kingdoms that had flourished in this part of the world, because far away, in the north, a new power was stirring: the Assyrians.

III

THE ASSYRIANS: SHOCK AND AWE IN ASSUR

Out of the wreckage of the Bronze Age collapse, there emerged one of the most awesome and terrifying military machines that the pre-industrial world was ever to know: the Assyrian Empire. The Near East at that time was a place where violent conflict and the horrors of war were commonplace but even by these blood-drenched standards the Assyrians stood out. It took utter ruthlessness to carve out an empire that included Iraq, Iran, Arabia, Turkey, Syria, Lebanon, Egypt and Cyprus. These were a people who deported over 4 million other people from their homelands and who practised a scorched earth policy that was so extreme that millions more simply starved to death. It is hardly surprising that in the Bible the Assyrians were considered to have been sent by the devil himself.

If geography is fate, the Assyrians learned how to overcome both. In the aftermath of the catastrophe that was the Sea Peoples, Assyria found itself with a small triangle of territory wedged between the plains of Mesopotamia and the mountains to the north. Cramped and land-locked, it had to fight for space. The Assyrian expansion, beginning in the tenth century BC, seems to have inaugurated new levels of violence and a new 'Iron Age' spirit of brutal efficiency: innovative siege engines, the merciless slaughter of captives, avid plunder, mass deportations, crushing tributes exacted from the conquered, and a disregard of the sanctity of ancient sites.

War underpinned the Assyrian economy, their society, their civilization, but

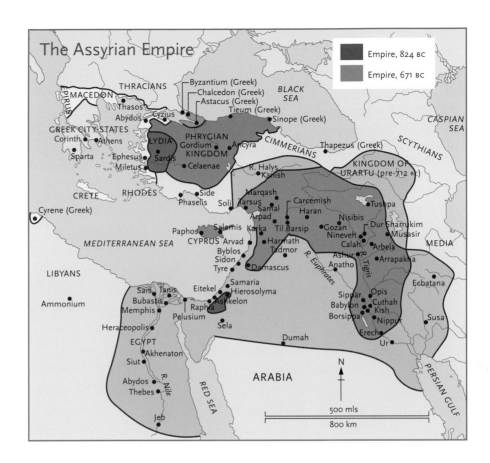

The Assyrian Empire

Empire, 824 BC
Empire, 671 BC

this wasn't mindless violence. Far from it: their reputation for savagery was the product of carefully managed statecraft. On their personal and public memorials the Assyrian kings proudly displayed their barbarous acts. These were often inscribed on the great palaces and monuments of their capital cities, and sometimes even on cliffs and mountains. The horrors of the battlefield and the siege were illustrated with explicit detail on the bas-reliefs of the Assyrian palaces. The desired effect was to make the terrible power of the Assyrian kings seem even more real and credible. For instance, the flaying alive of one treacherous client king was faithfully depicted on the walls of King Sargon's palace at Khorsabad in northern Iraq. It is not difficult to imagine the effect that these beautifully rendered images would have had on visiting ambassadors. There would have been no need for the king to spell out the consequences of opposing him. The parade of courtiers of the defeated kings of Kundu and Sidon through the streets of Nineveh wearing the heads of their masters around their necks like ghastly baubles would be replayed again and again in the minds of those who saw this gruesome pageant recorded on the walls of the imperial palace.

This was the ancient Near Eastern equivalent of 'shock and awe'. It was designed to inspire total panic among their enemies. The Assyrians had a word for it: *melammu*, literally the shining radiance that flashed forth from the king and placed terror in the hearts of his enemies. Time and again the importance of *melammu* is emphasized in the inscriptions, annals and bas-reliefs through which the Assyrians monarchs recorded their mighty deeds. By inflicting the maximum psychological terror on their opponents the Assyrian kings hoped to conquer them with the minimum amount of actual fighting.

This was carefully directed violence as an instrument of state policy, an economy of terror because after the shock and awe came the plunder. A raid by Ashurnasirpal II, king of Assyria from 883–859 BC, on a kingdom in what is now south-eastern Turkey netted the following booty: 40 chariots complete with trappings and horses; 460 horses, 2,000 cattle, 5,000 sheep; silver, gold, lead, copper and iron in varying but large amounts; fine linen and various pieces of fancy furniture including 'couches made of ivory and inlaid with gold'; the ruler's sister, the daughters of his nobles 'and their rich dowries'; and 15,000 subjects who were 'snatched away and brought to Assyria' as slaves. Ashurnasirpal II also imposed an annual tribute of sheep, grain, gold and silver. And these were the proceeds from just one of fifteen victims in that year's campaign season. Sometimes, it seems, war crimes did pay.

Despite the dire warnings, some kingdoms dared to rebel against the Assyrians' self-proclaimed 'universal empire'. One was the northern Jewish kingdom of Israel. In 737 BC it threw off its subservient vassal status and allied itself with Assyria's great rival to the south, Egypt. Vengeance came inevitably and decisively: within a decade the northern kingdom was no more: its cities destroyed, its territories confiscated, and its people deported en masse to Assyria. The 'ten tribes' of Israel became the 'ten lost tribes' of Israel.

But one kingdom's loss is another kingdom's gain, and with the more power-ful northern kingdom obliterated, the southern kingdom of Judah now came into its own. Under Ahaz, king of Judah, Jerusalem developed from an insig-nificant hill town into the capital city of an important Assyrian vassal state. And so it might have continued if Ahaz's successor had stuck to the same policy of keeping the Assyrian masters happy. But his next in line, Hezekiah, had other plans. He also made the fateful decision to defy the Assyrians, to stop paying tribute and to ally himself with the Egyptians. With the fate of the northern kingdom still within living memory, he clearly understood the consequences: massive city walls, 6 metres thick in places, were rapidly thrown up around Jerusalem, with the houses that stood in their path pulled down. Hezekiah also ordered the construction of a subterranean conduit, half a kilometre long, cut through the bedrock of the city. It was designed to carry fresh water from the Gihon spring, which was outside the city walls, to a reservoir inside them. It is a remarkably precise feat of Iron Age engineering because the height difference between spring and reservoir inside is about 30 centimetres. Hezekiah had done all he could, he had built his wall and dug his tunnel; now he just had to wait.

In the Book of Deuteronomy there is a very detailed description of the terror which was about to be unleashed. It must count as one of the most gruesome descriptions of the consequences of war ever written:

The Lord will raise up against you, a distant nation, strange of speech, grim of face, from the far ends of the earth, a nation like a vulture in flight, ruthless toward the old and piti-less toward the young. He will besiege you inside all your towns until your loftiest and most strongly fortified walls collapse. The siege and terrible distress of the enemy's attack will be so severe that you will eat the flesh of your own sons and daughters ... a mother newly delivered of a child will hide the afterbirth from her husband and children so that she can eat it herself.

And that is more or less what happened when the Assyrian king, Sennacherib, marched into the kingdom of Judah looking for payback, but it did not happen in Jerusalem itself. Sennacherib was content to leave Hezekiah behind his wall, 'like a caged bird' as the Assyrian account so patronizingly put it.

Instead Sennacherib and his army headed south to Lachish, Hezekiah's second city. Not many events from this period come down through the histori-cal record complete with illustrations, but the siege of Lachish is an exception. Relief sculptures taken from remains of Sennacherib's palace can be seen at the British Museum. They show in vivid, horrible detail what happened sometime around 701 BC. With archers and some advanced siege technology, the Assyrians tore into the defences of this formidable city. They built a siege ramp hard up against the city, and in the friezes you can see the tank-like siege engine that they ran up it, with a huge spear projecting out of the front. The city fell, of course, with the inevitable consequences: on the western slopes archaeologists found a mass grave with the bodies of more than 1,500 men, women and chil-dren, some of them, as the frieze shows, the victims of impaling and flaying alive. As for the survivors, the frieze also depicts their fate: deportation in their thousands to Assyria, where the men were put to work raising monuments to the glory of the mighty Assyrian Empire.

There is a sequel to the story of Hezekiah's defiance of Assyria. When he died, his son Manasseh succeeded him, and Manasseh reversed his father's

policies. He declared himself a loyal vassal of the Assyrian king, he paid tribute and, most important of all, he made himself useful. The Assyrians were tough, but they were not psychopaths. If you could offer them something then they would let you survive. Manasseh offered oil from olive trees. In fact he turned the town of Ekron into an oil refinery. More than a hundred olive-oil presses were found there, indicating the huge scale of oil output with which this little king kept the big Assyrian beast at bay.

Although keen to present its relationship with other Near Eastern states as a simple matter of total submission brought about by brute military force, the Assyrian kingdom was also engaged in a subtler strategic game involving the control of inter-regional trade networks. The soldiers, weavers, leatherworkers, farmers, ironsmiths and other craftsmen needed to keep the Assyrian state functioning required raw materials and payment. Courtiers and high-ranking royal officials were granted estates and tax immunities as a reward for their service and loyalty. The Great Kings represented themselves as the great providers of both. They would boast that the vast spoils that flowed back to Assyria from their conquests were used to bring prosperity to even their most humble subjects. Precious materials were also required on a vast scale, in order to keep up with the ambitious programme of magnificent royal building projects designed to engender both awe and obedience. Of particular note was the 'Palace without Rival', built by the Assyrian monarch Sennacherib at Nineveh in the early seventh century BC. It was massive, over two and half acres in area, and opulently decorated with ornamental scented woods covered with silver, copper and intricately carved ivory. The exterior walls were decorated with a mass of coloured glazed bricks. Every inch of the structure was covered with detailed narrative scenes outlining the king's triumphs (such as the siege of Lachish). Even the furniture was made of materials of the highest quality, for it was inlaid with ivory and precious metals. To function successfully the Assyrian state required a regular supply of high-quality materials and luxury finished goods on a scale that only trade, not conquest, could provide. It was their insatiable desire for raw materials that led directly to the rebirth of Greece and the discovery of the western Mediterranean.

The continuing independence of the Phoenician port-cities depended on their ability to supply the Assyrians with eye-watering quantities of raw materials, in particular silver. This burden was the catalyst for a huge Phoenician colonial expansion overseas as they sought out new sources of metal ore. First they established settlements on Cyprus before travelling ever further westwards to set up new colonies in Malta, North Africa, Sardinia and Sicily. It was only when the Tyrians reached the westernmost extent of the Mediterranean that they

RIGHT
Relief from the palace of the Assyrian king Sargon II (721–705 BC) at Khorsabad (northern Iraq). It shows the transportation of lumber by Phoenician sailors on 'hippos' boats (given that name by the Greeks on account of their horsehead-shaped prows). Assyrian kings required vast quantities of precious woods for their ambitious building projects, and the Phoenicians as skilled boatmen and sailors were the obvious choices to handle the logistical aspects of this enterprise.

found such abundant seams of silver in southern Spain that visitors believed it oozed in its molten form out of the ground. In partnership with the local Tartessian people, who controlled the mining and smelting operations, the Tyrians managed to maintain a constant flow of silver to Assyria, extracting enough ore to leave a phenomenal 20 million tonnes of slag in the Spanish countryside.

Gades (modern Cadiz) was founded by the Phoenicians in the late eighth century BC, just beyond the Pillars of Hercules on the south-western Atlantic coast of Spain, so they had a port from which to transport the metal ingots back to Tyre. Gades would be only the first of many Phoenician colonies in the western Mediterranean. The favoured route from Tyre to Gades took ships over the northern Mediterranean, first stopping at Cyprus, then on to the southern coast of what is now Turkey. The fleet would then travel on to the islands of Rhodes and Malta, Sicily and then Sardinia. The final leg of the journey went from Ibiza through the straits of Gibraltar to Cadiz. The least complicated return route was to hug the coast of North Africa, then on to Egypt and the Levantine coast. This meant that in essence the Mediterranean acted as an anti-clockwise conveyor belt for the Tyrians, disgorging product at either end of its expanse. Such a long and dangerous journey required that there be pit-stops for the ships to take on supplies and carry out essential repairs. Like footprints across the Great Sea, new Phoenician colonies sprang up to serve this need. Some of these original Phoenician settlements, such as Palermo (Sicily) and Cagliari (Sardinia) are famous working ports to this day.

However, it would be the very success of this new enterprise that would spell the fall of the dynamic entrepreneurs of Tyre. In a classic tale of the dangers of oversupply, one Assyrian king at the end of the eighth century BC boasted that he had managed to hoard such vast amounts of silver in his palace that copper was now the same price as silver: this was very bad news for the Tyrians. As the silver mountain in Nineveh and Nimrud rose, so Tyrian influence declined. Their territory was gradually annexed as Assyrian officials were drafted in to administer Tyrian political and economic activities. In the end, the Assyrians stepped in and took over completely. They didn't kill the golden goose – they simply plucked the feathers of its hard-won independence and dignity, one by one.

Soon after that, though, the imperial wheel turned, and the Assyrians found themselves on the losing side against a new force that had risen in old Mesopotamia: the Babylonians. Weakened by internal disorder and division, the Assyrian Empire started to disintegrate in the late seventh century BC. In 612, following a bitter three-month siege, Nineveh fell to Nabopolassar, the king of the Babylonians, who had formed a coalition with Assyrian vassal kingdoms. Ideologically, the Babylonians distanced themselves from the Assyrians by attributing their victory to their gods rather than the supremacy of their royal leaders. But the effects on the small kingdoms within striking distance were the same: during a punitive campaign by the Babylonian king, Nebuchadnezzer, imperial armies followed the well-trodden invasion routes west. Tyre and Jerusalem were sacked, and the populations deported to 'the rivers of Babylon'. But within a generation the wheel turned once more. Now it was the turn of the Persians, led by their 'high king' Cyrus. They overthrew Babylon, pushing the borders of their new empire to the coast of Asia Minor, a natural boundary which in the 500 years since the collapse of the unified Bronze Age world had become a cultural and political frontier that had grown and hardened between East and West. And across this divide, in the West, staring back at the empires and kingdoms of the old East, were the Greeks.

IV

THE REDISCOVERY OF GREECE

The Dark Age collapse had hit the Mycenaean kingdoms of ancient Greece hard. It had always been on the periphery of civilization; with the Bronze Age catastrophe it fell off the edge. Since the tumultuous breakdown of the Mycenaean civilization in the twelfth century BC, Greece had become the scene of a startling regression. In the last centuries of the second millennium BC, the population dropped by a staggering 75 per cent. Its inhabitants had abandoned sophisticated settlements and forgotten many of the facets that we associate with civilized life: monumental architecture, figurative art and even the ability to write. Farming practices reverted from agriculture to pastoralism, and almost all contact with the outside world ceased.

Very little historical evidence has survived from these centuries of darkness, but the archaeological record does contain the occasional vivid flash of light that suggests that not everything lay dormant. In Lefkandi, a coastal village on the Greek island of Euboea, archaeologists have found a tomb dated to around 1000 BC, about 120 years after the Bronze Age collapse. Both the structure of the tomb and its content are without precedent in this period. One female was buried with gilt hair coils, dress pins and other bronze objects. Her bleached and brittle finger bones, covered in an assortment of nine gold rings, were placed

over a finely crafted gilded bronze bowl. Where did these opulent goods come from? Certainly not Greece itself; the Greeks had long ago lost the knowledge of how to make anything that fine.

In Pithekoussai, in the Bay of Naples, there is another lightning flash and another clue, in the form of the so-called Cup of Nestor, a drinking cup found on the island, which has been dated from around the eighth century BC. Scratched on to its side is a poem, which reads:

I am Nestor's cup, good to drink from.
Whoever drinks this cup empty,
Straight away desire
for beautiful-crowned Aphrodite
will seize him …

Beneath the heady feeling that the cup describes, there is a more sober point: this little poem is written in Greek using an alphabet. Before the great Bronze Age collapse Greek was written using Linear B, an unwieldy system based on more than 200 different symbols and signs, and good for little more than book-keeping. Now, just a few centuries on, we have Greek speakers employing an efficient, concise alphabet system of less than thirty characters – and using it to write poetry. Clearly in the course of the Dark Age the Greeks had received enlightenment from somewhere – but where?

The getting of wisdom is all about the company you keep, and in Pithekoussai and elsewhere we know that the Greeks were rubbing shoulders with the inventors of the alphabet, the Phoenicians. Both groups had come here to exploit the region's iron, silver and tin mines and seemed to have ended up as partners rather than rivals. This allowed the Greeks to sit at the feet of the 'Purple People' and to re-learn the lost arts of civilization. A few centuries after that little poem was scratched on the side of a drinking cup, a Greek called Herodotus would carve out a monumental multi-volume work called *The Histories*. In it he acknowledged the debt the Greeks owed to the Phoenicians for the alphabet, and since then other historians have added more items to this debt of honour: the cultivation of olive trees and vines, the use of weights and measures, interest-bearing loans and banking, gods like Heracles or political concepts like kingship – all are said to have been carried west by those industrious Phoenician traders. They may have gone in search of profits, but, like honey bees, they unwittingly carried with them the pollen seeds of civilization – and the Greeks were the prime beneficiaries.

Through these links with the Phoenician cities, Greece was dragged out of its Dark Age. Long-lost skills were brought back to Hellas by the Phoenicians. By the ninth century BC, the local elites on the island of Crete could once again be buried, like their illustrious ancestors, with fine jewellery courtesy of immigrant Phoenician goldsmiths. Large amounts of Near Eastern pottery and artefacts, the telltale signs of Phoenician trading activity, have also been found on the islands of Crete and Rhodes. There are even tantalizing clues that the Phoenicians, particularly potters and metalsmiths, might have settled in Greece, and passed on their skills to native apprentices. At Kommos, in southern Crete, the remains of a particular type of Phoenician shrine have been found, suggesting that they had actually established a settlement there or at least that the inhabitants had been strongly influenced by them. Local imitation also had an important role to play. The famous Attic and Corinthian schools of ceramic ware both show strong Phoenician influences in motifs, iconography and style. Delicate ivories found all over Greece were either directly imported from Phoenicia or local imitations of Phoenician ware. Away from the mainland, the inhabitants of Rhodes had soon built up a thriving business manufacturing perfume flasks copied from the Phoenician originals.

By the tenth century BC, a quiet revolution had begun. The goods, skills and ideas brought by the Phoenicians essentially revived Greece. The resumption of trade in Greece had a seismic effect on society and culture. A dramatic rise in the population meant that some Greeks took to sea and became involved in trade themselves. Trading networks would be set up that spanned from Syria in the east to Italy in the west. The resulting influx of wealth brought about new ideas about social status. Previously, status had brought wealth: the Dark Age Greeks had followed a system of reciprocity that meant that those who held high status attracted gifts of property, goods and foodstuffs. Surpluses would then be redistributed amongst the wider community. Now, as individuals generated wealth outside their communities, steadily the people of Greece moved away from the old models of communal territory and instead began to accrue private property. It would be these growing economic and social distinctions that would provide the foundation stone for the Greek *polis,* or city-state, the political unit that would eventually spawn so many social, cultural and political innovations, including what we know as democratic government.

In recent years some historians and archaeologists have argued that there was a fairly extensive and sophisticated Greek trading network in the Mediterranean that functioned independently of the Phoenicians by the eighth century BC. Al Mina, a settlement at the mouth of the river Orontes in Syria, where a large amount of Greek pottery from this period has been found, is held up as an early Greek trading station. For some this would provide a far more satisfactory reason as to why so much Near Eastern pottery and goods ended up in Greece. Rather than the Phoenicians, it was the Greeks themselves who brought it back, and what was more they were trading their own wares in the Phoenicians' backyard. We should, however, be wary of such claims. At Al Mina as much local pottery has been found as Greek, suggesting a large Near Eastern component in the population. What is more, it is well documented that in the Near East, Greek goods had long been prized as being exotic. Large amounts of similar Greek pottery have been found in Phoenician cities such as Tyre but nobody is suggesting that they were Greek trading colonies. What is much more likely is that it was Phoenician merchants who transported Greek goods to Al Mina.

This nascent Greek trading network could not have prospered without the co-operation and goodwill of the Phoenicians, who controlled access to these markets. However, that was not all. The debt that ancient Greece and indeed the

modern Western world owes to the Phoenicians is even greater than one might first imagine: the greatest gift that the Phoenicians bestowed on the Greeks was their alphabet.

In the modern world, we associate ancient Greece with great literature and learning: Plato, Aristotle, Archimedes and Homer, to name just a few practitioners. But, a few hundred years before these great writers and thinkers, the Greeks could not even read or write. It would take the Phoenicians to show them how. Indeed, the Greeks called their alphabet *phoinikeia grammata* (Phoenician letters). It was not only the Greeks who owed a huge debt to the Phoenicians for teaching them an alphabet. Hebrew, the language of Israel and the original language of the Old Testament, was also directly derived from the Phoenician alphabet.

The Greeks took the Phoenician alphabet and developed it, devising five new letters to represent vowel sounds. No longer confined to the abbreviated

text-speak of the Phoenician alphabet, the Greek alphabet became an even more expressive tool, better at capturing the melodies and rhythms of speech – poems as well as cargo manifests. It was used to create a piece of writing so monumental and so profound that it would shape the destiny of the Greek-speaking world, the *Iliad*:

Sing, goddess, of the anger of Achilles, son of Peleus, the accursed anger which brought uncounted anguish on the Achaians and hurled down to Hades many mighty souls of heroes, making their bodies the prey to dogs and the birds' feasting: and this was the working of Zeus' will. Sing from the time of the first quarrel which divided Atreus' son, the lord of men, and godlike Achilles.

These are the opening lines (in the brilliant translation by Robert Fagles) of the unmistakable war music of the *Iliad*; 16,000 lines of hexameter verse that plunge you straight into the heart of the 'strife and havoc' that is said to have raged before the walls of Troy, some 3,200 years ago. The very first word of this epic poem is *menin*, meaning rage, and that is what the poem explores, with unflinching clarity and insight: the rage of men fighting for honour, vengeance and personal gain, for victory, survival and the intoxicating adrenaline rush of licensed savagery.

Achilles drew his sharp sword and struck him on the collar-bone by the neck, and the whole length of the two-edged sword sank inside him. He fell forward and lay stretched on the earth: and the dark blood ran from him, soaking the ground. Achilles took him by the foot and flung him to float in the river, and spoke winged words in triumph over him: 'Now lie there among the fish. They will lick the blood from your wound and give you no loving burial. Your mother will not lay you out on the bier and lament for you ... Death take you all, all the way till we reach the city of sacred Ilios, you Trojans running in flight and I behind you cutting you down.'

'Homer' is the name attached to this poem without precedent. He is variously described as its author, composer, performer or compiler. But was he one man or many? Was he an individual genius, a tradition, or a guild of poets? Some people argue that 'he' was a 'she', others that he or she never existed. Claimed by seven different cities as their native son, Homer has been called the Cheshire Cat of world literature, always disappearing without even the trace of a smile. What we do know is that sometime between 750 and 700 BC the *Iliad* was written down, using the new technology of the Greek alphabet. The language, though Greek, was like nothing heard before or since, a jumble of different dialects and vocabularies. The poem is also a patchwork of weapon technologies, battle tactics and political institutions, drawn from periods ancient and modern. But to the Greek audiences it clearly all made sense. More than 180 different manuscripts of the *Iliad* have survived, twice the number of its sister epic the *Odyssey*, a crude but telling measure of a work's popularity and relevance.

One reason for the centrality of the *Iliad* to the Greeks is that it gave them a conceptual framework with which to think about themselves and the kind of societies they were creating. Alongside all the blood and guts, it poses profound questions about the nature of society, the qualities of leadership, the rules by which people consent to be governed. 'Well-walled' Troy, with its 'lofty gates', 'wide streets' and 'fine towers', is in many ways the ideal city-state to which the Greeks aspired. And Hector, the noble, doomed warrior who fights and dies for its survival, is civilization's champion and the true hero of the *Iliad*. His fate, which foreshadows the fate of his city, is tragic but somehow serene. It is the Greeks, the wolves at the gates, who are troubled and troubling. They wrangle about their reasons for being there, the justness of their cause, the motives of their leaders. This is what puts the politics as well as poetry into the *Iliad*.

According to legend, the Greek camp was near the mouth of the Scamander River, which flows through modern north-western Turkey. The camp was thrown up around the black ships drawn up on the beach. With a rampart and ditch surmounted by wooden walls, it was a makeshift, vagabond place compared to 'well-walled' Troy. This was where Achilles, the hero, sulked in his tent; where Agamemnon blustered and strutted trying to maintain his authority as 'high king'; and where wily Odysseus, the unscrupulous piratical aristocrat, the model for tyrants of the future, plotted and schemed. It was here, too, that a debate took place that asked, but did not answer, a question that would preoccupy the Greeks in the centuries to come.

The moment comes when Greek armies have been gathered together to hear the decision of their leaders as to whether or not to abandon the long siege and return home. They are there to listen and obey rather than debate, but one of them, Thersites, dares to speak up. Thersites is a common soldier, a spear-carrier, one of the poor bloody infantry, and Homer clearly disapproves of him, describing him as hunchbacked and bandy-legged, 'the ugliest man who ever came to Troy'. But though it comes through broken teeth, Thersites' speech is also 'fluent and flowing', and he uses it to abuse King Agamemnon and to call for an immediate withdrawal to Greece. With morale at a low point, this is a critical moment in the long war.

It is Odysseus who puts a stop to the subversive rant. 'Who are you to wrangle with kings?' he demands and then beats Thersites with his rod of office. The mutinous moment passes, the war goes on, but the question is left hanging in the air: 'Who are you to wrangle with kings?' Homer's audiences would come up with very different answers to that question, and in doing so would change the future of their world and lay the foundations of our own.

ANCIENT GREECE:
THE TYRANNY OF FREEDOM

WORDS AND IRON: THE DEVELOPMENT OF THE *POLIS* IN ARCHAIC GREECE

It's not always easy to define what civilization is, but (in the words of the art historian Kenneth Clark) we think we recognize it when we see it. In the West some of the strongest visual images we associate with the concept come from ancient Greece: superb statues of the human body at its most powerful and beautiful, perfectly proportioned buildings, rationally ordered cities. And these are just the visual tip of a cultural iceberg that also includes poetry, drama, philosophy and science. The Greeks had a word for all this: *to Hellenikon*, meaning 'Greekness' or 'the Greek thing'. It was first used by the historian Herodotus to sum up everything the ancient Greeks had in common: language, religion, customs, blood. Today, 'the Greek thing' has become a kind of shorthand for the values and ideals that we like to think lie at the root of who we are: rational, cultured, humane and civilized. But beneath the cool marble skin there was a fierce pulse that gave 'the Greek thing' its energy and passion, and also its capacity for sudden, shocking violence.

In Argos, in 370 BC, you would have seen the violent side of Greekness. That year, a plot by disaffected aristocrats to overthrow the city's fledgling democracy was uncovered. Seizing the political opportunity, demagogues from the democratic faction whipped up a mob with fiery speeches directed against the city's wealthiest citizens. What followed was a reign of terror: trumped-up charges, summary trials, confiscation of property and execution, the victims handed over to the mob who beat them to death with clubs. It was only when the body count reached 1,200 or more that the democratic leaders began to have second thoughts about this cull of the city's elite. But when they tried to scale back the trials and executions, the mob turned on them and clubbed them to death as well. Eventually, the city woke from this nightmare of self-inflicted violence. The dust settled, the corpses were cleared away and the city consoled itself with a statue of Zeus the Merciful commissioned from a fashionable local sculptor – an act of collective remorse, or a cultural band-aid to cover a gaping civic wound.

The Argos massacre was notorious but not unique – just another sorry episode in a seemingly endless cycle of brutal wars between Greek cities, and civil wars within them. Friedrich Nietzsche, the German philosopher, may have been a bit crazy at times, but he did have some sensible things to say about the Greeks:

The most humane men of ancient times have a trait of cruelty, a tigerish lust to annihilate that really must strike fear into our hearts … Why must the Greek sculptor give form again and again to war and combat in innumerable repetitions, distended human bodies, their sinews tense with hatred or with the arrogance of triumph; writhing bodies, wounded, dying bodies, expiring? … I fear we do not understand these in a sufficiently 'Greek' manner – indeed that we should shudder if we were ever to understand them 'in Greek'.

In the story of ancient Greece, from the evolution of the city-states to their wars with Persia and then with each other, there is as much to shudder at as there is to admire: the blossoming in art, philosophy and science went hand-in-bloody hand with political discord, social unrest, endless wars and, ultimately,

the complete failure to forge a common political identity, despite, or maybe because of, all that shared 'Greekness'. In its staggering achievements and moments of violence and desolation, ancient Greece shows us, with absolute clarity, the polarities contained within the concept of 'civilization'. The Greeks themselves were aware of the gap that separated high ideals from grim reality. It was, after all, the Greek philosopher Aristotle (384–322 BC) who observed: 'Man, when perfected, is the best of animals, but, when separated from law and justice, he is the worst of all.' The story I have got for you now is the 'Greek thing', for better or worse.

The last time we met the Greeks they were a long way from home, a predatory army camped out before the walls of the fabled city of Troy, intent on vengeance and plunder. Homer's *Iliad* invested the heroes who fought in the Trojan War with epic grandeur and immortal fame, and left the Greeks who came after with the feeling that they had a lot to live up to. To understand these Greeks who lived so self-consciously in the shadow of the Heroic Age, you have to leave the killing fields of Troy behind and come to Boeotia, on the Greek mainland, where the fields are more mundane and everyday life has rarely been heroic, then or now. But the landscape of Boeotia has its poetry too, though of a sort very different from Homer's:

Hunger is always the companion of the man who does not graft. And gods and men have little time for the man who loafs ... Wealth brings excellence and acclaim. Whatever your luck, work is better, if you turn your foolhardy heart from the possessions of others towards work and pay attention to your livelihood as I instruct you.

The lines are from *Works and Days* by Hesiod. Hesiod was the poet laureate of the new down-to-earth Greece that followed the age of Heroes. We are not sure when Hesiod lived exactly, and some are even sceptical about his existence, but most experts believe that he *did* live, and that he owned and worked a small farm somewhere in the area near the village of Askra in Boeotia, in the period immediately after Homer.

That puts Hesiod sometime after 700 BC, when the Greek world was emerging, blinking, from the six centuries of historical darkness that had followed the collapse of Bronze Age Greece. After a long period of stagnation, things were changing fast. The tribal systems that the Greeks had reverted to during the Dark Age broke down as the more impersonal mechanisms of civilization returned. New technologies, most importantly metalworking and the alphabet, accelerated these processes as, willingly and unwillingly, the Greeks reconnected with the 'modern world' of the Iron Age.

In *Works and Days*, Hesiod's most famous poem, you get the authentic voice of the conservative farmer during a period of radical change: grumbling, gloomy and disillusioned, sceptical about the way things have changed and critical of leaders who seem to have turned their backs on the old ways.

For now indeed it is a race of iron ... justice is in their fists and one will sack the other's city, nor will there be any respect for the man who keeps his oath, or for the decent or good man but more respect will be granted to the wicked man and the reprobate.

To drive his point home, Hesiod tells the parable of the nightingale struggling in the claws of the hawk. 'Why do you cry out stupid bird?' asks the hawk. 'One much more powerful than you has you in their grip. You will go wherever I take you.' But Hesiod does cry out, railing like an Old Testament prophet against the corruption of this new age of iron and threatening divine retribution.

There is angry uproar when Right is dragged off wherever the kick-back merchants choose to take her as they give their judgment with bent verdicts ... but for those who concern themselves with only outrageousness and wicked deeds, far sighted Zeus, the son of Cronos brings punishment from the heavens.

The struggle between elite privilege and ancient rights would be a theme for politics as well as poetry, the battleground between *hoi oligoi* ('the few') and *hoi polloi* ('the many'). But the arena where this battle would be fought was not in out-of-the-way places like Askra, but in the *poleis*, the city-states, the nuclei around which the new Greece was crystallizing.

The city-states of ancient Greece were created when scattered tribal communities surrendered their local autonomy and acknowledged a single location as their political centre. They started to emerge during what is known as ancient Greece's Archaic Period – the stretch of time between the end of the Dark Age that followed the Bronze Age collapse (twelfth century BC) and the Persian Wars of the early fifth century BC. The formation of a *polis* was usually achieved by a strong leader with the charisma and muscle to shut down rival power centres and transfer their functions to the political heart of the city-state. (Athens would later claim Theseus as its founder-king and would fight a war to recover his bones and bring them 'home'.) These new political centres often owed their prominence to powerful strategic locations – a pinch-point along trade routes or a defensible citadel on a rocky hill which both protected and controlled the townships at its feet. Crucially, the political, urban centre was embedded in the surrounding farmland, and its citizens had one foot in the street and the other in the fields.

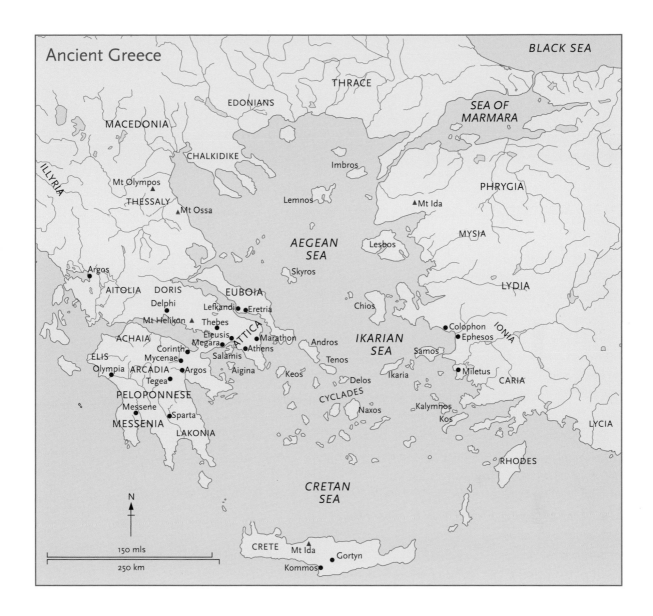

Ancient Greece

The *poleis* ranged in size from giants like Athens, Sparta, Argos or Corinth, with populations that topped 10,000 and territories to match, to tiny Belbina, a fly-speck of an island with a territory of just eight square kilometres. The average city-state had a population of around 1,000 with a territory of 100 square kilometres, so these were small, intimate places; people knew each other and there were few secrets. Even the biggest and most sophisticated *polis* clung to village instincts – strong prejudices against outsiders, a powerful shame culture, long-running feuds and vendettas, and an enduring collective memory. In Athens, the Alcmaeonidae, one of the great aristocratic families, earned the nickname 'the accursed' because of a sacrilegious murder committed by their ancestors. This *miasma*, or stain, was never forgotten, and at times of crisis, centuries later, the old story would be dragged up and clan members subjected to suspicion, hostility and even banishment.

Cities, too, found themselves saddled with reputations that were hard to shake. Sybaris, a Greek colony in southern Italy, was infamous for its refinement and luxury: it was said that its war horses were trained to dance into battle. Sparta was the opposite, of course – puritanical and sober-sided to a fault – but also notorious for its opinionated, sexually liberated women and its contempt for rival cities that cowered behind defensive walls. The hardest label to shake was 'Mediser'. It was hung around the necks of cities accused of collaboration with the Persian Empire, most notoriously Argos and Thebes. This was the ultimate offence against 'the Greek thing', and an all-purpose excuse for anyone who felt so inclined to declare war on these states.

Passions in a *polis* ran high. This was not just the place that you came to buy and sell or do business. It was the place where you learned to be a 'politician', a creature of the *polis*, a political animal. Of course your *polis* provided an economic hub and security in troubled times, but it went deeper than that: the *polis* was something you belonged to, the place that gave you an identity. In fact, according to Aristotle, the *polis* completed you as a human being: 'The man who in his self-sufficiency has no need of others,' he wrote, 'is like a beast – or a god.' Love of *polis* was so intense it was sometimes described as *himeros*, meaning sexual desire. The famous funeral oration attributed to the Athenian leader Pericles is nothing less than a love letter to Athens: 'Feed your eyes on her from day to day,' he told his fellow citizens, 'till love of her fills your hearts.'

Alongside love went hate. Opposition was central to the Greek way of making sense of their world. The best way to define anything was by saying what it was not: cold was the opposite of heat, dark the opposite of light, peace the opposite of war, Athens the opposite of Sparta. This black and white view of the world brought with it great clarity and became the foundation for the philosophical and scientific advances that would revolutionize the Greek-speaking world. But it also gave politics its noisy, rancorous edge: us and them, white hats and black hats. Stoked up by powerful, contradictory passions, the city-states of Greece were not rational, well-ordered utopias. They were more like test-tubes full of combustible material in an experimental laboratory that was always threatening to blow up. But although the body politic could be a volatile mix, the great genius of 'the Greek thing' was the way in which it often managed to control the explosions and even to harness the dynamic energies that were generated.

At the very start of his great poem *Works and Days*, Hesiod tells a revealing parable about the goddess Eris, or 'Strife', and her meddling with mankind. As the daughter of Night and the sister of Resentment and Despair, you would not expect to hear much in her favour, but Hesiod tells us that there are actually two Strife goddesses active among humanity. One promotes fighting and conflict, and is essentially destructive, but the other promotes rivalry 'that is good for mortals'.

When someone whose work falls short looks towards another
Towards a rich man who hastens to plough and plant
Then neighbour vies with neighbour as he hastens to wealth.
This Strife is good for mortals:
So potter is piqued with potter, carpenter with carpenter
Beggar begrudges beggar and singer, singer.

The idea that rivalry could act as a dynamic force in society leads us on to one of the most radical propositions at the heart of 'the Greek thing': individuals mattered. And not just rich and powerful individuals, but potters, carpenters and singers too. Even beggars mattered, if only in the eyes of rival beggars.

It is hard to pin down the status of the individual in the history of the ancient world. The historic record, up to this point, focuses almost exclusively on the high and mighty, and they are usually treated in a generic way, an endless succession of identikit kings processing down the centuries, being Great and All Conquering, until conquered by someone greater. What is striking about Iron Age Greece is that, from the start, there are strong, individual voices. Heroic Homer and grumpy Hesiod are soon joined by others, who are equally distinctive; a cacophony of individuals all clamouring to be heard on their own terms. There is the worldly wise Archilocus (the seventh-century BC mercenary and one of the first lyric poets), who says it is better to throw away your shield than your life – you can always get another shield. There is the ecstatic Sappho, who yearns to rest her head on the breast of her various girlfriends. There is the sardonic aristocrat Mimnermus, who eloquently bemoans the onset of hateful old age. Some of these voices may just be poetic personas – fictional constructs but even they must be products of a culture that prized pungent individuality. You see something similar at work in the visual arts too: Greek sculpture, which begins by sticking closely to the conservative blueprint of Egyptian art, soon develops an interest in exploring in detail the bones, muscle and sinew of idealized individuals.

Just as the Greeks defined themselves as different to the non-Greek, 'barbarian'

world, so each city-state insisted on its own distinct identity in the Greek-speaking world. And within the city-states, those with the means to devoted energy and resources to setting themselves apart from their fellow citizens. The Western cult of the individual begins here. Rather than the steep-sided pyramid hierarchies of Bronze Age societies, the social structure of Iron Age Greece was shallower and flat-topped. In other words, there was room at the top for a lot of those who, in the words of the poet Simonides, had been 'rich from of old'. By the eighth century BC, nearly all the city-states of Greece had done away with kings, the ancient world's default position for political leadership. The prestige and power that had once been in the hands of an individual was divvied up among the elites – the oligarchs. Oligarchies (oligarchy literally means 'rule by the few') broke down the job of 'king' into its component parts – war, justice,

religion and so on – creating a range of public offices for ambitious aristocrats to fill. Time limits were often placed on length of service, introducing the hallowed principle of 'Buggins's turn' into politics: 'My turn to be *archon* this year, your turn next.' Sharing out the spoils in this way was smart politics. It encouraged members of the elite to work together against the common enemy – the *demos*, the people, the grumbling Hesiods of their city-states who were always ready to challenge the claims of *aristokratia* – 'the rule of the best'.

Because of the small size of city-state populations, and the relatively small gap in wealth between rich and poor, there was a balance of impotence in this struggle between the classes. All the city-states had to tread the difficult line between the demands of the collective to work for the common good and the instincts of the elite to have things their own way. *Eunomia* – 'good order' – was recognized as the greatest good, but it was also understood that 'good order' depended on *dikte* – 'justice'. Perhaps recalling the 'natural justice' that prevailed in the tribal communities from which they had evolved, there was an expectation in the Greek city-states of fairness in the distribution of the efforts that went into building and maintaining a society and the rewards that flowed from it. Needless to say this applied only to males who were full citizens: foreigners, slaves and women were excluded. So the aristocrats were under continual pressure from below to deliver on the terms of a simple social contract – consent for their rule would be forthcoming only if the people felt they were getting a fair deal. When they felt they were being short-changed they evidently knew how

to make their voices heard. The aristocratic Mimnermus complains about the 'pitiless criticism' of the lower orders towards their betters.

Bearing in mind the fate of those aristocrats clubbed to death by the mob in Argos, solidarity among the upper classes was obviously a sensible strategy: if the oligarchs did not hang together they knew they would hang separately. But there were other pressures at work that put this unity under stress, creating cracks in the glass ceiling of class that would ultimately allow the people from below to fight their way up into the inner circles of power. You could say that the problems all began with an idea personified in a goddess: Arete, or 'excellence'. On the façade of the Hellenistic library in Ephesus she looks like a rather sedate matron, but in archaic Greece the pursuit of excellence was a red-blooded affair. All Greek males, but especially aristocratic ones, were haunted by the ghost of Achilles, the matchless warrior of the *Iliad*. Achilles taught them the lesson that he himself was said to have learned on his father's knee: 'always to be first and to excel the others in all things. Glory cannot be shared.'

The Achilles principle was at the heart of the games that took place every four years at Olympia. There was nothing playful about what went on there. Olympia was a sacred place, and the games, held in honour of Zeus, were spiritual as well as athletic. Two of the five days of the festival were set aside for religious rituals, but the focal point was provided by the competitive games. It was for these that a pan-Hellenic truce was declared, allowing males from all over the Greek-speaking world to make their way there and sort out the best from the rest.

The first Olympic Games were held in 776 BC and the first event was a 200-metre sprint. Over the next thousand years other events were added – more foot races, boxing and wrestling matches, jumping and throwing competitions, horse and chariot races – but this was the essence of the games, a mad dash from here to there to decide who was the 'best'. For the Greeks, there was no pious nonsense about 'it's not winning, it's the taking part that counts.' Winning was all that mattered. Victory, symbolized by an olive branch at Olympia, could be traded for more concrete benefits back home. The *kudos* of victory brought material rewards and political power. For the losers there was no silver or bronze – all they could expect were derision and ignominy. The poet Pindar describes them slinking back home, spurned by their mothers and girlfriends, 'lurking in byways, hoping to avoid their enemies, stung by their ill fortune'.

The risks associated with losing were all the greater because the games were open to all-comers, as long as they were Greek males. We are told that the winner of that very first Olympic race was Koroibos, a humble baker from Elis. So it was not just a matter of losing the race: if you were an aristocrat, you risked

losing face too, to some upstart from a no-horse town. And yet catastrophic loss of face is precisely what the Greeks were prepared to risk at the games, for the chance to inflict it on others. Given the high stakes, it is not surprising that some athletes were prepared to cheat. Bribery and race-fixing were common. Those who were found out were fined and the money used to make bronze statues of Zeus, which lined the road to the stadium. The statues named and shamed the cheats, a warning to others to stay on the straight and narrow, but as the number of statue bases suggests, the message did not always get through.

Victory, however it was achieved, was sweet, and it brought with it the usual bragging rights. For example, at the Olympia Museum there is a 150-kilogramme lump of sandstone carrying the inscription, 'Bybon, son of Pholos, threw me over his head with one hand'. The temples at Olympia were stuffed full of mementoes of athletic prowess, dedicated to the gods and to the undying fame of Bybon and the other meat-heads. But the temples were also hung with military gear: helmets, body-armour, shields and spears, many of them showing unmistakable signs of active service. With their Homeric blinkers on, Greeks clearly saw a direct link between prowess on the sports field and on the battlefield. In practice, though, they were very different things. Greek athletes competed as individuals. They did not represent their city-states, though they could expect a hero's welcome if they returned victorious, and there were no team events. It was every man for himself, just as Achilles would have wanted.

But when it came to warfare, the Greeks had travelled a very long way from the heroic individualism of Achilles. A new and hugely effective military technique had first been pioneered by the city-states of Corinth and Argos in the seventh century BC, and it quickly spread throughout Greece. It was based on the hoplite soldier, a citizen soldier, taken from the civilian population of the city-state rather than using mercenaries or a professional standing army (the city-states were too poor to afford either). The hoplites formed into densely packed ranks known as a phalanx, their round shields overlapping, protecting their neighbour rather than themselves. Committed to mutual protection, a phalanx advanced as a unit in carefully choreographed movements, each fighter a small but essential part of a formidable fighting machine. When two phalanxes butted up against each other there was no room for the kind of heroic man-to-man combat described in the *Iliad*. No one could break ranks, the line had to hold. This was unheroic push-and-shove: brutal, collective and anonymous, a rugby scrum with spear-points. And so while the Greeks may have had their heads in the clouds, dreaming of Achilles, their feet were firmly planted on the dusty ground of the battlefield, as they grunted and sweated alongside their neighbours in the phalanx. Hoplite warfare maximized the fighting muscle of a city-state: at the battle of Marathon, in 490 BC, Athens would deploy 9,000 hoplites – nearly one third of the city's population at the time.

Warfare was an inescapable fact in the story of the Greek city-states. Plato, who lived in the aftermath of decades of destructive inter-city war, wrote bluntly: 'Peace is nothing more than a name; every State is, by a law of nature, engaged in a war with every other State.' According to tradition, the first significant battle between city-states took place on the Lelantine Plain on the island of Euboea, some time in the late eighth or early seventh century BC. Then, as now, it was a broad and fertile table of farmland. In this land of steep mountains and narrow valleys, elbow-room like this was hard to find; it promised *autarchy*,

RIGHT
Bronze Corinthian helmet. Arms and armour were often dedicated as offerings at the sanctuary of Olympia.

'self-sufficiency', to anyone who could possess it. Since time immemorial, the cities of Chalcis and Eretria had shared the riches of the plain, but at some point in the seventh century BC, as their populations grew, that understanding broke down. They went to war, but they did not entirely forget their former friendship. They drew up an agreement in advance that no missiles, slingshots or arrows would be used by either side. In pre-Classical Greece, war was a curiously civilized affair, seasonal and ritualized. It was timed for when the harvest had been gathered in, and there were rules of engagement designed to minimize casualties. One scholar has even compared it to a cricket match between rival villages, which might be a bit of a stretch, but it captures something of the 'holds barred' atmosphere that seems to have prevailed. It certainly contrasts with the wars that lay ahead in the centuries to come, when the Greeks, according to the historian Thucydides, 'would become like beasts to each other'. Fighting for your *polis* was a privilege rather than an obligation, but the introduction of hoplite tactics made it possible for more people to take part than ever before: a spear, a helmet, some body armour, and most importantly a shield to protect your neighbour – if you could bring those to the battlefield you could expect a game.

The 'hoplite revolution', as it has been called, was not just about military tactics: it brought with it profound political changes too, because, as Aristotle would later observe, 'The class that does the fighting wields the power.' With more and more ordinary citizens finding their place in the phalanx, standing shoulder to shoulder and shield to shield with the well-to-do, the unequal distribution of power within a city-state would have been called into question every time the battle flutes sounded.

II

SPARTA AND ATHENS: FOSSILIZED *EUNOMIA* AND APPEASING THE *DEMOS*

Given the ever-present threat of war from without and the danger of civil war from within, it is not surprising that by the end of the seventh century BC the critical question for the city-states was: how should we best be governed? The Greeks, being Greek, could never agree on a single answer, but the ones they did come up with were test-runs for many of the political concepts we still live with today: totalitarianism, collectivism, tyranny, oligarchy, democracy – all of them were tried out in the test tubes that were the city-states. The Greeks seemed prepared to consider any system that might deliver the blessings of *eunomia* and *autarchy* – good order and self-sufficiency; anything, that is, except monarchy. All over Greece, royal dynasties were out. Kings were a relic of the past, or for the barbarians. But there was one exception: on the Greek mainland, in the heart of the Peloponnese, was a city-state that did not just have one king, it had two – and that was just the beginning, for Sparta was the strangest test tube in the laboratory.

Sparta was a looking-glass world: all the ingredients you would expect to find in a city-state were absent here. It had no single political centre, no city walls, no public buildings to speak of, no written laws, no money and a constitution apparently designed by Heath Robinson. There were two royal dynasties, who could be relied on to undermine each other, a council of elders, all of them over 60, a public assembly that voted but rarely debated and five annually elected *ephors* who squabbled over the levers of this ramshackle political machine. Partly radical and democratic, partly conservative and authoritarian, Aristotle called it a 'mixed constitution'. Mixed up seems more accurate. Sparta's complex constitution was designed to defy the laws of political gravity: its aim was to create and sustain a stable society based on the absolute equality of all its male citizens, known as the *homoioi*, or the Equals. This ideal was reinforced by strict codes of behaviour that suppressed all outward displays of wealth and status, from food to clothes to houses. There was to be no 'us and them' threatening the unity of this totalitarian Utopia, where anything not forbidden was of course compulsory.

There was a reason for all this extreme social engineering: the Spartans believed they had already achieved the twin goals of good order and self-sufficiency in the Eurotas valley, and they were prepared to do all they could to hang on to them – as their neighbours had learned to their cost. Sparta's rise had been at the expense of Messenia, whose territory lay about sixty kilometres west, on the other side of the Taygetos mountains. Sometime in the eighth century BC, Spartan hoplites had marched west and begun a long, bitter war against their neighbours. It took them twenty years, but they finally defeated the Messenians and reduced them en masse to the status of *helots* – feudal slaves.

The radical reordering of Spartan society that followed turned Sparta from just another city-state into a full-time military training camp, where the needs of the individuals were sacrificed to the good of the collective. The legendary law-giver Lycurgus was said to be the leader of Sparta's barmy cultural revolution of the early eighth century BC, which centred on the principles of extreme egalitarianism, excruciating austerity and obsessional physical fitness. The Spartans were prepared to do all they could to preserve their Utopia, at whatever cost, to

them or their *helots*. The *helots* served the Spartans as servants, shield-carriers, potters, cooks, agricultural labourers and breeding machines. They surrendered half their harvest to the military elite, whose prime objective was to keep them in subjection. They had no rights and were obliged to wear dog-skin caps and animal skins, making them objects of mockery. To the Spartan poet Tyrtaeus, the *helots* were 'donkeys suffering under heavy loads'. Every year, Sparta declared war on their donkeys, allowing them to be killed with impunity. Its trainee warriors waged a campaign of terror and assassination against them, infiltrating their territory and striking at night – the ancient equivalent of shooting fish in a barrel.

But the Spartans were also tough on themselves. They practised eugenics at birth, killing off any male child deemed to be weak or infirm. Those that survived were sent, at the age of seven, to the *agoge* – the brat camp to end all brat camps. Here they would begin thirteen years of savage training to prepare them for a lifelong vocation as full-time warriors. There were no hyphenated farmer-soldiers in Sparta and no part-timers in the Spartan phalanx. Fighting was what the Spartans lived for, and died for. With their men training or fighting or just hanging out together in their all-male messes, where homosexuality was obligatory, Spartan women were free to enjoy economic, educational and sexual freedoms unheard of in the ancient world, and indeed, in many parts of the world today. When Spartan men and women did come together to procreate, their unfamiliarity with each other was said to be eased by a series of bizarre marriage rituals that would keep a team of sex therapists in jobs for life.

The rest of the Greek world looked on all this with a mixture of horror and fascination, but they accepted the Spartan assertion that this peculiar way of life was 'traditional'. In fact, many non-Spartans would be seduced by this fantasy of the 'good old days' being played out in the Eurotas valley, although they were always a little uncomfortable with the idea of Greeks enslaving Greeks – a fate usually reserved for barbarians. But despite its reputation for conservatism, Sparta was really no more stable than any of the other city-states. In the name of preserving what it had won it had embarked on one of the most radical political experiments the ancient world had ever seen. And in its passionate desire to 'keep things the way they had always been' it was constantly having to tinker with its traditions. In periods of manpower shortage, it was forced to admit different grades of warrior into the ranks of 'Equals': *mothakes*, whose fathers were Spartans and whose mothers were *helot* slaves, and the *neodamodais*, the 'new men', *helots* who had been granted citizenship in return for long military service. Even in the land of absolute equality, some were more equal than others. What these pragmatic adjustments make clear is that the Spartans, just like

everyone else, were struggling to come to terms with a fundamental but unsettling truth about civilization, in whatever form it took. It would be articulated for the first time by the Greek philosopher Heraclitus, whose teachings could be summarized in two words: *panta rhei* – 'everything changes'. In other words, not even the most conservative society could step into the same river twice.

In Athens, the river of change flowed just as forcefully as it did in Sparta, but here there was greater willingness to go with the flow. Like most of the other city-states, Athens had shrugged off its hereditary kings early on, replacing monarchy with oligarchy, which is when things began to get complicated. Although there do seem to have been rules controlling displays of wealth, they were nothing like the ones in Sparta, and they soon lapsed. As the Greek city-states emerged from the Dark Age and began to reconnect with the rest of the ancient world through colonization and trade, the rich inevitably got richer. In Athens and elsewhere these enterprises were financed by private wealth rather than the common purse, and the profits were distributed accordingly. The old law of 'them that's got shall get' came into play with a vengeance.

In Athens, as the poor got poorer, many were forced to sell themselves and their families into slavery to service their debts. Towards the end of the seventh century BC, the Athenian poor were in danger of becoming the *helots* of the Athenian rich. In Sparta, the destabilizing effects of inequality had been neutralized by Lycurgus' social revolution. In Athens, the ruling class chose the path of gradual reform. Solon, a statesman who lived from about 638 to 558 BC, was the first of a series of cautious aristocratic reformers who conceded by inches protections, rights and privileges to the *demos*, the people. Over the next 200 years, piecemeal reforms would ultimately lead to the establishment of a form of democracy in Athens. During Solon's rule as *archon*, or chief magistrate, debt slavery was abolished and the city's class system overhauled, with wealth replacing birth as the deciding factor of your place in the hierarchy, your voice in the community. Solon was a poet as well as a law-giver. He described his thankless role in the no-man's land between the rich and poor in heroic terms:

I girded myself, my mighty shield protecting both sides and allowed neither to win an unfair victory.

In the stories we tell ourselves about Athens, reformers like Solon are inevitably the good guys, far-sighted visionaries fighting the good fight, paving the way for the ultimate triumph of 'democracy'. But of course it was more complicated than that. Solon's reforms were as much the product of the fears of the ruling class as the idealism of a proto-democrat. Appeasing the *demos* was one way to lay the spectre of *stasis* – civil war – to rest. The trick, for the elite, was to buy stability as cheaply as possible, retaining as much real power as possible, feeding the democratic beast with tidbits without getting swallowed by it.

But in the political jungle of ancient Greece there were other animals on the prowl, and their influence was just as significant as that of the reformers. Today in the democratic West we do not look on them kindly, but the tyrants of ancient Greece are as much part of this story as the reformers. There was once another Parthenon standing where the present one now stands, and it was every bit as iconic as the one we are familiar with. The first Parthenon was built by Peisistratos, one of the most interesting characters from the early days of Classical Athens (the late sixth century BC). He was a *tyrannos* – a tyrant – which in Greek-speak meant a ruler who has come to power by illegitimate means and who maintains his power by appealing to the people over the heads of the elites. Peisistratos was guilty on both counts, but it was during his twenty-year rule (from 546 to about 527 BC) that Athens first came of age as one of the dominant city-states of ancient Greece.

It was evidently hard to resist Peisistratos; although they were miles apart politically, Solon, the solemn law-giver, was apparently in love with him in the way that older Greek men so often were with younger ones. Plutarch would later say of Peisistratos: 'He was so good at simulating faculties that he did not possess that he was credited with them more than those that already had them.' Aristotle called him an 'extreme democrat'. To me he sounds like a chancer. We have heard a lot about the shadow cast by the warrior Achilles over the imagination of the ancient Greeks, but the hero whose example really counted in the cut and thrust of their contemporary politics was Odysseus. Resourceful, nimble-witted, a trickster who could cheat a one-eyed giant out of his sight and leave him telling the world that 'no Man has hurt me', Odysseus was the

BELOW
A depiction of what is thought to be the Athenian tyrant Peisistratos' (c. 605–527 BC) club-wielding bodyguard. In a cunning ploy, Peisistratos had slashed himself and the mules of his chariot and made a dramatic entrance into the *agora* (marketplace) of Athens to show how his enemies had wounded him. The people voted for him to be given the use of a bodyguard of citizens armed with clubs, with the aid of which he seized the Acropolis and held power briefly in 560/559.

model for all successful tyrants. Peisistratos first came to prominence by allying with the 'hill dwellers', the lowest of the low in the pecking order of Athenian politics, turning them into a formidable powerbase. He then faked an attack on himself which persuaded the Athenians to vote him a bodyguard corps. He used this personal militia to stage his first coup, occupying the Acropolis and declaring himself tyrant. The Athenians eventually dislodged him and threw him out of the city, but he was not finished. In a move taken straight from the Odysseus play-book, Peisistratos drove back into the city in a chariot with beside him the tallest woman he could find, kitted out as the goddess Pallas Athena. She commanded the citizens of her city to take back her prodigal son – and the stunned Athenians obeyed.

The protection of this fake Athena did not last long, and Peisistratos was exiled for a second time. So he went to Laurion, nearly sixty-five kilometres from Athens, where silver mines had been discovered. He spent a decade getting filthy rich and then, in 546 BC, he returned to Athens, this time with a mercenary army at his back to do the persuading for him.

What followed was not bloodshed or revenge but a renaissance. Peisistratos embarked on a series of very public grand projects. He embellished the scope and number of the city's cult celebrations, important bonding sessions for all Athenians. He also commissioned the first definitive edition of the *Iliad*, an event of huge cultural significance for the Greeks – and for the world. And he built the first Parthenon, the remnants of which can be seen today in the new Acropolis Museum.

That is what tyrants, at their best, did: short-circuiting the stagnant impasse between rich and poor, galvanizing things through strong leadership, getting things done. Tyrants were the first politicians in the modern sense of the term, adept at the black arts of spin and triangulation, working the angles, building alliances. But as with all dynastic systems, complications arose with the question of succession. Who would take over when the old tyrant died? Without the sanctity of monarchy to protect them, second or third generation tyrants made legitimate targets for would-be freedom fighters.

In Athens, the dynasty founded by Peisistratos was brought down by Harmodius and Aristogeiton, honoured by later generations of Athenians as 'the liberators'. They assassinated Hipparchus, son of Peisistratos and brother of the tyrant Hippias, who was then himself deposed. But the motives of 'the liberators' were personal rather than political. Hipparchus had tried to seduce Harmodius away from his lover Aristogeiton, and the pair resolved to strike back at him and his brother. They bagged the would-be lover but not his tyrant brother. But the attempted assassination really brought out the tyrant in Hippias.

The Athenians eventually rebelled against his increasingly oppressive regime and he was forced to flee to the court of the Persian king Darius.

After the collapse of tyranny in Athens, the final churn in the political cycle that had begun with the reforms of Solon came with the rise to power of Kleisthenes. Like Solon, Kleisthenes was one of those canny aristocrats who recognized the need to sacrifice the privileges of his own class in order to preserve the good order of the city-state as a whole. In the last decade of the sixth century BC, Kleisthenes laid the foundations of the first recognizably democratic system in Athens. Tribal allegiances to old aristocratic families were replaced by geographic ones. The *deme*, or district, where you lived now gave the Athenians their political identity. Kleisthenes thoughtfully provided each *deme* with a mythical hero, and their statues were prominently displayed on a public altar in the *agora*. Election to public bodies, political and judicial, was thrown open to all citizens chosen by lot ('democratic' Athens always favoured the randomness of the lottery to the consciousness of the ballot box – chance rather than choice). Members of the *boule*, or council of citizens, swore an oath 'to advise according to the laws what was best for the people'. Kleisthenes called his reforms *isonomia* – equality before the law. Hesiod would surely have approved.

Kleisthenes is also credited with the introduction of *ostraka*, in 487 BC. If you earned 6,000 of these pottery shards with your name scratched on them, you would be ostracized, exiled, from Athens for ten years. The system was supposed to guard against the return of tyrants like Peisistratos, but it soon became a political weapon directed against anyone deemed to have become too prominent. One of the first to fall foul of this tall-poppy syndrome appears to have been the father of democracy himself: Kleisthenes.

By the beginning of the fifth century BC the Greek city-states had evolved their own distinctive set of characteristics, like Darwin's finches on the Galapagos Islands. They were all Greek, but they were Greek in their own peculiar way. It would take an external threat of apocalyptic proportions to force these birds of a feather to stick together.

III

PERSIAN WARS

In the centuries since the Dark Age, during which the Greeks had slowly groped their way back towards the light of civilization, the mighty empires of the East had come and gone: the Assyrians, the Babylonians and the Medes. Each had their moment in the sun, and each had in turn been eclipsed by the rising star of a new empire. By the time of Kleisthenes' reforms, the Persians ruled in the East. The Persian Empire was a monster: thirteen million square kilometres spanning three continents, from Afghanistan in the east to the west coast of Turkey, from Libya in the south to Macedonia in the north. Forged by Cyrus the Great in the mid sixth century BC, it became the greatest empire the ancient world would ever know. On its hem, Greek colonists on the coast of Asia Minor had stitched a dozen or so city-states. The threads would entangle the fate of the Persians and the Greeks for centuries to come.

The Great Kings of Persia, Xerxes and Darius, certainly had the territorial wherewithal to justify their claim to be a 'universal empire', but it was not just the vast resources at the disposal of the Great King that made him such a formidable power. This was no old-school Near Eastern power, doomed to a constant route march through its territory to keep all the bits in place. And it didn't bother overmuch about the inaccessible parts of its imperial map, so long as the locals were quiescent and its envoys and messengers could travel the Royal Road without disruption. The Persian Empire had learned not to sweat the small stuff. Rather than stamping a centralizing authority on their vast dominions, Persian kings embraced the cultural and political diversity

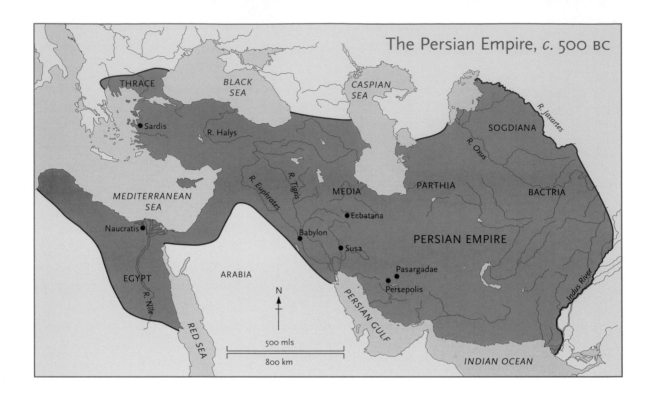

The Persian Empire, *c.* 500 BC

of their subject peoples. Nowhere was this better symbolized than at their magnificent new capital, Persepolis, in what is now western Iran. There Darius built his new city from materials sourced from all over his empire, using crafts-men from all his subject peoples. To emphasize the point, the walls of the giant stairway leading to his royal audience hall, which could hold over 10,000 people, were adorned with meticulously drawn reliefs showing representatives from all of the royal dominions. At its centre was a depiction of the Great King himself sitting on a huge throne, carried aloft by the leaders of his subject peoples.

Darius would construct a powerful new ideology of absolute kingship to bolster his rule. By appropriating the traditional Zoroastrian moral concepts of truth (*rta*) and lies (*drauga*), Darius was able to categorize the latter as anything that opposed his divinely sanctioned right to rule. It was his mission to root out *drauga* wherever he found it. Yet the Persian king was far more than a mere power mad autocrat. Later Athenian writers would, for good propaganda reasons, paint the Persian wars as a straight fight between Greek liberty and the darkness of the Orient. In fact, nothing could have been further from the truth. As long as taxes were paid and military levies met, the constituent parts of the Persian Empire were left pretty much to their own devices. Even Greek authors were moved to praise the Persian regime for its enlightened attitude towards its subject peoples. Here is Herodotus, the so-called 'Father of History':

And although it [the Persian empire] was of such magnitude, it was governed by the single will of Cyrus [the king]; and he honoured his subjects and cared for them as if they were his own children; and they, on their part, revered Cyrus as a father.

The Greek cities of western Asia Minor (known as the Ionian cities) became part of this hands-off empire with the defeat of the legendarily wealthy Lydian monarch Croesus in the 540s BC. The story of Greek relations with Persia would be recast later into one of total resistance against the incursions of a barbarous power. In fact, even the famous rebellion of the Ionians against Persian rule was not as clear cut as later historians would have us believe, with many Greeks choosing to abstain and even siding with the Persians. Records found at Persepolis show that large numbers of free Greeks were employed there. Even the Persian army, which would eventually attempt to invade Greece, was full of Greeks. Most of the Greek states seem to have had no problems maintaining friendly relations with their new neighbours. Deposed or aspiring rulers of Greek city-states (like the deposed Athenian tyrant Hippias) often travelled eastwards to the Persian king seeking asylum, military assistance or a well-paid 'consultancy' as resident expert on the Greeks.

Persia had no immediate argument with their puny, puzzling neighbours, though no doubt the logic of empire would have eventually entailed an attempt to add their territories to the imperial trophy cupboard. In the end it was the Greeks who provided the provocation and the justification for Persians to march west. It was, almost inevitably, a tyrant, one of those catalysts of the Greek world, who sparked the first great war of civilization between East and West. His name was Aristagoras, tyrant of the city of Miletus, one of the Ionian cities in Asia Minor that paid tribute to the Great King. Restless and ambitious, like all tyrants, Aristagoras' first move had been to offer to annex the Greek island of Naxos for the Persian Empire, in 499 BC. When this enterprise failed and he was threatened with imperial displeasure, he decided to go for broke and to foment rebellion among the Ionian cities. Aristagoras, imperial lackey turned pan-Hellenic freedom fighter, headed for the Greek mainland looking for military support for his plans. The Spartans, conservative and wary as ever, turned him down, but he had more luck in Athens, a city always ready to give a silver-tongued demagogue a hearing.

First he appealed to their greed, telling them easy pickings were to be had in the east; then he appealed to 'the Greek thing', wrapping up his opportunism in the cloak of a 'pan-Hellenic crusade'. Athens liked what it heard. It sent twenty-five ships to support the rebellion. 'These ships,' says Herodotus, 'were the beginning of all evils for Greeks and barbarians alike.' Having defeated the Ionian Revolt, Darius sought to secure his empire and punish the cities on mainland Greece for the destruction of Sardis, a major Persian city that the Greeks had burnt down during the revolt. The first Persian invasion of Greece took place in 494 BC but, after early successes in Macedon and Thrace, was pushed back.

In 490 BC, the Persian fleet set sail for Greece. They landed in the shallow, sheltered bay of Marathon, 40 kilometres east of Athens. On the plain of Marathon they were met by a mixed force of 9,000 Athenian and 1,000 Plataean hoplites. Against all the odds, the Persians were defeated and driven back. Greece had been saved, and the Athenians (ignoring the contribution made by the Plataeans) never allowed any of their rivals to forget it. After Marathon, one of Athens' generals, Themistocles, worked hard to convince his fellow citizens that sooner or later Persia would be back. Revenues from new silver mines found at Laurion were diverted towards a trireme-building programme to meet the threat of the gathering storm.

RIGHT
Marble statue thought to be of
Leonidas I, king of Sparta.

Themistocles would be proved right. It would take a decade for the Persians to return but, when they did, it was with 150,000 men and a fleet of 600 ships. Xerxes, the new Persian monarch, wanted to prove his mettle to his new subjects by dealing once and for all with these insolent Greeks. He took command of the campaign personally. Flanked by the 10,000 crack troops of his 'immortals' bodyguard, Xerxes crossed from Asia into Europe by way of an enormous floating pontoon, which his engineers built to bridge the Bosphorus. This second round of the conflict with Persia would draw in more Greek states, most notably Sparta. At the narrow pass of Thermopylae, 300 Spartan hoplites under the command of the Spartan king Leonidas would go on a suicide mission, attempting to keep the Persians at bay for as long as possible while the remainder of the Greeks tried to organize themselves. The Spartans were eventually vanquished through treachery, but Leonidas would win his place in the hall of fame for his gallows humour when he encouraged his men to breakfast well as they would be having their dinner in the Underworld. (The 700 Thespians, 400 Thebans and Sparta's shield-carrying *helots* who also got their dinner there would be routinely overlooked in the retelling of this glorious defeat.)

The Spartans would not be the only Greeks to make sacrifices. As the Persian juggernaut advanced, the Athenians evacuated their city and had to watch as the Persians burnt the Acropolis to the ground. But once again the Persian field commanders and admirals underestimated the determination of the Greeks.

At a great sea battle near the island of Salamis, Themistocles, realizing that the Greek ships were too slow and clumsy to face up to the state-of-the-art Persian fleet in open water, decided instead to turn them into stationary fighting platforms. The decks were filled with soldiers who would fight the enemy hand to hand. The Persians, who were unprepared for such tactics, were soundly defeated and retreated. Xerxes, sensing a total public-relations disaster, returned home but left his army to fight on. The job would be finished the next year when the Persian land army was destroyed and their commander Mardonius was killed by a huge Greek army led by the Spartan king Pausanias at Plataea, in 479 BC. The Persian army retreated in disarray, never to return to the Greek mainland, although hostilities rumbled on in Thrace and the Aegean until 449, when peace finally came.

The Persian Wars were the making of Greece – the story of heroic resistance and the ultimate victory over a regional superpower clearly showed that 'the Greek thing' produced a different and altogether superior class of human being. In Athens, always the most receptive amplifier of the Hellenic *zeitgeist*, there was an outpouring of literature and art that did much to crystallize what Greekness meant (and what it did not): Aeschylus would write the first tragedy, *The Persians*, which marks a critical break between a reconstituted 'Greek' culture and the Near East that had spawned it. Greece would default on the cultural debt that it owed to the East, insisting that like the goddess Athena, who sprang fully formed from the head of Zeus, it owed nothing to anybody. The virtues of Greece – liberty, reason, civilization and virility – were now juxtaposed with the supposed oriental barbarity of the East as represented by Persia, who were routinely portrayed as effeminate, hen-pecked, treacherous and cowardly. In the instinctive polarizing mindset of the Greeks, the 'East' would come to stand for everything Greece was not – an anti-type to be despised and parodied.

IV

THE GOLDEN AGE OF ATHENS AND THE DESOLATION OF GREECE

But the end of the Persian Wars did nothing to ease the eternal dynamic of 'the Greek thing': inter-*polis* rivalry. You would have thought that the time was now right for the Greeks to develop some kind of political and economic union – an alliance, a federation, a united states of Greece. But it did not happen. The two

dominant city-states, Athens and Sparta, sniffed around each other for a while, but in the end they and their allies went their separate ways for a generation and more. The next time they would come together, they would be at each other's throats in a destructive war that would ultimately cost both sides everything they had: the Peloponnesian War.

The truth is that Sparta and Athens had evolved into such different societies that they had trouble understanding one another. Sparta distrusted Athenian democracy, fearing it would infect their *helot* slaves with the virus of freedom. Unwilling to seize the opportunities that came with victory, it was said that after the Persian Wars 'Sparta slept'. Athens was very different: galvanized by the adrenaline rush of victory, she embarked on ever more radical experiments in democracy, culture and empire-building.

During the Persian invasion, the Athenians had done a daring thing: they had voluntarily abandoned their city to the Persians. The elderly, women and children were evacuated to the island of Salamis and other safe locations from where they watched their city burn. Given the centrality of the city to the security and identity of its citizens, this move was about as likely as a snail giving up its shell, but perhaps the bold spirit that powered post-war Athens was born at this moment of crisis. By abandoning their city, the Athenians discovered that it was more than just its walls or buildings. Athens became an idea, a 'city of the head'.

Politics was never very far from the surface of things in Athens. When Athens had been evacuated, men of fighting age had taken their places on the rowing benches of the triremes moored at the port of Piraeus, from where they set out to face the enemy in the bay of Salamis. On the rowing benches, the richest citizens sat next to the poorest (the *thetes*), and the sweat of *hoi oligoi* mixed with the sweat of *hoi polloi*. At Salamis the Persian Wars became a people's war, and afterwards the *thetes* expected that to be remembered. Like the hoplite revolution, the transformation of the *thetes* into the heroic protectors of the city would have profound political consequences in Athens, demonstrating once again Aristotle's dictum: 'The class that does the fighting wields the power.'

Post-war Athens was the scene of one of the most radical experiments in government that the world has ever witnessed: by the middle of the fifth century BC, the city was no longer ruled by a single autocratic, or even a narrow aristocratic, elite like other states, but by its whole citizen body, whether they be young or old, rich or poor. Admittedly, this did not include anyone who was under sixteen, female or who could not prove that both their parents were

LEFT
Sexually engaged couple.

Athenians, but it was still an extraordinary departure from the way that other states had organized their affairs. Unsurprisingly, the elite found plenty to moan about when it came to democracy. For a start, it allowed the people far too much power. How could it possibly be right that those who had been carefully and painstakingly prepared to rule be accountable to those who had not? These misgivings would later be fully articulated by Aristotle, who would argue that democracy could lead directly to tyranny if the rule of law was ignored. In his famous treatise the *Politics*, Aristotle likened the general citizen body to a mercurial despot whose unrealistic dreams were fuelled by unscrupulous tub-thumping politicians, defining for ever the conservative's nightmare of an unholy alliance between the ignorant mob and the manipulative demagogue.

In some important ways, it could be argued that Athenian democracy changed very little. The educated elite were now accountable for their actions to the general citizen body, but they continued to hold most of the executive offices of state. Although reforms had been passed that paid ordinary citizens a day rate if they served in the law courts or the assembly, it was not enough to live on. Many of the poor were still excluded from participating in the political process because they had to work. The same was true of Athenian citizens who worked the land and lived too far away to travel into the city each day. The truth about Athenian democracy is that it left the hands of the rich firmly on the levers of power. After all, democratic politics required a specific skill set which was usually possessed only by those who had received an expensive education – oratory, legal training and sophism (the ability to argue any case) would remain the rich man's choice of weapons in the ongoing class war.

But for all its hidden inequalities, there is no doubt that democracy brought about huge intellectual and cultural advances. It is not without reason that the second half of the fifth century BC is known as the Golden Age of Classical Greece. In Athens, arts and literature, philosophy and science flourished. Democracy not only allowed, but actively encouraged, the citizens of the Athenian *polis* to question the premises on which their society and institutions were built. Philosophers such as Plato and Aristotle (despite their anti-democratic sympathies) could have been produced only in a democracy. The development of drama could have thrived only in an environment where freedom of speech was enshrined in law, and where the audience was itself involved in the political process.

Whilst democracy enormously enriched the lives of the citizens of Athens, it came at a terrible cost for others. Slavery had existed right from the creation of the very first cities in Mesopotamia, but it was in fifth-century BC Athens that slavery would first be intellectually justified. To us it seems a contradiction that any democratic state could promote and profit from the denial of liberty to other human beings, but that is fundamentally to misunderstand the intellectual underpinning of democracy as a political institution in the ancient world: just as Sparta's warrior society could exist only because of the *helots*, Athenian democracy could exist only because of slavery. For Aristotle and other Athenian intellectuals it was self-evident that freedom for the few could be built only on the slavery of the many.

This was not some abstruse academic point; it was a clear economic reality. Radical democracy was expensive. Money was needed to pay for the poorer citizens to skip work and exercise their democratic rights in the assemblies and law courts. But even with slaves to work it, the land surrounding Athens was good for little more than growing olives. Virtually all the city's food had to be imported, making it vulnerable to military blockade. The solution was slavery of another kind: Athenian freedom would be underwritten by the financial, political and military enslavement of Athens' Greek allies.

The original anti-Persian alliance, the Delian League, was forged in 478 BC. It was an alliance of 173 city-states, led by Athens, but Sparta was not a member. When they signed up, League members had thrown lumps of iron into the waters of the Aegean to represent the permanence of their relationship. Many would later have reason to look back on this solemn ceremony with regret. Even after the Persian threat had subsided, the Athenians would hold them to their pledge. Victory over the Persians did not secure their liberty but instead sealed their descent into servitude. The bitter irony was that their subjugator was not some perfumed oriental king but their Greek comrades in Athens.

The Athenians persuaded their allies to contribute money to their mutual defence league rather than warships or warriors. It was a Faustian bargain – the more the allies paid, the more militarily powerful the Athenians became. Before long none of the allied states could mount any resistance to Athens. They were forced to adopt Athenian coinage, weights and measures. Their populations became diluted as the Athenians set up new colonies on their territory, and their autonomy was compromised as Athenian garrisons followed. Although nominally independent, allied governments were packed full of pro-Athenian quislings who thought nothing of privileging the interests of Athens over those of their own citizens. Some historians have argued that Athens promoted democracy throughout Greece, but it is a strange sort of democracy where the people are not free to make their own decisions. 'Allies' that stepped out of line soon felt the force of the Athenian trireme diplomacy. The fathers of democracy would use threats, economic embargoes, political indoctrination, murder, rape and starvation to keep their fledgling empire intact. Nothing would

ATLANTIC OCEAN

Tartessos
Gades
Carteia
Malaca
Sexi
Tingis
Calpe
Abdera
Lixus
Sala
Rusadir

Greece
Greek colonies
Phoenicia
Phoenician colonies

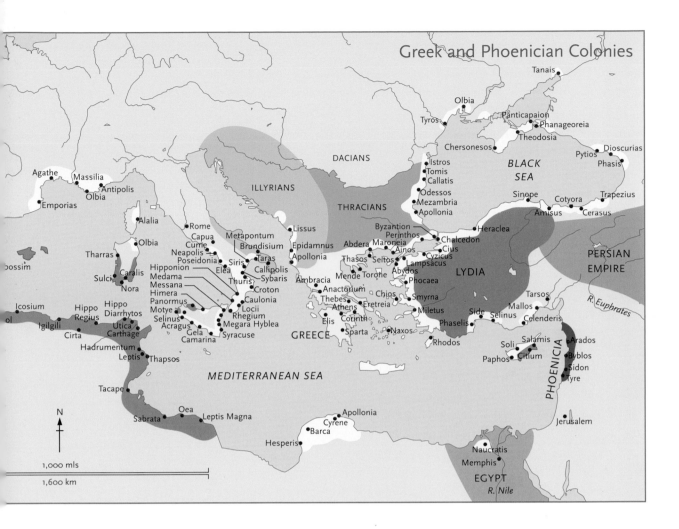

Greek and Phoenician Colonies

be allowed to threaten the precious democratic freedoms that the citizens of Athens enjoyed.

One of the most notorious examples of the ruthlessness that governed Athenian imperial policy took place in 427 BC, after a revolt by the city of Mytilene, an Athenian 'ally' that attempted to defect to the Spartans at a critical point in the Peloponnesian War. Once the uprising was suppressed, the Athenian populist politician Cleon (a tanner by trade, a butcher by nature) proposed that every man, woman and child there should be slaughtered. The motion was passed and a ship was sent, carrying the orders for the massacre. The next day, the debate was revived and, mercurial as ever, the Athenians decided that only the ringleaders should be put to death (though with a thousand names on the list, the Athenians cast the ring pretty wide). So a second ship was dispatched with the new orders. The historian Thucydides gives a vivid description of the scene on this second boat, with the anxious Mytilenean envoys supplying the Athenian rowers with barley mixed with oil and wine to keep them going so they could overtake the first ship. They only just made it in time, but the people of Mytilene were saved. Mercy had its own propaganda value: this dramatic story crisscrossed the Aegean and mainland Greece and served as yet another emphatic reminder of the disaster that awaited any city tempted to try to leave the alliance. The episode was the final instalment in the Delian League's transformation from mutual protection alliance to Athenian protection racket.

Why were the Athenians so ruthless when it came to keeping the League together? The answer lies in the nature of radical democracy and its reliance on a fragile consensus of its richest and poorest citizens. To keep everybody happy and on board, democratic governments had to control the resources of others.

For much of the second half of the fifth century BC, Athens was mired in an increasingly destructive and unwinnable war with the other great power of ancient Greece, Sparta. In 460 BC, only twenty years after the end of the Persian Wars, the first Peloponnesian War broke out between Athens, dragging the rest of the Delian League along with it, and Sparta, Thebes and other members of Sparta's rival alliance, the Peloponnesian League. So widespread was suspicion of Athenian acquisitiveness that Sparta, hardly a fount of altruistic benevolence itself, was successful, at least initially, in presenting itself as protector of Greek freedoms. The first war ended in something of a stalemate, in about 445 BC, but reignited in 431 and went on until 404, and Sparta's ultimate victory. In the process, though, the 'village cricket match' culture of inter-*polis* warfare was well and truly jettisoned. As we have seen, according to the historian Thucydides the Greeks became 'like beasts to each other'. The truth was that both sides increasingly stood for nothing but their own self-interest. A revealing episode occurred in 423 when Sparta and Athens, both exhausted by the heavy toll in both manpower and resources, signed a peace treaty. The town of Skione had made the unfortunate decision, a short while before the agreement, to go over from the Athenians to the Spartan side. Now the Spartans merely stood aside whilst the vengeful Athenians captured Skione and slaughtered its entire population.

The Spartans made particularly poor liberators, and the goodwill felt towards them was soon squandered as their allies became disenchanted by their violent and high-handed behaviour. A particular case in point was the colony of Heraclea, set up by the Spartans at Trachis in central Greece in 426. Heraclea was, to start with, a fantastic propaganda coup. The Spartans proclaimed that the new settlement, named after Heracles, the Greek hero from whom the Spartan kings claimed to be descended, would be a refuge for all those threatened by Athenian aggression. The colony was initially a huge success, with people flocking to it from all over Greece, but the arrogant and harsh actions of the Spartan governor soon alienated the colonists and Heraclea ended up a flop. The problem was that the Spartans' xenophobic and inward-looking tendencies made them completely ill-suited to accommodating the 'Greekness' of their fellow Greeks.

Sparta's other great obstacle to swiftly bringing the war to an end was its lack of resources and manpower, the result of a political system no longer suited to the demands that it faced. The exclusive definition of who was a genuine Spartan, and therefore able to serve as part of the main core of their army, led to a serious shortage of fighters. Just how serious this problem had become is demonstrated by the fact that the shocking capture of just 120 of Sparta's key warrior class, the Spartiates, by the Athenians in 425 forced Sparta to the negotiating table. Although more forward-thinking commanders tried to get around this problem by recruiting *helots* into their army, the Spartan government remained deeply suspicious and did all in their power to resist any move to politically enfranchise them.

Painfully aware of their lack of Spartiate hoplites, Spartan generals were often cautious in how they deployed these troops, knowing that they could not bear heavy losses. In fact, for much of the Peloponnesian War, Sparta pursued the unambitious and ultimately unsuccessful strategy of annually invading Attica and waging a scorched-earth policy in the hope of starving Athens out. Lack of money was also a serious impediment to a decisive victory over Athens. Sparta tried to make up the shortfall by raising a levy from its allies, but it was eventually forced to look further afield for funds. The Spartans might have presented their war against Athens as one of Greek liberation, but it did not stop them in the 420s appealing to the Persian king, who still ruled over a large number of their Greeks in western Asia Minor, for money. The resources of the mighty Persian Empire dwarfed the combined wealth of all the Greek city-states, and the Great King and his subordinates were more than ready to finance discord among the Hellenes.

The Peloponnesian War spread over nearly sixty years, punctuated by ineffectual peace treaties signed in bad faith. In Athens, war fatally destabilized the fragile political consensus on which its democracy had long relied. In fact, for much of the fifth century BC, the political tensions that had existed between mass and elite in democratic Athens had been a source of dynamic energy from which the city had benefited. The same could not be said in the last years of that century. Radical democracy, with its often harsh penalties for failure and propensity for scapegoating, had never been particularly conducive to the acceptance of either corporate or individual responsibility by its citizens.

The disappointments, false hopes and disasters of the Peloponnesian War

merely exaggerated these tendencies. Each reverse was met with a predictable rerun of the blame game. Mutual recriminations would be eventually replaced by active attempts by the members of the aristocratic elite to replace democracy with an oligarchic regime. Their indignation grew as they were increasingly expected to shoulder the financial burden of the war now that some of their allies were refusing to pay tribute.

In 411 BC, a group of 400 wealthy citizens, taking advantage of the turmoil, mounted an oligarchic coup. Although they managed to seize power, it did not take long for the oligarchs to show that they were themselves divided on a number of key issues. Some argued for a peace with Sparta, but their position was transparently governed by self-interest, as they thought it gave them a better chance of maintaining their own political pre-eminence. Others saw an alliance with Persia as a way of defeating Sparta. The most serious disagreement was about just how exclusive the Athenian state should be. Although the hardliners in their leadership promised to hand power over to a larger group of 5,000 citizens, they seem to have had no intention of doing so. They were opposed by the moderates in the new ruling group, who argued that all those who can serve the state with horse and shield, in other words both the wealthy elite and the hoplite class, should be included in a power share.

With support for their government quickly falling away, the rule of the 400 was replaced by a more inclusive oligarchy made up of 5,000 wealthier citizens. Dressed up by the anti-democratic Athenian historian Thucydides as a 'moderate blend of the few and the many', the truth was that it still rescinded the democratic rights of the *thetes*, descendants of the oarsmen who had manned the triremes at Salamis. The 5,000 would soon, however, go the same way as the 400: in a time of war, Athens could hardly exclude the very rowers on whom they were so reliant, despite their efforts to bribe them with offers of increased pay in exchange for their constitutional rights.

The return of democracy to Athens resulted in a fresh bout of political infighting that seriously impaired the city's war effort. In a self-defeating move that was clearly part of a concerted campaign to reassert the political muscle of the masses, a number of Athens' generals were successfully prosecuted after bad weather forced them to leave survivors and the bodies of the dead in the water after a naval battle. This was despite the fact they had won an important victory. Athens had to fight on without some of its most experienced and talented commanders. Once again short-term internal score-settling trumped long-term strategic goals in democratic Athens.

Another key development occurred in 407, when Darius II, the Persian king, decided to bring this seemingly endless, disruptive war to a conclusion because he had a number of other serious rebellions and wars to deal with across his vast realm. He sent his son Cyrus to Asia Minor to energize the ever-cautious Spartans. With Sparta reinforced by the Persians and the Athenians having shorn themselves of their best commanders, a resolution was in sight. The last significant battle of the war came at the mouth of the Goat river on the Dardanelles in 405 BC. The cunning Spartan general Lysander dealt the final blow, trapping and destroying the Athenian fleet on the beach. The battle of Aigospotamoi was a fatal blow for the Athenians. Losing the Hellespont also meant losing the corn supply from the Black Sea on which they heavily relied. Faced with starvation, Athens had no option but to surrender in 404. It was a deeply destructive war, finally brought to an end by political instability and starvation in Athens and by the Persian king deciding that his interests were best served by bringing it all to a close. Prostitutes played flutes as the walls of Athens were torn down by the Spartans, but it was a barbarian king who was calling the tune.

The peace terms were severe. Apart from twelve ships, the entire Athenian fleet had to be surrendered. What remained of the Athenian empire across Greece was lost, and the city was forced to join the Peloponnesian League under the leadership of Sparta. A reactionary oligarchic regime of Thirty Tyrants was installed with a garrison of Spartan troops to protect them. Just under eighty years earlier it had been a Persian army that had occupied the city, now it was an army of fellow Greeks. Some of their enemies thought that even this was too lenient a punishment, and argued that the city should be completely obliterated.

The Peloponnesian War pitted Greek against Greek in a pitiless struggle that in the end corrupted the ideals of all those who took part. And it ended with a foreign king, a Persian barbarian, pulling the strings while Greek slaughtered Greek in the name of democracy, freedom and justice. In the long term there were no real winners: the Spartans might have emerged victorious, but the victory itself began to appear increasingly hollow. During the war the precious moral capital that Sparta had initially enjoyed had been quickly squandered by its ineffectual and crass leadership. Its reputation as a great warrior power had also been damaged by its failure to land any kind of knockout blow on the battlefield, while its increasingly desperate attempts to secure the support of Persia had made Sparta look weak and its claims to be the liberator of the Greeks appear ridiculous. But perhaps most corrosive of all was the corruption of Sparta's anti-materialistic warrior code. Persian silver may have paid for their victory, but it also changed the way the 'Equals' saw the world. Gylippus, the architect of Sparta's decisive victory over the Athenians in Sicily, was exposed as an embezzler when a shipment of Persian 'archers' (the symbol with which Persian coins were stamped) was discovered hidden in the roof of his house.

A period of Spartan expansion followed the end of the war, but it proved to be a false dawn. Within a few years the Spartans found themselves fighting a coalition of their former friends and enemies – Athens, Corinth, Thebes, Argos and Persia – in the Corinthian War of 395 to 387 BC. Sparta was able to emerge victorious only because the Persian king swapped sides after becoming alarmed at the prospect of a resurgent Athens. This was a Pyrrhic victory for Sparta, merely marking the beginning of a serious decline brought on by long-term structural defects within the state. Spartan ambition had outstripped the fragile human resources of a city-state built on the exclusivity of its warrior class. Old problems such as a low birth rate, the result of the tradition of late marriage as well as the Spartans' liberal attitudes towards women inheriting property and choosing their own husbands, had a cumulative effect. More and more property appears to have fallen into the hands of heiresses, with the result that by the fourth century BC two fifths of Spartan land was in female hands. This state of affairs had a disastrous effect on Spartiate numbers, as their status relied on them holding enough land to produce an agricultural surplus to pay their mess bills. Consequently the number of Spartiates declined when these impoverished warriors were forced to drop down to an inferior class. With restrictions in place that made upward mobility into the Spartiate class virtually impossible, all the conditions were in place for self-inflicted extinction. As the number of Spartiates dwindled, so Sparta's fighting capacity fell. The watershed moment came at the battle of Leuctra in 371, where the Spartans were heavily defeated by a Theban army: 400 out of the 700 Spartiates there were killed. With a full fighting strength of only around 1,000 Spartiates, this reverse was a knockout blow. The Theban commander Epaminondas subsequently invaded the Peloponnese and liberated the *helots* of Messenia, destroying for ever the economic cornerstone on which the Spartan state rested.

In Athens the bloody rule of the Thirty Tyrants was swiftly curtailed, but it did not bring to an end the political tensions that had beset the city. The returning democrats embarked on a settling of accounts against those who were suspected of having collaborated with the Thirty Tyrants. Their most celebrated victim was Athens' best-known highbrow celebrity, the philosopher Socrates. In 399 he was put on trial for impiety and corrupting the Athenian youth, but the charges had as much to do with his well-known antipathy towards democracy: he argued that it was not majority opinion that produced correct policy but rather genuine knowledge and professional competence, which was possessed by only a few. Ironically the philosopher was also accused of promoting sophism – considered

LEFT
So-called hemlock pots. Hemlock (*Conium maculatum*), native to Europe and the Mediterranean region, contains the neurotoxin coniine, which disrupts the workings of the central nervous system. For an adult the ingestion of just six to eight fresh leaves can lead to respiratory collapse and death.

by many Athenians as the unacceptable by-product of their democracy, a training that might have taught their youth intellectual flexibility and eloquence but also encouraged a cynical and nihilistic attitude towards justice and truth. Found guilty by a majority verdict, Socrates was sentenced to death, euthanizing himself with a cup of hemlock.

Nine decades of conflict had turned the Greeks into a mercenary people, schooled in war and survival. With their own cities in crisis, many now became hired swords for whoever would pay them. The Athenian aristocrat Xenophon, a soldier and writer who lived from around 430 to 354 BC, signed up to fight for the Persian prince Cyrus, who was trying to usurp his brother, King Artaxerxes II, who had succeeded Darius II in 404. When they were deep in the Persian Empire, Cyrus their paymaster was killed and their Greek generals were murdered at a peace conference. The 10,000 stranded Greek mercenaries, facing imminent destruction, turned around and marched back westwards, fighting their way through hostile Persians, Armenians and other local populations until finally making it back to Greece.

The exploits of 'the Ten Thousand' were written by Xenophon in his work the *Anabasis*. Under his descriptive pen they took on a Homeric lustre (with a starring role for a wise, unflappable Athenian called Xenophon). The reality, however, was that this was an inglorious and shabby episode: 10,000 rootless mercenaries retreating through the back of beyond, surviving on plunder, debating whether or not to found a new colony by abducting women from local tribes; and when they finally made it back, they were threatened with permanent exile by the neurotically hostile Spartans.

It was not just soldiers who hired themselves out to the highest bidder. With Athenian political and economic capital at such a low ebb, a brain drain took place with many of the cream of its intelligentsia, artists and craftsmen leaving – following the money and power. Some went off to the Greek cities of Italy and Sicily, where there were wealthy autocrats ready to spend vast amounts on self-aggrandizing projects. Others headed for the courts of the Persian satraps, where work could always be found. There was also another destination – a growing centre of wealth and power in the north – where an ambitious and talented Greek might find employment and preferment.

The kingdom of Macedon, to the north of Greece, had long been considered a barbarous backwater but in the first half of the fourth century BC under the brilliant leadership of its king Philip II had increasingly replaced Persia as the power broker to which the squabbling city-states of Greece turned to in order to seek help against their enemies. It was here that a number of Athens' brightest intellectual stars congregated at the court of Philip. Among them was the philosopher Aristotle, who in the late 340s became head of the Macedonian Academy and tutor to Philip's son, Alexander. Aristotle, like many Greeks of his time, still looked back with regret at the wasted opportunities of the fifth century. He wrote: 'If only the Greeks could achieve a single *politeia*, or constitution, they would rule the world.'

It had remained the big 'if only' of ancient Greece. Neither the democracy of Athens nor the warrior code of Sparta had been able to weld the Greeks into a single *politeia*. And it had not escaped the notice of Aristotle and other fourth-century BC Greek writers and thinkers that a much older institution, which had been extinct in their own land for centuries, had provided enviable cohesion and stability for some of their near neighbours. Under the rule of kings, Macedon and Persia had become major powers, while the city-states of Greece remained mired in inter-communal violence and endless wars. The Peloponnesian War had not only damaged the belief that oligarchy or democracy could produce a well governed state but also made many in Greece re-evaluate the relative merits of political freedom against those of personal security. Kingship was about to make a spectacular comeback, and it would be under the leadership of the most brilliant and charismatic of their number that Greekness, if not Greece, would at last come to rule the world.

4

AGE OF KINGSHIP: ALEXANDER
AND THE HELLENISTIC AGE

THE RETREAT TO KINGSHIP: THE RISE OF MACEDON

It is tempting to see civilization as incremental – not without its difficulties and setbacks, but fundamentally a steady progression. In fact, the onward march of civilization was one that was full of blind alleys, cul-de-sacs and dead-ends. Periods of retrenchment often followed hard on eras of brilliance and innovation. Yet what might initially appear to be reverse, regression or worse was often merely a necessary process of thinning and pruning from which new stronger ideas would eventually force themselves through.

By the early fourth century BC the high-octane political experimentation that had turned Greece into the cultural epicentre of the ancient world had descended into mutual recrimination, cynicism and inertia. It had become clear that, however good the product, the Greeks were singularly ill-equipped to export the fruits of their brilliance. It would take a people from a barbarous northern land – a place where the *polis* was a stranger, where kingship, a form of government that the Greeks thought they had left long behind in the distant heroic past, still held sway – to turn the 'Greek thing', or at least part of it, into a global brand.

Greece was suffering from a power vacuum. The rival city-states of Athens, Sparta and Thebes were at each other's throats, and the main beneficiary of the ruinous Peloponnesian and Corinthian wars had been the old enemy, Persia. With Greece as weak and divided as it had ever been, for many ancient Greeks it was a time for sombre reflection as they surveyed the wreckage of the ambitious pan-Hellenic dreams of their forefathers.

In Athens, the humiliating defeat in the Peloponnesian War coupled with the self-destructive political ructions that had followed it led many among its intelligentsia to rethink the concept of the city-state. Their problem – how to achieve order and stability among diverse constituents – was as old as the city-state itself. Long and bitter experience had shown that the most destructive

PREVIOUS PAGE
Mount Eryx, Sicily.

element within the Greek city was *stasis*: political or ideological disputes that descended into ghastly inter-communal violence. Reading Thucydides' account of the internecine carnage that occurred between democrats and oligarchs on Corcyra (Corfu) in 427 BC, it is easy to see why *stasis* cast such a dark shadow:

Death was present in every which way. As usually occurs in such circumstances people went to the brink and beyond. Fathers butchered their sons, men were dragged from the temples or even murdered on the altars themselves, some were actually walled up in the Temple of Dionysius where they died.

In the *Republic*, the philosopher Plato, a pupil of Socrates, attempted to establish, at least on paper, the perfect state, one that would withstand the political storms that had long buffeted the cities of Greece. In the process, Plato (who lived from about 428 to 348 BC) created one of the most influential works of philosophy ever written. What terrified Plato was instability, and he attacked democracy because it privileged equality and freedom over the knowledge and experience that good leadership needed. Radical democracy so disturbed Plato that it led one of the great minds of the ancient world to sarcasm; he described democracy as 'a delightful form of government, anarchic and motley, assigning a kind of equality to equals and unequals alike'.

Plato's great ambition was to save the city from *stasis* by establishing an ideal society, built on justice, reason and order and at the same time strong enough to defend itself from outside enemies. His ideal state would be led by individuals of the highest education and philosophical training, for only they had sufficient knowledge of what was good and true. At the heart of this vision of the perfect state stood the philosopher-ruler, an idealized figure, the recipient of long years of rigorous training and combining supreme talent with a perfect education. While uniquely placed to govern, this ruler should not crave power, but rather understand the duty to take on the burden of leadership. Although Plato himself often warned about the distinction between reality and theory in his work, it is clear that he saw a philosophical education, at the very least, as an essential part of the training of any successful ruler. With this in mind, he established the Academy, a school for aspiring statesmen, in Athens in 386 BC. He also became involved, with very mixed results, in the attempted re-education of contemporary autocratic rulers. Plato advised Dionysius II, the young tyrant of Syracuse in Sicily, at the request of Dionysius' chief minister and uncle, Dion. After making a number of visits to Syracuse, Plato discovered how much harder practice is than theory. Dionysius was not only arrogant and dissolute but, already in his late twenties, hardly a blank canvas. While becoming increasingly

hostile towards his critical uncle Dion, Dionysius was also keen to win the approval of his learned tutor, but without putting in any effort or bothering to implement anything he had learned. Plato's Republic was a utopia, its elitist purity completely and self-consciously out of step with the hurly-burly world of early fourth-century BC Greek politics. Many modern commentators have seen Plato's main motivation as political escapism rather than a true desire to reform.

It was not just in the rarefied intellectual stratosphere of Plato and his peers that this questioning of the whole concept of the *polis* was going on. Xenophon, a far simpler soul, looked for real examples of the perfect ruler rather than trying to test out his theories in a human laboratory. For Xenophon and others like him, the solution to the political instability that had long paralysed the city-states of Greece already existed – in fact it had been in existence for almost as long as the cities themselves. Although kingship had been dormant, their most powerful neighbours to the north and east, Macedon and Persia, were monarchies. Many of the Greek states in Sicily and southern Italy were also ruled over by autocrats, some of whom had taken on the trappings, if not the titles, of royalty.

Xenophon wrote *Cyropaedia*, a eulogy of Cyrus – the founder of the Persian empire – as a way of exploring the virtues of kingship. Cyrus, who lived in the sixth century BC, might have been long dead, but Xenophon clearly thought his qualities had contemporary value and relevance. Cyrus, according to Xenophon, was a servant of his subjects rather than a tyrant. He ruled not by force or divine right but by the virtue of his own actions. According to Xenophon, the ideal ruler 'is the first to execute what is appointed by the whole state, and submits to what is appointed; his own inclination is not his standard of action, but, the law'. In another piece of writing, this time about his friend the Spartan king Agesilaus, Xenophon covered similar themes about compassion, generosity and service:

His family members found him a relative of exceptional generosity. To his close companions he was an intimate friend. To the man who had performed good service, he had a long memory. A champion to victims of injustice, he was a saviour second only to the gods to those who risked danger at his side.

Times had certainly changed: just one century on from the Persian Wars and a few decades on from the Peloponnesian War, we find an Athenian looking to the old enemies, Persia and Sparta, for examples of ideal leadership. After the political violence and self-destruction of the previous half-century, the certainties of autocracy, although one enlightened enough to meet the needs of its subjects, appeared preferable to the insecurities of more representative forms of government.

It certainly seemed that the oligarchic and democratic regimes that dominated the Greek city-states had learned little from the Peloponnesian War. War and strife still stalked Greece; both democrats and oligarchs thought nothing of trying to draw powerful non-Greek neighbours into their conflicts, a practice that often prolonged rather than shortened these debilitating disputes. And now feuding Greek city-states seeking advantage over their enemies had another foreign power besides Persia to whom they could turn.

The kingdom of Macedon on the northern marches of Greece had traditionally been the victim of the city-states, rather than an aggressor towards them. The region had long been a target for Athenian imperial ambitions, mainly because of its vast forests, which were a ready source of timber for their fleets. It was always a moot point as to how Greek the Macedonians were, and the Greeks would change their position on the issue according to current political relations with the kingdom. In the mid fifth century, the Macedonian king, Alexander I, had earned the title Philhellene, or lover of the Greeks, because of his immersion in Greek culture. He had even won several victories at Greek athletic competitions held at Delphi and Olympia. The Macedonian language was a Greek dialect and, as we shall see, members of the royal family were often given a rigorous education in Greek literature and the arts. To many in Greece, however, the Macedonians would always be nothing more than northern barbarians, no matter how accomplished they became. As one, admittedly politically hostile, Athenian orator let rip into the Macedonian king Philip II, the father of Alexander the Great:

Not only not a Greek, nor related to the Greeks, but not even a barbarian from anywhere that can be named with any admiration, but a dishonorable troublemaker from Macedonia, from where it is still impossible to buy a decent slave.

Even Alexander I, the lover of Greece, had had to prove his Hellenic credentials before he was allowed to compete in their Games.

Those, however, who cast Macedon as an uncouth barbarian realm were avoiding an uncomfortable truth: Macedon was part of Greece. Not the Greece of Athens, Sparta, Argos and Corinth, but an older Greece that had always existed in the lands of the north. Entering Macedon in the fourth century BC would have been like stepping back to a time before the emergence of the citizen-led Greek city-state, to the tribal, warrior society described in the epic myths of Homer. Although the influence of Greek literature, art and architecture had long reached Macedon, the political systems that were such an important aspect of Classical Greece held no sway. This was not a civilization of politicians and orators, but of ruthless autocrats. High-minded concepts of citizenship mattered less than ethnic loyalties and tribal horse trading. The *polis* was a stranger to Macedon, a kingdom of powerful clans ruled, often precariously, by a single monarch. Kings, surrounded by their bodyguards, were judged on their military prowess as much as their political acumen. The Macedonians excelled in hunting, horse riding and fighting; they were a warlike people. The army was kingmaker and a symbol of national unity. This was a culture of Big Man-ism writ large.

Philip II, father of Alexander the Great, was the king who led Macedon's dizzying ascent from peripheral barbarism to regional supremacy during his reign from 359 to 336 BC. In the process, he reunified Greece into a formidable imperial power. One of his first acts as king was to rebuild the Macedonian army, inspiring the unity of both the military and the people as a whole through a series of morale-boosting speeches at assemblies across the kingdom, and recruiting his army from both upper and lower Macedon. Upper Macedon was a world of minor mountain kings and petty princes akin to the feudal baronies of fifteenth-century Europe. There was a whiff of pine forests and mountain air to it all. This is 'the North', above the 'olive line', a long way from the world of the citizen-hoplites of Greece. But when it got to the brutal realities of warfare, the Macedonians really came into their own. Philip himself revolutionized the hoplite style of fighting by introducing the *sarissa* – a pike up to 6 metres long. Deployed en masse and swished up and down the infantry phalanx (another Macedonian innovation), they were, according to one eyewitness, like 'the quills of a giant porcupine'.

Macedon had long suffered from the interferences of Greek city-states, most notably Thebes and Athens, in its internal affairs. But in the 350s, it became strong and united, and its influence began to spread over northern Greece. Using new military strategies, like the infantry phalanx, Philip's armies proved irresistible as a series of Greek armies were swept out of the way. Philip was greatly aided in all this by the Greek penchant for inviting larger foreign powers to attack their enemies and the Macedonian king was canny enough to play the 'divide and rule' card to maximum effect. Between 355 and 346 BC, the Third Sacred War had gone on between a Theban-led alliance of Greek states and the Phocians, who hailed from central Greece. The dispute centred on the Phocians' refusal to pay a very large fine for supposedly cultivating crops on sacred land. The fine was imposed on them by the Delphic Amphictionic League, an ancient panel of different Greek states charged with the protection and oversight of the famous sanctuaries of the god Apollo, among others. Correctly interpreting this punitive fine as part of a Theban campaign of persecution, the Phocians reacted by seizing the sanctuary at Delphi and making free use of the god's enormous treasury to fund their war effort. Philip was called in to help. It was too late by the time the Greeks – particularly the Athenians and Spartans – realized what they had unleashed. By 346, Philip had much of the land to the north of Greece, Illyria, Thrace and Epirus, either under his control or in alliance. He had also subjugated the resource-rich region of Thessaly, in northern Greece. Macedon was now so powerful that there was little that the Athenians and the other Greeks could do but join an alliance with the Macedonians. Philip had arrived.

Some observers appreciated the danger that Philip posed to the autonomy of the city-states and their political systems. The Athenian statesman and orator Demosthenes (384–322 BC) warned against any kind of detente with this northern king and argued for resistance against the 'barbarian' from the North, even if it meant making an alliance with the 'barbarian' from the East, Persia. For Demosthenes, one of the greatest threats facing his fellow citizens was complacency:

Consider for a moment. The minute this court rises, each of you will return home, quickly or leisurely, unstressed, not looking around, unconcerned whether he is going to run into against a friend or an enemy, a big or little man, a strong or a weak man, or anything of that sort. Why is that? Because in his heart he knows, and is confident, through his trust of the State, that none shall seize, abuse or beat him.

Demosthenes attempted to alert the Athenians to the threat that they faced from Philip by spelling it out in the baldest possible terms.

First, my fellow citizens, you have to understand, that Philip has declared war on our state, and has broken the peace treaty; that, whilst he is antagonistic and hostile to the whole of Athens, to the territory of Athens, and I may add, to the gods of Athens (may they wipe him off the face of the earth!), there is nothing which he struggles and machinates against as much as our constitution, nothing in the world that he is so concerned about, as its obliteration.

Demosthenes' alarmist rant does show that he was alive to the danger that Philip posed to Athens, but it also highlights the fact that he, in his own way, was as out of touch as his fellow citizens who had put their heads in the sand. What both Demosthenes and his detractors had in common was a misplaced sense of Athens' importance to Philip. That is not to say that Athens was not important; it was still one of the most powerful cities in Greece. But it was a long way from its fifth-century BC zenith. As an Athenian, Demosthenes could not possibly imagine that his city was not at the heart of Philip's plans.

Athens was trading on former glories, and everyone apart from the Athenians knew it.

Philip was unburdened by the insularity of the *polis* and by the inflexibility of its ideologies. He could afford to take a broader and more flexible view, and this pragmatism meant that he would accept almost any type of government as long as it was friendly towards Macedon. Philip also knew that radical democracy stopped Athens from acting decisively. Referring to the fact that Athenian generals served on a panel of ten, were appointed only for a year, and were susceptible to political interference, Philip was said to have ironically commented, 'I congratulate the Athenians for finding ten generals each year; I have only ever found one.'

The parochialism of the *polis* meant that there was a collective failure by the major Greek states to understand that the issues that mattered most to them were not Philip's priorities. The city-states also failed to see that Philip was taking advantage of their over-inflated sense of importance. But once invited into Greece, Philip was never going to leave. In the second phase of his campaign to dominate Greece, he would use the same strategy, this time by aligning himself with Pan-Hellenism, the great holy grail of ancient Greece.

There was a growing body of opinion in Greece that the only way to bring a halt to the disastrous infighting that had dogged the region for over a century was another great expedition against their common enemy, Persia. At the vanguard to this revived Pan-Hellenic movement was the Athenian statesman Isocrates, who with others had spent forty years calling on various contenders to launch the first fully articulated Western 'crusade' against the 'East'. None of the main candidates to lead such a campaign, Agesilaus of Sparta, Alexander of Pherae or Dionysius of Syracuse, had risen to the challenge, so Isocrates turned to the next best thing: Philip. Isocrates argued that Philip was just the man (and Greek enough) to kick-start that great unfulfilled Greek dream of Pan-Hellenism. Philip and Macedon had come a long way from northern hill-billies to leaders of the Greek world. The Greeks had long known what the problem was but did not know how to solve it: it was the giant paradox that the *polis*, the very thing that made them great, also made them weak and divided. Only a barbarian 'king' with no stake in the *polis* could unite them.

Philip's agenda was never going to be the same as that of Isocrates. He was a proud Macedonian monarch, only really interested in using Pan-Hellenism to cement his own political power in Greece and beyond. The Greeks might have thought that they were too clever for Philip but really it was he who played them. Ominously, the Macedonian-led Pan-Hellenic League came about only after Philip had comprehensively routed a combined Athenian and Theban force at

the battle of Chaeronea in 338. Instead of laying siege to Athens, as its citizens feared, Philip made no further effort to crush Greece. He did not need to; the battle had proved that resistance to Macedonian military might was futile. Philip would now subjugate Greece by alliance rather than the sword. The League of Corinth, established by Philip in the following year, was a confederation of Greek states, excluding Sparta, with the underlying purpose of a unified Greek campaign against Persia. It also guaranteed peace and the freedom and autonomy of its members – although in reality it was underwritten by Macedonian military might. It was sworn at the site of the Isthmian games, where cities had taken oath to resist the Persian king Xerxes in 481 BC. An apparent symbol of peace, in reality the League of Corinth was an instrument of Macedonian control in the familiar pattern of the Delian League. The Pan-Hellenic dream had become the Trojan horse for Macedonian domination. However, before any expedition against Persia could be launched, Philip was assassinated, in 336. It was a sign of how toothless the Greek city-states had become that his murderer was a Macedonian psychopath with a grudge rather than a knife wielding democrat, or even oligarch, striking a blow for freedom.

II

THE ALEXANDER ENIGMA

If the Greeks thought that the assassination of Philip II heralded the demise of Macedonian power, they were to be sorely disappointed. By the age of 31, his son and successor, Alexander, had gone from being the disputed monarch of the small kingdom of Macedon to master of an empire that took in Greece, Turkey, Egypt, Syria, Iran, Afghanistan and Pakistan. How was it possible for one man to achieve so much in such a short space of time? And was he really that great, or merely, as St Augustine described him in *City of God*, 'a rogue with a global appetite for plunder'?

Philip had ensured that his son was given a thorough Classical Greek education under the tutorship of the most brilliant of Plato's students, Aristotle – who shared his old teacher's dislike of Athens' radical democracy (although he did approve in majority decision taking as long as it was carefully controlled). Aristotle already had experience of working for an autocrat, having spent time at the court of a minor tyrant in Asia Minor and had even married his daughter. The move to Macedon in 343, however, was a step up into the major league, and secured Aristotle's fortune. Aristotle shared his fellow Greeks' disdain for barbarians but he also understood that Philip represented something different. Aristotle's critics would snipe that he was consigning himself to a house of 'mud and slime', but for a keen student of politics the move north to where the real power now lay must have been irresistible. As for Philip, he could not have made a better choice of tutor. Aristotle's intellectual range was unsurpassed. His interests included philosophy, politics, poetry, music, astronomy, medicine, science and natural history.

Frustratingly, we know very little about the relationship between the soon-to-be-famous philosopher and his soon-to-be-even-more-famous pupil: Aristotle appears to have maintained a discreet silence on the subject. It has been speculated that some of Aristotle's later general observations about young men as 'not a proper audience for political science; he has no experience of life, and because he still follows his emotions, he will only listen to no purpose uselessly' might be an autobiographical allusion to his days of tutoring Alexander. There were areas of learning where Alexander certainly paid attention; it was said that such was Alexander's love for Homer's *Iliad* that Aristotle helped prepare a special text of the poem, which Alexander kept under his pillow along with a dagger.

Throughout his short life the *Iliad* would serve as an inspiration and personal guide to the Macedonian king. Alexander's identity and ambitions were defined by Homeric values: he self-consciously lived by the heroic quality of *philotimo*, the competitive urge to win honour and glory. To base your life round the *Iliad* would have seemed hopelessly anachronistic to the Greeks; at half a millennium old, the text would have been seen by most as rather out of date. Alexander was ridiculed as a gauche buffoon and boorish simpleton by Demosthenes, who made him out to be a kind of village idiot from the barbarous north. Demosthenes actually did have a point, but the cultural chasm between Alexander and the likes of Demosthenes also reveals how peripheral the precious polities were to the man who held their collective fate in his hand. To a young prince in a land where the *polis* had never taken hold, and where the power of life and death was in the hands of an autocratic monarch served by a close group of heroic warrior companions, and whose authority was very much centred on his personal prowess, the *Iliad* must have had a powerful resonance.

Alexander's expensive education meant that he could walk the walk and talk the talk when it came to 'the Greek thing', but he had no investment in the political institutions that had spawned them. At the heart of Greekness, the *raison d'être* for the brilliant plays, the philosophical treatises, the art and the architecture, was that indispensable political organism, the *polis*. For Alexander, no matter how well versed he was in Greek culture, the *polis* was fundamentally an alien concept. In his lifetime he would found many cities but to most Greeks cities were more than bricks and mortar – they encapsulated the crucial principles of communal responsibilities and freedoms, albeit to varying degrees. The education that Alexander received made him dangerous because, like Philip, he was able to appreciate how important concepts like the *polis* and Pan-Hellenism were to the Greeks. Just as his father had done, Alexander would proclaim support for these ideals until his political objectives had been met, and then he would discard them. Alexander would ruthlessly take Greekness and bend it to his own autocratic ends while leaving its creators, the Greeks, behind. The conquests of Alexander brought about the triumph of Greece over much of the known world, but they also represented the watershed moment when the city-states of Greece lost control of Greekness.

After securing the succession from Philip with the customary round of bloodletting against the other prospective claimants to the throne, Alexander turned his attention back to Greece, where the powerful city of Thebes had revolted. If the other Greek states had any doubts about the mettle of the 20-year-old Alexander, then they were surely dispelled by the brutal treatment that he meted out on the Thebans. The city was completely destroyed and turned over to farmland, except for the sacred precincts and the house of the poet Pindar. Many of the inhabitants were massacred and 30,000 survivors enslaved. This brutal liquidation was committed under the authority of the League of Corinth, which had elected Alexander as leader. This was not the last time that Alexander would raise the convenient banner of Pan-Hellenism when suppressing the political freedoms of the Greeks. The terror unleashed by Alexander gained him the total submission of Greece, for the time being at least. Alexander's contempt for the hard fought liberties of the city-states was confirmed by his decision to leave one of his Macedonian lieutenants, a governor in all but name, to look after 'the freedom of the Greeks'. With Greece united under his control, Alexander could claim inheritance of the Pan-Hellenic 'crusade' and he used this as the launch-pad for a ten-year blaze of glory: five years to defeat Persia and make himself 'King of Asia' and another five to take him to the edge of the known world on a quest for personal glory. It was empire by blitzkrieg.

Alexander's flirtation with Pan-Hellenism was short-lived. It was another sort of Greekness that fascinated Alexander, the long-gone, mythical past of the Homeric era. As he crossed the treacherous waters of the Dardanelles from Europe into Asia to take on the Persian army for the first time, in 334 BC, he took the helm of the royal trireme, wearing a suit of glistening armour, and he made sure he was the first man to step on Asian soil. As he did so, he thrust his spear into the ground, just as the Greek hero Protesilaus had done, according to the *Iliad*, as the Greek expeditionary force arrived in Troy. Right from the outset of the expedition it was clear that despite his Pan-Hellenic rhetoric, Alexander had the Trojan rather than Persian Wars in mind.

Alexander's lack of genuine interest in the Pan-Hellenic dream was further exposed by his treatment of the Greeks once he had arrived in Asia. The Athenian fleet was sent home during the first winter of the campaign and there were very few Greeks in his army, except when they had some specialist skill, such as in engineering. Hardly any of Alexander's close companions or senior subordinates were Greek. The Greeks furnished Alexander with a cause for attacking Persia and a fleet to transport his army across the sea; after that they were simply left in his slipstream, the first of many.

After routing the Persian army at the battle of the Granicus river in May 334 BC, Alexander arranged a political settlement for western Asia Minor, a region with many Greeks inhabitants, whose liberation had been an important issue for the Pan-Hellenic cause. Even this reorganization merely highlighted the steely pragmatism that lay behind all Alexander's major political decisions. He proclaimed the restoration of democracy and the old laws, but he did this to undermine the pro-Persian regimes in the Greek cities in the region that had traditionally been oligarchies, certainly not for any ideological reasons. It is highly instructive that Alexander also maintained the satrapy system of imperial governors that had been established by the Persians, merely appointing his own men into post.

An exposé of Alexander's real motivations for attacking Persia can be found in a letter he supposedly wrote to Darius, the Persian Great King. It started off toeing the usual Pan-Hellenic line:

Your forefathers attacked Macedon and the rest of Greece and harmed us greatly although we had not done you any previous wrong. I have been appointed commander-in-chief of the Hellenes and it is in order to punish the Persians that I have crossed into Asia, since you are the aggressors.

The last paragraph, though, stands as an ominous testament to the real extent of Alexander's ambitions:

In future whenever you communicate with me, address me as king of Asia; do not write to me as an equal, but state your demands to the master of all your possessions.

Kingship, with its emphasis on the personality of one man, offered flexibility and pragmatism in the way that the thousands of voices of the democratic *polis*

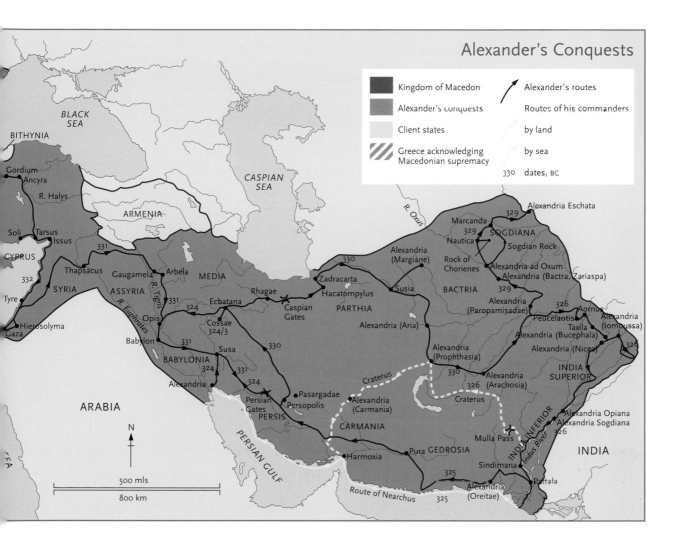

and even the more limited ones of an oligarchic regime could not. Alexander embodied the mercurial possibilities of charismatic kingship at its most extreme. He never really promoted a cause or an ideology, just himself. Like the Homeric heroes, his aim was to win as many battles, as much prestige and the greatest share of spear-won territory as he possibly could. That was why the *Iliad* exerted such a strong influence on the young king.

Throughout his short but stellar career, Alexander modelled himself very closely on two of the most celebrated figures of the heroic age, the legendary strong man Heracles and the most dazzling warrior of the *Iliad*, Achilles. Conveniently, Alexander could claim family links with both. He also encouraged the idea that he, like his two famous forebears, was the son of a god – in his case none less than Zeus, the king of the gods. Stories of his celestial parentage swirled around the towns and cities of the ancient Mediterranean and Near East. Some said that Olympias, Alexander's mother, had fallen pregnant on her wedding night after her belly was struck by celestial lightning. Others whispered that it had been Philip himself who had discovered a snake stretched out beside his sleeping wife. The tale was further spiced up with the suggestion that Philip had actually been spying on his wife, and had witnessed his 'son's' divine conception. Adding insult to injury, Zeus had later punished him for his voyeurism by causing him to be blinded in the offending eye during battle. It did not to do to cross the gods even when they were impregnating your wife. Rumours abounded that Alexander was a celestial cuckoo in the Macedonian royal nest and these stories would provide the foundation stone of the 'Alexander legend'. Alexander understood the power of a good story.

His long march across Asia was punctuated by a series of brilliantly choreographed events that made it appear that he was literally following in the footsteps of his celebrated forebears. To start with, after he had crossed the Hellespont into Asia, Alexander made straight for the legendary city of Troy. Troy's glory days had long since passed; it was now an insignificant backwater trading on its illustrious history. Past glories meant that this ancient version of a heritage centre was an essential stopping-point for such an image-conscious monarch. Alexander stripped naked, covered himself in oil and ran to the tombstone of Achilles and placed a garland on it. His lover, Hephaistion, did the same at the tomb of Patroclus, Achilles' companion. At an altar to Zeus, Alexander sacrificed and prayed to Priam, the legendary king of Troy, another 'ancestor', and followed this up by offering his suit of armour to the goddess Athena. The ever-enterprising priests then presented him with a shield and weapons supposedly left from the days of the Trojan War which they had conveniently 'found' – a clear reference to the divine armour that Achilles had been given by his mother, the goddess Aphrodite. As he travelled east Alexander took a little piece of the historical and divine authority of Troy with him, as extra insurance.

Incidents such as this abound in the ancient accounts of Alexander's conquest of the Persian Empire. On another occasion, while campaigning in northern Pakistan, he was determined to capture a particularly inaccessible mountain peak called Aornus, where some enemies were holed up. He proclaimed that this was no ordinary mountain refuge, but a place that the great Greek hero Heracles himself had, not once, but twice, failed to capture. Ptolemy goes on to explain that Alexander felt a 'longing' to outdo Heracles. After heavy fighting, two parties of 700 men climbed the highest peak at night in an almost insanely risky operation. Alexander was, of course, the first to reach the summit.

Alexander's self-consciously heroic antics did not always sit easily with the fourth-century BC world that he inhabited. At best some of his exploits made him look like a shallow ventriloquist and at worst, a barbaric psychopath. A case in point was his treatment of Batis, the Persian governor of Gaza, who had made the mistake of taking just a little too long to surrender the city after Alexander had put it under siege. Once Gaza had fallen Alexander had the still very much alive Batis hitched to the back of his chariot and dragged him around the walls of the city. It was, of course, an allusion to Achilles' brutal treatment of Hector's body outside the walls of Troy; Batis, though, was a fat eunuch who had surrendered, not a great warrior. What was intended to strengthen the association between Alexander and Achilles had descended to nothing more than brutal parody.

Alexander would not just adopt the persona of a Homeric hero. Throughout his career as conqueror of most of the known world, he would play a bewildering array of different roles: Greek liberator, Egyptian pharaoh and Persian autocrat. The essential point about him was not his commitment to, but rather his detachment from the numerous causes which he espoused. There was more to these role changes than mere ego, although that certainly played its part. Liberated from the political ideologies for which the Greeks would live and die, Alexander preferred the 'pick and mix' approach, adopting customs and practices that he discovered during his great march eastwards if they helped further his own ends.

The abandon with which Alexander dropped one identity and picked up another was most apparent when he arrived in Egypt, which, by this time, was the oldest living civilization on earth. The Persians had controlled Egypt for the last two centuries and were deeply unpopular because of their harsh exactions and high-handed behaviour. Alexander played on Egyptian antipathy towards Persia by once again taking on the role of liberator. He was shrewd enough to realize that he needed to win over the priesthood, which effectively ruled the country for the pharaoh. The Persians were Zoroastrians and believed other gods were demons; they had alienated the Egyptian priests by not respecting their gods and customs. And so Alexander went to Memphis, the old capital of Egypt, and made a sacrifice to Apis, the Egyptian bull god, to win the favour of the all-powerful priests. It seems to have worked, because subsequently Alexander was crowned pharaoh of both Upper and Lower Egypt, although it is difficult to know how much this warm welcome from Egypt's priesthood can be put down to Alexander's act of piety or the large and apparently unbeatable army he had with him.

Alexander was later referred to as pharaoh in temples around Egypt. A bas-relief in the temple at Luxor in Upper Egypt shows him as pharaoh paying homage to the native god Min. He was also worshipped as Horus, a living god,

ABOVE
Temple of Amun, Siwa, Egypt.

the son of Amun, who was the divine creator of the universe. Later, Alexander marched his troops to the remote Libyan oasis of Siwa, about 600 kilometres south-west of Cairo. It was a dangerous journey through the waterless desert, and he and his entire army nearly died from thirst after getting hopelessly lost in this most hostile of environments. The prize was, for Alexander, worth the dangers. Siwa was the site of the fabled oracle of the god Amun; it had been built by the pharaoh Amasis in the sixth century BC. When Alexander reached the front gate of the temple he was met by the high priest who took him inside while Macedonian companions were told to wait outside.

Once inside, Alexander witnessed an ancient ritual. The priests carried a symbol of Amun in a gilded boat with silver cups dangling from the side. They were followed by virgins singing hymns. A temple servant collected holy water from the well to offer to Amun. Alexander then approached the oracle to ask three questions. The first was whether he had punished all of his father's murderers. To which the convenient reply was that Amun was his father, not Philip. And then true to form, Alexander asked whether he was going to rule over the whole world. To which the answer was yes. And lastly he asked which gods he should worship when he reached the outer ocean, the supposed edge of the earth. The obvious reply to this was Poseidon, the sea god.

Although couched in terms of family duty and religious piety, Alexander's questions give us a fascinating glimpse of his towering ego and limitless ambition. But his visits to Siwa and other important Egyptian religious centres also reveal his willingness to immerse himself in an alien religion and culture in order to cement his control. It was a freedom that kingship afforded: to be worshipped as living god was politically, culturally and religiously unacceptable to the Greeks. But Alexander could write his own script.

A couple of years later, in the autumn of 331, after a decisive victory at the battle of Gaugamela near Nineveh in modern-day Iraq and the subsequent murder of King Darius, the mammoth Persian Empire effectively fell into Alexander's hands. Here, too, his extraordinary capacity to adapt to new situations is strongly in evidence. The barbaric destruction of Persepolis, the magnificent Persian capital, the year after the defeat of Darius was shocking, but in many ways it was also a blind alley. Alexander had needed to put on a 'spectacular' so that his millions of new subjects understood what would happen to them if they resisted him. Some sources even explain this apocalyptic onslaught on one of the most sophisticated cities of the ancient world as nothing more than a drunken escapade that got completely out of hand. As far as the Zoroastrian holy books of the Persians were concerned, Alexander was an evil servant of the destroying demon Ashemok. Whatever the underlying reasons for this wanton vandalism, Alexander's subsequent actions show that he was also willing to engage with Persian customs, just as he had adapted himself to Greek and Egyptian traditions.

Unsurprisingly, it was the Persian emphasis on the divine right to rule, and the concept of a universal empire, that most attracted Alexander. Over time he took on many of the trappings as well the ideology of the Persian royal court. His Macedonian veterans resented all this, particularly rituals such as prostrating oneself in Alexander's presence. It ended, almost inevitably, in bloodshed, with the murder in a drunken rage of one of his father's loyal lieutenants, Cleitus, who had dared to remind Alexander of his Macedonian roots. A plot against Alexander's life was also discovered. Among the victims swept up in the wave of arrests and summary executions was Callisthenes, the historian 'embedded' with the Macedonian army to record the conquests of the great Alexander.

We should, however, resist the temptation to paint Alexander as some kind of Colonel Kurtz-like figure who had lost himself in foreign lands and 'gone native'. The Macedonian old guard were the past. If Alexander wanted to remain Lord of Asia then the future lay with the disparate peoples who made up his vast new

ALEXANDER M DARIVM VIC : SVPERAT
CÆSIS IN ACIE PERSAR : PEDIT ; C M. EQVIT
VERO.A M. INTERFECTIS. MATRE QVOQVE
CONIVGE.LIBERIS DARII REG.CVM.M. HAVD
AMPLIVS EQVITIB : FVGA DILAPSI. CAPTIS.

empire. Hence the Moonie-style arranged mass weddings between Macedonians and Persians, as well as the promotion of Persians into the highest echelons of his administration. Alexander was a true autocrat: systems and precedence were often discarded as he imposed ad hoc solutions to short-term problems before moving swiftly on. It was no way to create an enduring empire, let alone a lasting civilization. No episode exposes that aspect of Alexander better than the famous story of the Gordian knot. In 333 BC he had stopped his army at the ancient city of Gordium in Asia Minor, where he encountered a sacred chariot attached to its yoke by a rope. The story went that nobody had been able to solve the intractable problem of the Gordian Knot and whoever could would be destined to seize all of Asia. Alexander tried to untie it, and failed. So he took his sword and sliced through the rope. It was typical Alexander: decisive, impulsive, theatrical and ultimately missing the point. Alexander always took the short cut.

LEFT
The Battle of Issus, by Albrecht Altdorfer – one of the great Renaissance visions of the ancient world. At Issus (333 BC) Alexander the Great secured a decisive victory over the forces of the Persian king Darius III.

Serious empire-builders made alliances, forged diplomatic and political ties and put down the roots of a new civilization through the promotion of trade and cultural exchange. In other words, they allowed politics, diplomacy and commerce to follow conquest. Alexander's personal, whirlwind pursuit of world domination left no room for such banalities, and produced an empire of breath-taking extent but terrible fragility. The only constant in Alexander's world now was himself. He had created a world in which he was at the centre of everything, a system that depended entirely on his supposedly godlike genius. Without him the whole thing would fall apart. And that is what almost happened after a further seven years of increasingly aimless conquest for conquest's sake that had taken him into Afghanistan and then on to what is now Pakistan. After his exhausted troops mutinied at the Hyphasis river (now known as the Beas river), south of the Himalayas, he had to turn back.

Alexander returned to Persia, where he spent his final years attempting to bring order and stability to his fractious kingdom through violence and forced marriages, and preparing for the invasion of Arabia. But his quest for personal fulfilment and world domination had to come to an end sometime, somewhere. It did; on 10 June 323 BC, in Babylon, he died, not a hero's death in battle, but probably of a mosquito bite. Alexander was 32 years old. A weather-watching Babylonian chronicler would mark the king's passing with the laconic comment, 'The king died. Clouds.'

The brevity and detachment of this statement appears curiously at odds with what we know of Alexander's huge legacy. In Alexander, after all, we have the first comprehensive case of the 'Great Man' theory of history in action: his example rippled down the millennia from Caesar to Napoleon to Hitler. It would be hard to overstate the impact that Alexander the Great had on the ancient world. He was its first truly iconic historical figure. You have only to walk around the sculpture collection of any classical museum or flick through any book on Hellenistic and Roman art to understand just what an idol Alexander was for the emperors, kings, princes and warlords who followed after him. Whether in the portrait of a Hellenistic or Afghan princeling or a Roman emperor, time and again you are confronted by the same youthful, almost boyish face with its tousled hair but hard, calculating eyes. The reasons for this adulation are not difficult to understand. Quite simply, Alexander changed everything for those who came after him.

Like the loyal Macedonian veterans who followed him, it is hard not to get dragged into the slipstream of this charismatic demi-god as he fights his way across Asia into the realms of myth and legend. But the legend should be resisted, because the journey that Alexander made was as singular as the man himself, a restless personal quest to find some kind of limit by which to define himself. Rich territory perhaps for the psychologist, but from a historical perspective, it was ephemeral, quixotic and ultimately futile.

If you were sitting in Babylon in 323 BC, Alexander's legacy would have seemed far from clear or secure. History had, and would continue to produce, plenty of charismatic conquerors whose achievements would quickly turn to dust after their death. The truth was that Alexander's enduring legacy was as much the achievement of the mere mortals who followed him as his own spectacular exploits. It was his successors who, conscious of their own limitations in a way that Alexander never was, became the founders and real heroes of the Hellenistic Age.

III

THE HELLENISTIC KINGS: PICKING UP THE PIECES

In the aftermath of Alexander's death, an odd assortment of generals and confidants were fated to be the ones to tidy up after their irrepressible leader. The question of succession was a very complicated one. Immediately after he had died, they met in the tent where the empty throne of their dead hero stood, and debated what should be done next. It is said that when they spoke they imitated Alexander's voice and even the way he held his head. According to one account, 'they felt as if a god was leading them on'. The political reality, however, was a good deal less celestial. Alexander had left no immediate successor. There was an unborn son to a Bactrian princess, and a half-brother, Philip, but the son was half-barbarian and the brother half-mad. So anybody with sufficient military muscle at their disposal grabbed what they could, while piously declaring they were just holding it in trust until a rightful heir emerged.

On his deathbed, Alexander was asked to whom he left his kingdom. He cryptically replied: 'To the strongest', before predicting, with impressive wit for a dying man, that 'all his foremost friends would hold a great funeral contest over him'. His prophecy turned out to be correct. Thirteen years of intrigue, infighting and outright bloodletting followed, during which his son and half-brother were murdered. After four major wars in as many years, Alexander's transient empire had split into four massive territorial units, divvied up along the old tectonic plates of the ancient world: Greece and Macedon were taken by Cassander, the son of Antipater, Alexander's old viceroy in that region; western and northern Asia Minor was ruled by Lysimachus, a former bodyguard; Ptolemy, a childhood friend and one of Alexander's more thoughtful generals, got Egypt; and lastly Seleucus, an infantry commander and former satrap, ruled over a vast realm which centred on Syria and stretched from eastern Asia Minor to northern Pakistan.

It did not take long for these successors to proclaim themselves kings. Always caught in the mighty shadow of Alexander, their authority was often reliant, in the case of the first generation of successor kings, on their connections with him. Ptolemy even went so far as to pretend that he was Alexander's bastard half-brother. It is unsurprising that these kings self-consciously modelled themselves on their dead royal master. Like Alexander, they cultivated a Homeric veneer, surrounding themselves with a band of aristocrats to serve as dinner companions, bodyguard, confidants, advisors and assassins. Monarchs would present themselves as living embodiments of the old heroic virtues: personal skill and courage in battle, military leadership and conquest and the right to distribute the spoils of war were all presented as central aspects of Hellenistic rule.

The seemingly endless series of conquests achieved under Alexander had pretty much ground to a halt, but the successors had each other to fight, which they did with almost monotonous regularity The constantly fractious relationship between the Seleucids and their neighbours the Ptolemies culminated in the battle of Raphia in Palestine in 217 BC. This was one of the largest set-piece battles of the Hellenistic period, with the Ptolemaic army totalling 70,000 infantry, 6,000 cavalry and 73 war elephants (a shock-and-awe weapon picked up by Alexander during his invasion of the Indian sub-continent), while the Seleucid

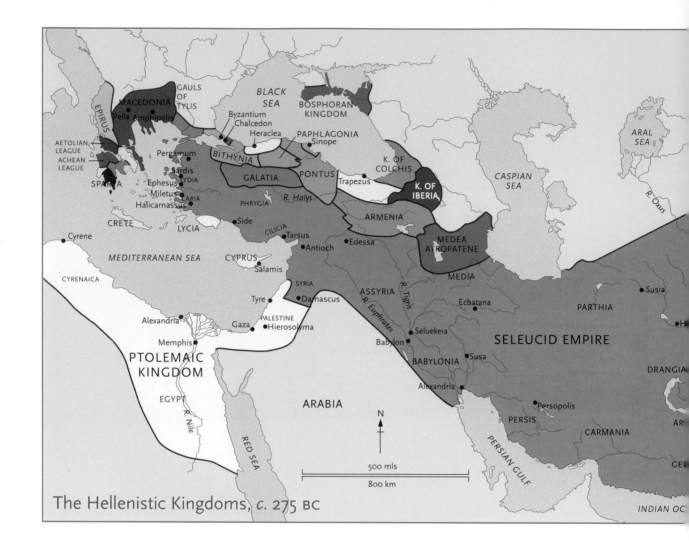

The Hellenistic Kingdoms, *c.* 275 BC

forces consisted of fewer troops – 62,000 foot and 5,000 horse – but more elephants (103). Some of the Hellenistic kings modelled themselves more closely on Alexander than others. There was the extremely gung ho Antiochus III (241–187 BC), who was determined to recapture all the vast territories that his great-greatgrandfather, Seleucus I, had held. This campaign climaxed in a terrific re-run of Alexander's *anabasis*, that took Antiochus and his armies on a march of conquest through central Asia – Media, Parthia, Bactria – and eventually through the Hindu Kush into northern India. Although Antiochus now claimed the title of Great King as Alexander had done, his great 're-conquest' was something of a mirage: after he and his army had left, these eastern lands quickly settled back down to doing their own thing.

There was more to these successors than being pale imitations of the mighty

Alexander. There had to be. Despite bullish posturing, these kingdoms were precarious affairs; usually with a small Macedonian or Greek colonial population ruling over much larger indigenous peoples with the help of a large mercenary army. As well as local revolts, they had to almost constantly contend with the threat of attack by one of the other successor kings or assassination by a member of their own family or entourage. If they wanted to survive, let alone thrive, they needed the skills of a wily Odysseus more than a heroic Achilles. They had to do what Alexander never would or could do himself: knuckle down to the prosaic business of administering their kingdoms, levying taxes, seeing off their rivals and establishing dynasties. And what they achieved was far more concrete than any mere legend. This was conquest not by brute force of the *sarissa* (the pike) but by the soft power of economic opportunity and cultural aspiration.

Ironically, the most potent weapon in the armouries of these 'barbarian' kings, besides their huge armies and piles of money, was Greek culture. In the old country, Greeks such as Demosthenes might not have recognized them as being proper Greeks, but in the Nile Delta, Syrian hills, Bactrian desert or the Hindu Kush the finer distinctions between Hellene and Macedonian, so important in Athens, were rather blurred. Alexander conquered the world, but it was these successors who Hellenized it. It was under their watch that Greek became the language of power from Cyrene in North Africa to the Oxus in Afghanistan and the Punjab in north-west India. And where power trod, business and culture were quick to follow. Just as the British would one day create an 'English-speaking world' so the successor kings created a 'Greek-speaking world', known as the Hellenistic *koine*, or community. Whether your trade was politics, poetry or import-export, if you wanted a line to the elite who were now running your country the first necessity was to be able to read and write Greek. In fact, the only Hellenistic monarch of Egypt to learn Egyptian was the final one, the famous Cleopatra. Learn Greek and you might just even become a 'cosmopolitan' – a 'citizen of the world' – able to fit in wherever Aeschylus was performed or Plato quoted.

This process had very little to do with any conscious missionary zeal on the part of the successor kings. These were hard-bitten soldiers, not Hellenizing evangelists, and they did not see the plays of Sophocles or the treatises of Aristotle as a way of pacifying restless local subjects. They had tax rebates and soldiers to do that. When the deeper thinkers among the Hellenistic monarchs showed an interest in Greek culture, it involved a far more ambitious and all-encompassing project: the creation of an ideological *raison d'être* for their new kingdoms, and a mandate for themselves to rule over their hard-won lands. Nowhere would that vision be more brilliantly realized than in the city of Alexandria, the greatest creation of Ptolemy, Alexander's heir in Egypt and the cleverest successor king of them all.

Alexandria had not been Ptolemy's idea but that of the man whose name it bore. Alexander had been passing through on the way to Siwa in 331 BC when he declared that a great city in his name should be built on Egypt's northern coast. He was no stranger to founding cities in his own name. At the age of sixteen he had led his first campaign and founded his first city, Alexandrupolis in Thrace. There would be at least fifteen Alexandrias founded by him, from Asia Minor to what is now Pakistan. But it was the Egyptian Alexandria that was destined to become one of the richest and most densely populated cities of the Mediterranean, on a par with Carthage and Rome, and a centre of ideas and learning that came to eclipse Athens. Fittingly, it was also in this Alexandria that Alexander's embalmed body (which Ptolemy had shrewdly snatched) lay in state in a gold coffin.

Alexander had personally gone over the prospective site with his Greek architect, Deinocrates, marking out the location of the *agora*, the temples and the line of the city walls. Aristander, Alexander's favourite seer, prophesied that the new city would possess 'most abundant and helpful resources and be a nursing mother to men of every nation'. The second half of Aristander's prediction would soon be proved to be correct but the 'abundant and helpful resources' would require the intervention of Alexander's able lieutenant Ptolemy. When Alexander decided to found a new city on the Mediterranean coast of Egypt, practical considerations seemed to have slipped his mind, like what the citizens of his new foundation were going to drink. The nearest source of fresh water is the river Nile; there was nothing for it but to bring the Nile to the city. Ptolemy delegated the task to his brother, Menelaus, who was the head of the army. He dug a twenty-kilometre canal to bring fresh water from the Nile at Schedia to the gates of the new city. A network of vaulted underground channels was then carved out of the rock on which the city was built to supply water to its inhabitants. In sorting out Alexandria's water problems Ptolemy once again showed his unerring ability to make real Alexander's often rather fanciful pipe-dreams. The water system reflects the annual habits of the Nile. Every year it flooded in August and September. The excess water flowed through the canal and into the cisterns, filling the city's wells for the year ahead. This provided Ptolemy's engineers with a challenge. Too much water could have flooded the city from beneath, so they built a system of dams and locks to regulate the flow. A traditional nilometer was put in to monitor the level of the waters to prevent flooding. Alexandria is commonly referred to as being Alexander's vision but it was Ptolemy who made it real. By addressing the practical implications of

ABOVE

The Lighthouse or Pharos of Alexandria by Hermann Thiersch (1909). Commissioned by Ptolemy II and built between 280 and 247 BC, the lighthouse was one of the tallest manmade structures of the ancient world (its height has been variously estimated at between 120 and 140 metres). It was built from large blocks of stone, the tower made up of a lower square section with a central core, a middle octagonal section and, at the top, a circular section. At its apex was a mirror which reflected sunlight during the day; a fire was lit at night.

Alexander's legacy Ptolemy and other Hellenistic rulers laid the foundations for their own regimes.

Ptolemy's vision for Alexandria was an extremely ambitious one. The new foundation would not only serve as his royal capital but also as the world centre for Greek arts, science and literature. Political calculation rather than ego-driven dilettantism lay behind this decision. Ptolemy made the judgement that the Greek cultural capital that had for so long lit up democratic Athens, would bring legitimacy, prestige and brilliance to his own nascent regime. Alexandria also helped get round the familiar but awkward problem of the Hellenistic kings looking like what they actually were: alien autocrats ruling over resentful populations whose lands had been conquered at the point of the spear. By setting up a self-consciously Greek city with a large Greek population swelled by large-scale emigration from other parts of the Greek world (over 150,000 Greeks are said to have arrived in the wake of the establishment of the city) and then making it the most famous city in the Hellenistic world, Ptolemy ensured that this little corner of Egypt at least appeared to be indigenously Greek. He was barely interested in his vast number of Egyptian subjects as long as they paid their taxes and did not rebel.

The centrepieces of the new city were two extraordinary cultural institutions: the Library and the Museum, based closely on Plato's Academy and Aristotle's Lyceum. The Museum was much more like the research centre of prestigious and wealthy universities in the United States than a modern museum. It contained research collections and residential areas, as well as communal dining facilities and pleasant spaces where scholars could discuss ideas. One key difference, however, was its religious dimension. The Museum was primarily a shrine dedicated to the Muses, the Greek goddesses of arts and learning, and its head was always a priest.

In order to staff his new research centre Ptolemy embarked on an extraordinary recruitment campaign scouring the Greek world for talent. Like the patrons of wealthy, new academic institutions throughout history, Ptolemy first turned to more established but less prosperous counterparts. An attempt to hire Theophrastus, the head of the Athenian Lyceum, failed, but Theophrastus recommended one of his star pupils, Demetrius of Phaleron, to advise Ptolemy on the setting up of this vastly ambitious enterprise. Demetrius had had a slightly chequered history and needed a fresh start. In 317 BC after a period of grave political crisis, the Macedonian prince Cassander had imposed a regime on the rebellious Athenians, with Demetrius at its head. Under his pious, philosophically purist leadership Athens had been turned into what was essentially a laboratory for the political ideas of its most famous sons, Plato and Aristotle. Unsurprisingly it was a dismal failure. What sounded good in the lecture hall was quickly exposed for the joyless, stifling, stagnant and unworkable system that it was. After ten years Demetrius, the Macedonian-backed philosopher-king, was kicked out. The Athenians, having seen the disastrous consequences of letting the lunatics run the asylum, banned the establishment of new Schools of Philosophy in their city.

Others were happy to come to Alexandria for a standard of living that was well above what they could expect anywhere else – a good tax-free salary, free, high-quality board and lodgings, and a powerful king who, even if he did not take their advice, still politely listened to them. All in all, it was a very attractive package for a group who were used to living hand to mouth and being routinely ignored. Although the Museum quickly picked up the usual reputation for vitriolic infighting, heavy drinking and obscure research topics among its resident academics, scholars did sometimes find themselves advising their monarch on far more worldly matters.

The successor kings, lacking the epic, improvisational confidence of Alexander, often rather less heroically tried to have their kingly status bolstered in political treatises written by the intellectuals who flocked to their courts in the hope of fame and preferment. The political philosophy of the Hellenistic world at this time promoted meritocracy, responsibility and noble service as the key elements of kingship. Demetrius himself obligingly wrote such a work for Ptolemy, and was even asked his opinion on the royal succession (not that this ultimately seems to have done him much good; when Ptolemy II succeeded to the throne in 283, Demetrius was exiled to Upper Egypt, where he died of a snake bite).

For many of the intelligentsia from the old Greek world, Alexandria represented a welcome escape from the moribund decline of their own cities. Foreign domination and violent political upheaval had left many deeply disillusioned with the *polis*. As well as providing superb facilities and welcome material comfort, Ptolemy's Alexandria liberated the philosophers, artists, poets, geographers and scientists who flocked there from the political responsibilities that usually came with being a citizen-intellectual in a *polis*. Superficially Alexandria and other new Hellenistic foundations such as Pergamon and Antioch in Asia Minor, might have resembled the old Greek polities with their voting, *demes*, elected magistrates, councils and assemblies, but the existence of these familiar institutions was often no more than window dressing. The senior city magistrates were usually appointed by the king, and opposition to his autocratic regime was simply not tolerated. In fact, these new urban centres were really a reversion to a much older model of the great royal cities of the Near East such as Babylon, Nineveh, Mari and Uruk. Freed from the burdens of political responsibility, the new intelligentsia of Alexandria could get on with pursuing knowledge for knowledge's sake.

Alexandria was not simply some immaculate but lifeless monument to totalitarianism, an ancient equivalent of some concrete Stalinist dream. It was a vibrant, dynamic and cosmopolitan environment. As we have seen before in this book, mercantile trade, the exchange not only of goods but of skills and ideas too, had always been the great engine of civilization. Alexandria, with its impressive set of deep water harbours, had quickly become one of the leading trading hubs of the Mediterranean world. Key exports were papyrus, glassware, grain, medicines, perfumes and exotic jewellery. Elephants from Somalia, horses from Cyrene, gold from Nubia, jewellery and exotic goods from Carthage, copper and timber from Cyprus and silver from Spain were just some of the goods imported into the city. Commerce also attracted an ethnically diverse population of Greeks, Macedonians and a large Jewish community, as well as local Egyptians. In this melting pot the exchange of ideas was bound to thrive.

Ptolemy and his eponymous successor Ptolemy II took care to blend this complex and potentially volatile ethnic mix in a number of imaginative ways. The most ambitious was the creation and heavy promotion of a hybrid Egyptian-Greek god, Sarapis. Sarapis had a strong Egyptian pedigree, with the bull god Apis and the god of the Underworld Osiris in his family tree. But in virtually every other respect, he represented everything that a Greek intellectual would have liked an Egyptian god to be. That was, of course, because he was primarily the invention of Greek intellectuals. His Zeus-like human appearance (Greeks, unlike the Egyptians, were very disturbed by animal-headed gods), with a beard and flowing locks crowned by a grain measure bowl (a symbol of fertility), was clearly aimed at a Greek audience. The image had been created by the Greek court sculptor Bryaxis. Sarapis' supposed healing properties were also shamelessly fabricated and then promoted by Ptolemy's coterie of philosophers; the ever-amenable Demetrius even claimed that the god had prevented him from going blind.

Despite these careful preparations, the cult of Sarapis got off to rather a slow start in the city of his birth. Royal officials, eager to please the king, jostled to show their devotion to Sarapis but the Egyptian population was not terribly interested; this was understandable given that the cult had not really been invented for them. Even Greeks outside the charmed academic and court circles took time to warm to Sarapis, perhaps put off by his Disneyesque artificiality. Eventually, heavy investment in the cult by successive Ptolemies paid off; none worked harder than Ptolemy III, who built the Sarapeum, a magnificent new temple and cult centre in honour of the god in the heart of Alexandria. By the time the Sarapeum was torn down by a Christian mob in the fourth century AD, the god and his temple had come to epitomize Alexandria.

The Library in Alexandria was also a colossal enterprise. At its height it contained around 490,000 volumes, an enormous number for the ancient world. Just as the Museum acted as a safe haven for the Greek intellectual community, the Library was designed as a kind of Noah's ark for works of Greek learning that were felt to be in danger of disappearing in those dangerous war-ridden times. The ancient learning of Pharaonic Egypt was not part of its remit. Ptolemy, like many before and after him, stood in respectful awe in front of the millennia-old literary culture of his new kingdom but then basically ignored it. The holy grail for those who worked there was to obtain editions of every known work – a kind of super copyright library. Scholars codified Greek literature, effectively creating the canon of Greek literature that we have inherited. It was

here that the Jewish holy books, or the Christian Old Testament, were translated into Greek. Agents combed the bookshops of Athens and Rhodes. In a move that would warm the heart of any bibliomaniac, Ptolemy III ordered that all the books unloaded on to Alexandria's docks were to be impounded and copied. The copies were then returned and the originals went into the great library. Other libraries soon learned not to lend their works, as the Ptolemies had an alarming habit of not returning rare works, preferring to forfeit the deposit however huge the sum was.

As well as the Library's massive collection, scholars had access to dissection rooms, laboratories, zoological and botanical gardens and an observatory. There were breakthroughs in medical science: Herophilus identified the links between the brain and nervous system and the function of the heart and blood circulation. Eristratos studied the digestive system and the effects of nutrition. The Library had its very own Leonardo da Vinci in Hero of Alexandria, who has been credited with inventing among other things hydraulics, the syringe and the robot. Hero described his prolific inventions in many works, including *Pneumatica*: in this book there are statues that played trumpets using compressed air; a one-way valve for a pump; and a set of temple doors that would open when a fire was lit on the altar and then close automatically once the fire went out. Hero's greatest invention was the steam engine, something he created as a little toy, an intellectual exercise whose real value would not be fully understood until the Industrial Revolution.

It was at the Library in Alexandria that Archimedes invented his screw-shaped water pump that is still in use today. Euclid discovered the rules of geometry here, and Aristarchus estimated the size of the sun and moon. But of all the brilliant minds that graced the portals of the Library, one stands out: Eratosthenes of Cyrene. He was the original Renaissance man well ahead of his time, a mathematician, poet, geographer, astronomer and athlete. The list of Eratosthenes' achievements is staggering. He calculated the circumference of the earth with remarkable accuracy (at a time when most people thought the world was flat) and worked out that a year had 365 1/4 days, making him the father of the leap year. Another of Eratosthenes' most important discoveries was that all the seas were connected together so that theoretically it would be possible to circumnavigate Africa, and also to sail from Spain in the west all the way to India in the east. Of course, there are no surprises for guessing what was absolutely at the centre of Eratosthenes' famous map: Alexandria.

Some of the best-known sculptures of the ancient world date from this time, including the *Venus de Milo*, *Laocoön and His Sons* and *Winged Victory*. There were two main reasons for the progress in style and technique at this time: patronage by the Ptolemy kings and the expansion of the known world. New inspiration from the East left the orthodoxy of Classical Greece in the shadows as Hellenistic sculptors mastered the art of carving drapery, that most demanding of disciplines. Marble was the perfect medium for expressing the human form, and in Alexandria sculptors finessed their work with extraordinary, life-like detail, perfectly capturing the bulge of muscle and vein and the tautness of the tendons. Such work also shows us how Alexandrian artists were working closely with anatomists, developing a much better understanding of the human body and how it worked. New techniques emerged, for example, in the bust of Socrates, where the marble is polished to accentuate the burnished beauty of the face and skin. Hellenistic sculpture was also far more expressive than its Classical Greek counterpart. It goes beyond a mere rendition of a subject's features into the realm of the emotions. *The Dying Gaul* – a Roman copy of which survives – is disturbingly realistic, from the detail of the Celtic warrior's wild hair and moustache, to the agonized expression on his face.

Under Ptolemy, knowledge rather than the sword would become the dominant currency of prestige and power. Battles still had to be fought and wars waged but knowledge conferred enormous authority because it bestowed upon the initiated the power to define themselves and the world around them. The idea was that the Library should stand as the new epicentre of Greek civilization and learning, placing Alexandria and, of course, Ptolemy at the very centre of this new Hellenistic world. Perhaps the most extraordinary aspect of the Great Library was that it was open to anyone who could read. Democracy might not have been a force to be reckoned with in Ptolemy's Alexandria but in the book stacks of the Great Library it was alive and well.

Ptolemaic Egypt is not the only place where we can witness the ingenuity and sheer grit that the Hellenistic kings used to cement their rule over alien and potentially hostile environments. Perhaps the most intriguingly persistent of the Hellenistic kingdoms lay far to the east, in Bactria, a region of central Asia that reaches into what we now know as Afghanistan, Tajikistan, Uzbekistan and Turkmenistan. A civilization first emerged in Bactria in the late third millennium BC; little is known about this world, but we know they practised irrigation, created impressive monumental buildings and produced elaborate ceramics and jewellery – all the hallmarks of Bronze Age civilization. Some believe that

LEFT

A Graeco-Roman glass vase from Alexandria (c. first century BC), found in Begram, Afghanistan. Even after the political disintegration of the Hellenistic world, trade ensured that economic and cultural links endured over the vast and diverse area that Alexander and his successors had ruled over.

Bactria was where the Indo-European tribes began, before moving on to south-west Iran and north-west India. The Indo-European language family is the common ancestor to all European languages; this is a mysterious, forgotten world, rediscovered quite recently by archaeologists, but it is a world to which the modern West is profoundly indebted, by language, culture and descent.

Its central Asian position made Bactria a stepping-stone between east and west for millennia, from the Indo-Europeans onwards, and the Graeco-Bactrian kingdom achieved almost text-book ancient cultural fusion. Bactria had been conquered by Cyrus the Great of the Persian Empire, in the sixth century BC, making it the easternmost swathe of the vast sweep of Persian territory. In the chaos following the defeat of the Persian king Darius III by Alexander at the battle of Gaugamela in 331 BC, Darius was murdered by Bessus, his satrap (governor) of Bactria. Bessus then seized the Persian throne and went back to his Bactrian homeland, where he organized intense resistance to Alexander's army. Bactria was subdued after two years of war and annexed into Alexander's territory; Alexander commanded that Bessus' ears and nose be cut off – in keeping with the traditional Persian punishment for regicide.

In the carve-up following Alexander's death, Bactria became part of the eastern empire that was handed over to Alexander's infantry commander, Seleucus. This eastern Hellenistic offshoot became the Seleucid Empire, but Bactria claimed its independence from this overextended eastern empire in about 245 BC. Cut off from direct overland contact with Greece by the Parthian Empire in Iran, the Bactrians followed an independent, but still identifiably Hellenistic, evolutionary path. They developed sea trading routes with Ptolemaic Egypt and also made contact with China: small statuettes depicting Greek soldiers have been found in south-west China and Bactrian coins have been discovered that contain metal alloys exported from China. The independent Graeco-Bactrian kingdom was elaborately Hellenistic; it was also the most prosperous kingdom in the region, widely urbanized and Greek in style. Greek was the dominant language of the region. The evolving Bactrian language – which has only very recently been deciphered – continued to be written in the Greek script, until it died out in the eighth century AD.

Demetrius I, a Buddhist Graeco-Bactrian king who ruled from about 200 to 180 BC, expanded his kingdom, conquering parts of Afghanistan, Pakistan and eastern Iran, and forging a new Indo-Greek kingdom that lasted for two centuries, until it fell in AD 10. This kingdom dominated the north and north-west of the Indian subcontinent, under different, competing – and often fighting – ruling dynasties. Despite political disunity, there was a peculiarly fertile blending of cultures and religions in the region as Greek and Indian languages merged and ancient Greek, Zoroastrian, Hindu and Buddhist religious ideas co-existed. The Graeco-Buddhist art that evolved in this cultural melting-pot is a particularly powerful example of how successful and vibrant this Hellenistic offshoot became. It is an artistic tradition that began with wonderfully fine and naturalistic stone depictions of the Buddha, and which dominated central Asian art for nearly a millennium. The immediacy and human empathy that make images of Buddha speak to us so powerfully to this day can partly be attributed to the ancient Greek artistic style with its emphasis on idealized but realistic depictions of the individual.

The Graeco-Bactrian and Indo-Greek kingdoms were among the most lasting, prosperous and culturally enriching of the Hellenistic outposts. This was multi-culturalism, ancient-world style, at its most successful. It was achieved through a fair amount of violence, but like the Ptolemaic Empire the Indo-Greek world was held together by the more lasting ties on which civilizations are built: trading and communicating, building cities, working out ways of worshipping your own and other people's gods. In forging relations with Asian civilizations, in the Indian subcontinent and in China, the Bactrians and Indo-Greeks disseminated and developed Hellenism in a way that gave this relatively short-lived kingdom an enduring influence that the Greeks, in their separately evolving homeland, could have barely known of or recognized.

RIGHT
A bust of Pyrrhus.

Not everybody had learned that the 'Big Man-ism' of Alexander was no way to secure a lasting kingdom or legacy. Throughout the three centuries of its existence the Hellenistic world also threw up plenty of warlords, adventurers and Alexander the Great wannabes. Unlike the Ptolemies and the Graeco-Bactrian kings they tended to come and go, leaving little of substance behind them apart from burnt cities, looted temples and corpses. Perhaps the greatest of these mini-Alexanders was Pyrrhus, king of Epirus, a small Hellenistic kingdom, roughly where Albania is now, in the first quarter of the third century BC. Pyrrhus had led an extremely eventful life as a young man, including several depositions and restorations to the throne, a spell as a hostage at the Egyptian court and a short-lived interlude as king of Macedonia; all this was a reflection of both his restless ambition and the insecurity of the times.

In 280 BC, a golden opportunity presented itself to Pyrrhus. At this time the wealthy cities of Magna Graecia (the area of southern Italy that had been colonized by Greek settlers) were being menaced by Rome, which had expanded its power on the peninsula in a remarkable way over the previous century. Casting around for a saviour, the Greek cities sent an invitation to Pyrrhus, who had already picked up a reputation for being a brilliant general. Pyrrhus also had a reputation for being an indefatigable troublemaker, so

other Hellenistic monarchs, anxious to see the back of him, enthusiastically supplied him with the troops, elephants, ships and money needed to set him on his way.

Pyrrhus landed in Italy with 30,000 men and thirty elephants and quickly made an impact. As the self-styled heir of Alexander, Pyrrhus successfully re-enacted a number of the great king's tactics and strategies. On the battlefield, his use of elephants (the first time that it had been done in the West) proved decisive in two battles fought against the Romans at Heraclea in 279 BC. The elephants caused panic and disarray among the Roman cavalry. Like Alexander, Pyrrhus was a brilliant self-publicist, and like his predecessor he too travelled with several writers in his entourage, charged with producing an 'official' account of his campaigns. Pyrrhus also penned several works himself; through a judicious mix of legend, speeches, pageantry and iconography, he successfully promoted himself as the saviour of the Greeks against the barbarians – in this case the Romans. The Romans meanwhile, in an effort to create an epic past that was gloriously in keeping with their present dominance over Italy, had started to claim that they were the ancestors of refugees from Troy who had fled the city as it fell to the Greeks at the end of the Trojan War. This set things up perfectly for Pyrrhus, who used the idea of the two legendary teams squaring up against each other again to marshal the Italian Greeks under his banner. Pyrrhus declared that he would follow the example of his famous ancestor, the great Greek hero Achilles (yes, another of Achilles' descendants!), by conquering the Romans, the descendants of the Trojans. The fine silver coins minted by Pyrrhus during this period carry portraits of the Greek heroes Heracles and Achilles just as the coins of Alexander had done.

LEFT
Silver tetradrachm of Demetrius I King of Bactria (*c.* 200–185 BC). On one side there is a portrait of the king wearing an elephant's skin headdress; on the other is Heracles holding a club. The headdress, a traditional symbol of Alexander the Great's conquest of India, and the portrayal of Heracles show that the influence of the great king as a source of royal authority in this far-flung region of the Hellenistic world remained strong long after his death.

In the wake of victory at Heraclea, Pyrrhus managed to advance within an imposingly short distance of Rome itself. After almost agreeing to Pyrrhus' peace terms, the Roman Senate at the last minute showed the defiant resilience for which its city would become famous: it rejected his demands and voted to continue the war. Although Pyrrhus won another victory against the Roman legions at Ausculum, it came at such a cost that he is said to have made the famous comment, 'One more victory like that and we are lost', which has earned him an undying reputation for wry cleverness. With his army seriously weakened, Pyrrhus had little choice but to retreat.

Despite this devastating 'Pyrrhic victory', the irrepressible king was not yet finished in the central Mediterranean. One of the advantages of being an Alexandrian adventurer (or sword for hire) was that new opportunities tended crop up. The Greek cities in Sicily were at that time hard pressed by the Carthaginians, who had long been militarily and politically involved in the island. Sicily was particularly attractive because Pyrrhus' wife was, conveniently, the daughter of Agathocles, the old king of Syracuse, the most important city-state on the island. This meant that Pyrrhus' son had a legitimate claim over the city and its territory at a time when it was weak and politically divided. The regency over the richest and most powerful city in Sicily, with the possibility of using its resources to seize the whole of that populous and well-resourced island, was a very tempting proposition for the king of a small and poor kingdom in the Balkans. In asking Pyrrhus for help, the Sicilian Greeks were playing with fire.

Although Pyrrhus had initially landed in Sicily in the summer of 278 BC with a very modest force, he was quickly provided with troops, money and supplies by the anti-Carthaginian group of Sicilian cities. After entering Syracuse in triumph – his mere appearance had led to a substantial Carthaginian fleet abandoning their blockade of the harbour – Pyrrhus was able to acquire a substantial army of 30,000 infantry and 2,500 cavalry for the campaign ahead. He quickly discovered that the Carthaginian army on Sicily did not present the same kind of stiff challenge as the Roman legions.

Once again, Pyrrhus showed himself to be an extremely effective propagandist. He quickly took on the mantle of a Hellenic liberator who would rid Sicily of the barbarous Carthaginians once and for all. In time-honoured fashion, he made a vow to institute games and a sacrifice in honour of Heracles if he captured the stronghold of Eryx, an important strategic and religious centre for the Carthaginians, with its temple to Astarte famous for its sacred prostitutes. This was a move that really seemed designed to compare Pyrrhus with Alexander, who had done exactly the same thing after capturing the city of Tyre.

It all fitted perfectly, because Carthage had originally been a colony of Tyre and the Carthaginians had long been called the Persians of the West by hostile Greek writers.

Eryx, though, was a daunting challenge for any army, however powerful. It was almost impregnable, rising 750 metres into the clouds from the coastal plains below. Triangular in shape, Eryx had precipitous cliffs on two sides and was protected all the way round by a huge defensive wall. Pyrrhus had little option but to attack from the south-west. It was still an enormous challenge. He moved in his siege machines and catapults to start with, to soften up the city. At first he faced fierce resistance, but he was ultimately victorious. Ever the self-publicist, Pyrrhus made sure that he was the first over the walls in a suit of magnificent armour; yet another reference to Alexander, this time his scaling of the sheer mountain fortress at Aornus in the Swat valley. The games and sacrifice to Heracles were then carried out, in duly magnificent style.

Yet, as usual with Pyrrhus, defeat was snatched from the jaws of victory. His increasingly high-handed behaviour made his Sicilian Greek allies suspicious of his true motives. Tougher Carthaginian resistance in skirmishes elsewhere on Sicily meant that the war degenerated into one of long sieges and attrition – not the kind of conflict that a restless glory seeker such as Pyrrhus was likely to remain interested in for long. In 276 BC, Pyrrhus decided to return to Italy where the desperate Greek cities, who had been falling one by one to the Roman legions, were ready to welcome him with open arms. This time, though, the Romans had his measure, and there would be no repeats of those great victories that he had won in the previous war. Rome was also helped by an effective alliance with the Carthaginians, who also wanted this mercurial troublemaker permanently dealt with. The next year Pyrrhus would leave the shores of Italy for good.

Pyrrhus' career, which promised so much but delivered so little, showed that this was no longer an age where all you needed to conquer the world were charisma, courage, tactical genius, limitless ambition and a copy of the *Iliad*. This was a new era of kingdoms and states patiently built on the sustained commitment and investment of their leaders, not grand dreams and unfulfilled promises. The problem for would-be Alexanders was that the story could only ever end in one of two ways: premature death, as with Alexander, which at least left your heroic legacy intact; or eventual defeat. A peaceful retirement was not an option. If you left it too long it was possible to suffer both fates. Three years after leaving Italy, Pyrrhus met a humiliating end while besieging a city in Greece. Stunned by a tile thrown from a roof top by an old woman, his head was cut off by an enemy soldier.

Even the irrepressible Pyrrhus had sensed the new political realities of the Mediterranean world. As he sailed away from Sicily for the last time, he was said to have remarked that the island was now destined to become the wrestling ground of Carthage and Rome. Pyrrhus might have been yesterday's man, but he was shrewd enough to glimpse the future.

5

THE RISE AND FALL OF
THE ROMAN REPUBLIC

I
EARLY ROME: A METEORIC RISE

The rise of Rome is one of the most familiar stories from the ancient world: a dynamic republic is transformed into a mighty empire, the greatest the world has ever known, and with it the foundations for much of modern Western civilization are established. But what was it that set the Romans apart from other powerful civilizations that had come before? One clue lies in that word 'civilization'. It comes from *civis*, meaning 'citizen', a Latin word – not Greek or Punic, not Persian or Egyptian, not Assyrian, Akkadian, Sumerian or Hittite, nor any of the mother-tongues of the other civilizations that we have encountered so far. Ancient Rome defines 'civilization' because the Romans did something that no one else had managed before: they created a civilization for export.

Civilization is not the same as culture. Culture is eminently exportable, and the Hellenistic kings that came after Alexander the Great had already demonstrated how to exploit its international appeal: the library, the theatre, the gymnasium, the museum – these components of the Greek franchise made every Greek-speaker into a 'cosmopolitan' – a 'citizen of the world'. But in the centuries that were to come, being a citizen of Rome would trump being a 'citizen of the world'.

By and large the Romans were often content to concede the cultural stage to the Greeks because they were grappling with something far more intractable: politics – the science, or perhaps the art, of civilization. After Alexander the Great, the Greeks had little chance to practise politics, except in a theoretical way, but the Roman Republic in the same period was actively, intensely and often violently political. The Senate, the hustings, the law courts and, when all else failed, the battlefield – these were the places where Roman civilization was forged.

Rome was no Utopia-on-the-Tiber, no philosopher-king had planned the civilization that was hammered out here. It was the familiar story of crude

PEVIOUS PAGE
The battle of Zama. This sixteenth-century painting, with the Carthaginians portrayed as Turks and the Romans as Europeans, is a precursor to the orientalization of Carthage that was so prevalent in the eighteenth and nineteenth centuries.

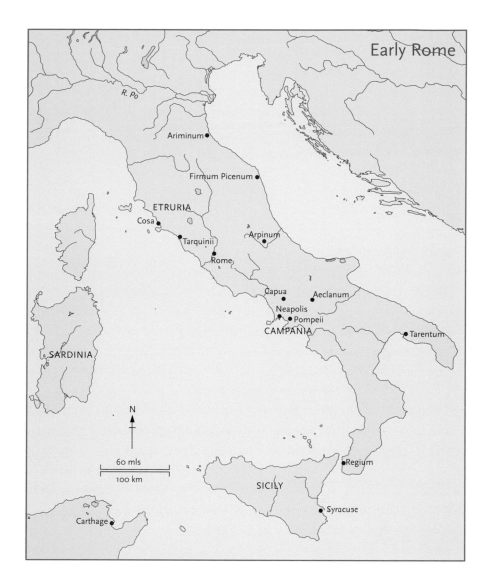

Early Rome

improvisation and blind panic in the face of crises, as elites clung to power, the masses seethed and boiled and external enemies threatened both. Yet the Roman response to the disasters, tensions and conflagrations that beset their city was entirely unfamiliar. Rome would not merely conquer the world but transform the world into Rome. The brutal realities of war and conquest were followed by an effective process of incorporation of new subject populations based on an overarching superstructure of shared political rights and responsibilities that still left room for all-important local identities and relationships. Under Roman stewardship, civilization as a tool of imperialism came of age at last.

The story begins with an insignificant collection of hill-top villages in the back of beyond and ends with a mighty Republican empire branded with the slogan: *Senatus Et Populusque Romanus*. But of course nothing is that simple. Having overcome the ancient world in the name of 'The Senate and the People of Rome', the only people the Romans had left to defeat were themselves.

Around 130 BC Polybius, a Greek historian, reflected on the spectacular rise of Rome, a city where he had been held hostage for sixteen years, but which he had come to regard as home:

Who is so unthinking or apathetic that he would not want to discover how and under what form of government almost all of the known world came under the single rule of the Romans in a period of less than fifty-three years ... an event for which previous history gives no precedent?

Polybius was perhaps the greatest historian of the ancient world. He was eyewitness to some of the key moments in the rise of Rome, including the subjugation of Greece and the final, brutal burial of its arch-rival Carthage, in 146 BC. He saw Roman ascendancy as the inevitable working out of a historical destiny; but in truth, as we shall see in this chapter, the rise of Rome was far from assured and her future never certain.

You can learn a lot from the stories that peoples tell about their earliest origins. It is striking that Roman mythology about the foundation and early years of their city involved fratricide, mass abduction and rape, a series of bloody wars and foreign domination. The clear message was that Rome had emerged from its infancy already hardened by adversity, a city-state with no reverse gear, programmed to resist any outside interference whatever the consequences. Surrounded by powerful neighbours, Rome had to be ready to fight if it was to preserve its independence. But what really distinguished Rome from other small Italian city-states was its out-and-out belligerence and acquisitiveness.

Most Romans believed that their city was founded by twin brothers, Romulus and Remus. The siblings had not had the best start in life: they were chucked into the Tiber to drown by their great-uncle, the king of a local city who feared that they would grow up to claim the throne. But the infants were washed up at the future site of Rome, where they were sheltered and suckled by a she-wolf. What might have ended as a heart-warming story of adversity conquered, as the twins went on to found Rome, had a sting in the tail. After an argument, Romulus murdered his twin, spilling his blood on the foundations of the fledgling city.

For later Romans, who knew of the tumultuous civil wars that had racked their city, that Rome should have come into being against the backdrop of bloody

murder must have seemed all too fitting. Certainly the story of Romulus and Remus highlighted a persistent and well-founded fear of the consequences of destructive strife within its ruling elite. The high-octane environment of competition that made Rome so successful also meant that it was always teetering on the verge of political instability and potential disaster. As we shall see, Rome was always driven by fierce and potentially combustible levels of ambition.

But who were the Romans? It is always tricky to piece together the earliest days of any city but we do know that Rome, in around the eighth century BC, was the usual post-Dark Age cluster of clannish villages, struggling for survival, fighting for pre-eminence and squabbling over cattle-rustling, ownership of water sources and land: the primordial soup from which all civilizations emerge. The people who first settled there picked a good spot. Situated in northern Latium (the region of western central Italy surrounding Rome), on a group of seven hills, it was the best crossing point of the Tiber river. Not only did it occupy a good defensive position but it was also blessed with a supply of fresh water and easy access to the sea. By the end of the seventh century BC Rome had begun to develop those indicators of urban civilization: planned streets, temples and a forum.

Rome is said to have been initially ruled by a succession of seven kings, starting with Romulus, the city's founder. Serious trouble between the monarch and his people seems to have begun under Servius Tullius, the sixth king, who tried to break the power of the nobility by reorganizing the traditional tribes into four new ones made up of equal numbers of individuals of each level of rank, status and wealth. In one bold move, old allegiances to aristocratic leaders were swept away, along with their power to mobilize dissent. It is said that Servius was murdered in 535 BC by his own daughter, Tullia, and her husband, Tarquinius Superbus or Tarquin the Proud, who became the seventh and last king. According to Livy, Tarquin threw his father-in-law down the steps of the Senate building and then Tullia ran him over with a chariot. This terrible, polluting crime was seen by the later Roman historian Livy as just cause for terminating Roman kingship, although ongoing tensions between the increasingly domineering monarch and the viciously ambitious families vying for power beneath may also have had something to do with it.

Cruel and tyrannical, Tarquin had quickly alienated everyone. The final straw was the rape and subsequent suicide of Lucretia, the virtuous wife of a Roman nobleman, by one of Tarquin's sons. This provoked widespread outrage and disgust (and inspired a swathe of artists and poets, including Titian and Rembrandt, Chaucer and Shakespeare). Rome's early experiment with monarchy ended abruptly with the expulsion of Tarquin in 509 BC. He did not give up his throne without a fight; Tarquin enlisted the support of the Etruscans and other powerful Latin kings with the persuasive 'domino effect' argument that surrounding kings might suffer a similar fate. But the rebels prevailed and the Roman Republic came into being, with two noblemen Lucius Collatinus (Lucretia's widowed husband) and Marcus Brutus (who had led the revolt against Tarquin) as the first consuls of Rome. The story of the expulsion of Rome's kings probably camouflages a familiar tale found in city-states from Bronze Age Iraq to Classical Greece: a vying for power between an aristocratic elite and an overweening autocrat. In Rome, the autocrat lost.

The Republic was not built for beauty, but utility and endurance. And it was durable: it lasted for over 450 years. It was a mix of monarchical, oligarchic and democratic elements. The king was replaced by two elected consuls, who could serve no longer than a year in office. This constitutional arrangement was designed to ensure that no individual could amass too much political power or influence. Each consul acted not only as a colleague but also as a check on his fellow consul. On election, the first act of the two consuls was to administer an oath, taken by all the Roman people, which promised never to accept another king. The Romans had had enough of kings, and throughout the long history of the Republic woe betide any man, however powerful, if there were suspicions that he wanted to restore the hated monarchy. Kingship came to be identified with foreignness, tyranny, internal dissension and external threats; hardly an attractive pitch for an ambitious politician. Only when the state was facing an extreme military crisis would the consuls hand over the reins of power to a dictator, who acted as head of state and supreme military commander; the dictator was given power for a maximum of six months.

Over time, as Rome grew, new roles, or magistracies, were added to assist the consuls: praetors, aediles and quaestors, each one with a fixed set of responsibilities and seniority. All these officials were elected from the sovereign law-making body of the state, the Senate. Lastly, there was a Popular Assembly made up of the whole citizen body, which, as in many other city-states, was essentially disempowered but would lend clamorous support to whoever promised to grant it favours.

It is not easy to get a strong sense of what the earliest Republican leaders were like. First of all, we need to put aside the pristine image, created by later Roman myth-makers, of the emergence of a perfectly formed and civil Republic. Early sixth-century BC Rome was basically still in the thrall of an aristocratic warrior class engaged in cattle rustling and attacking their neighbours. The early consuls were more likely to have been charismatic militia leaders than the toga-clad Republicans portrayed by later Roman historians.

The Republican system was a creaky, ad hoc, slightly crackpot mechanism of checks and balances designed to keep the show on the road. Rome might have got rid of its kings, but it always struggled to fill the void that they left behind. Like all oligarchies, the Roman elite strove to achieve good order by admitting the barest minimum of 'rights' to lower social classes while at the same time preventing any one of their own number from achieving pre-eminence by breaking ranks and recruiting the lower orders to their banner. Republican politics was like a bicycle race, everyone hanging back, jockeying for position until someone suddenly made a break for the front, and then all hell broke loose.

Somehow, the Republic was flexible enough to override these tensions. Despite ritual appeals to *mos maiorum* – the 'old ways' – Rome was always prepared to improvise when circumstances dictated. Bits and pieces of constitutional machinery, temporary and expedient, were added or refined, a kind of regular rearrangement of constitutional ballast to keep the ship of state on an even keel. Take, for example, the creation of the Popular Tribunate. In 495 BC, discord over debt and military recruitment between the Patricians (a closed group of aristocratic clans) and the Plebeians (everybody else) had reached a crisis point, with the Plebeians withdrawing from Rome and going to the Sacred Mount to the north of the city, where they elected their own officials. It looked like the Roman Republic, barely out of its honeymoon, was facing a painful divorce. The Senate realized it simply could not function if it lost almost its entire army, and agreed to the Plebeians' demands. From then on, two Plebeian tribunes, in what became known as the Popular Tribunate, were elected every year to protect the interests of the Roman people in the Senate as well as presiding over the Popular Assembly.

Along with their improvisational and implausibly complicated political system, another characteristic of the ancient Romans was their extreme attachment to the physical site of their city. Not since Athens had a single geographical location imparted so much to the identity and, ultimately, the fate of a state. Alexander's freewheeling conquests, the Phoenicians' merchant spirit, the peripatetic Persian court all reflect a portable attitude towards power: *L'état, c'est moi*. But Rome remained a fetish for the Romans throughout their history. This obsession can perhaps be pegged to one particularly humiliating event. In 390 BC a horde of Celts from the Po valley in northern Italy marched southwards and, on the very outskirts of Rome, crushed a hastily assembled Roman army before entering the defenceless city and sacking it. Only a small garrison on the Capitoline Hill managed to hold, saved by a flock of geese sacred to the Roman goddess Juno, which started cackling as the Celts were about to scale the citadel in the dead of night. Eventually even this last garrison was forced to surrender, and the Celtic war-band had to be paid off with a large amount of gold.

Until that point Rome had been doing well, expanding its influence and territory across Latium. In 396 they had even succeeded in capturing the important city of Veii, by tunnelling under its walls after a very long (supposedly ten-year) siege. Afterwards Rome had behaved towards Veii like any conqueror did, enslaving part of the population and handing out parcels of land to Roman settlers. Juno, the chief goddess of Veii, was then persuaded by a special prayer, the *evocatio*, to desert her old city and return to Rome with the victorious army. The outside world existed to be subdued and brought home as the spoils of victory.

The Celtic catastrophe changed all of that. Now Rome would be brought to the outside world. The remaining inhabitants of Veii were offered the chance to become Roman citizens, as were the populations of other cities in Latium that Rome had defeated. This dual process of military conquest followed by the skilful assimilation of conquered lands and peoples into the Roman state was repeated many times in the following centuries as Rome overran Latium. Rome strengthened its hold over Latium in other, more subtle ways. There was a legend that the Latins were descended from Trojans, refugees of the destruction of Troy by the Greeks, who had made their way to Italy under the leadership of Prince Aeneas. It was an idea that seems to have developed from the sixth century BC onwards, probably through contact with the Greeks. It was claimed that Aeneas had founded the town of Lavinium, and over time the town became something of a place of pilgrimage for the Latin people. An annual festival was held, where the *Penates*, sacred objects that Aeneas was meant to have rescued from Troy, were venerated. The Romans used this myth of a shared Trojan heritage to their advantage: Rome's chief priests and magistrates took a leading role in the annual pilgrimage to Lavinium. It also became an established part of Rome's foundation myth that Alba Longa, the city where Romulus and Remus had been born, had itself been founded by settlers from Lavinium, the city of Aeneas. Now the Romans could claim one of the major players in Homer's *Iliad* as an ancestor and justify the takeover of Latium with claims of a shared heritage. Italy would never be just a piece of conquered territory that could be evacuated if circumstances dictated. It was Roman land that was to be defended as if it were within the city limits itself.

It has been calculated that by the early third century BC, Rome occupied 14,000 square kilometres of land, nearly tripling the size of its territory in less than fifty years. The Roman domain spread right across the expanse of central Italy. Decades of war and conquest brought considerable wealth to the city: it was recorded that during the great triumphs of 293 BC to celebrate the final victory over the Samnites (of the region to the south of Latium), one consul brought back 830 kilogrammes of silver and 1,151,000 kilogrammes of bronze. There had been plenty of reverses along the way; the worst of these occurred in 321 at the Caudine forks in Campania, where the Roman army was trapped by the Samnites in a remote mountain glen. They gained their freedom only after being humiliatingly forced to process unarmed and semi-naked under a yoke of spears. But the Romans had a marked capacity to absorb the loss and shock of defeat. They responded to a setback not with offers of peace treaties and truces but by sending out new armies to make good what had been lost. It was this relentless pressure that Rome would exert on its enemies that often led to final victory.

Romans asserted their control over newly subjugated territory with extraordinary efficiency. Within a startlingly short time a network of roads was cut through the countryside, connecting the city to all the major settlements in the region. The first of these new thoroughfares was the Via Appia, built in 312 to connect Rome with Campania. Although much of it would soon be paved, to start with it was little more than a cleared and widened pathway finished off with a layer of gravel. Still, 'the queen of long roads', as it was known by later Romans, was an impressive feat of engineering. Spanning a distance of 210 kilometres, it cut through steep hills and required the construction of bridges and a causeway to cross the foul smelling Pomptine marshes. No longer would the troublesome Samnites be out of the reach of the iron fist of Rome.

OVERLEAF
Via Appia, photographed in the 1920s, with the ruin of the Ercole Temple and the Villa dei Quintilii.

Rome's great strength was its ability to integrate native populations, creating a large and stable swathe of territory that was not just temporarily cowed by defeat. Although Rome granted full Roman citizenship to virtually all the Latin cities, they also bestowed the old Latin legal status that guaranteed rights such as property ownership, intermarriage and migration on the populations of the new colonies that they established further afield across the rest of Italy. These Latin rights acted as a kind of halfway house between foreigner and Roman citizen. This was clever stuff: by using newly created legal statuses, rather than ethnicity or geography, as the basis for membership of their club, all sorts of very different populations could be quickly and fairly painlessly absorbed into the Roman state. They were good incentivizers too, because by maintaining a sliding scale of statuses, Rome could reward loyal allies with an upgrade. At the same time these communities were able to maintain their own local political offices and identities. It was a blueprint that would help Rome to hold together a vast empire for centuries.

For Rome, the most important benefit of this generosity with rights and citizenship lay in military recruitment: Latin rights brought with them an obligation to provide troops for military service. As Roman territory grew, so did the potential size of its army, giving it a huge advantage over other states with far more finite resources. By the second century BC, over half the Roman army was made up of Italians, not Romans. The conferral of Latin status also ensured that ties were kept up with communities that were of vital strategic importance in preserving Rome's hold over the rest of Italy. Rome was transformed from being just another successful Italian city-state into an irresistible force.

What drove this seemingly insatiable desire to expand? Certainly greed and fear played their part. But the greatest engine for Roman expansion was the extreme competitive ethos that was the hallmark of the ruling class. The aristocratic Roman male was hard-wired to pursue political and military glory. And if a budding Roman senatorial politician was in any doubt about the importance of such worldly achievements, then he only had to look at the deeds of those who had gone before him. It was the past that provided a model for how a life should be lived and a career managed. For a Roman noble, winning high political office was not just about patriotic duty or individual ambition, but a matter of maintaining or promoting the stature of his family. It would have been very difficult for any scion of a Roman noble family to forget what was expected of him: he lived surrounded by his illustrious ancestors. Wooden cupboards in the atrium of each aristocratic house held the *imagines*, realistic wax masks of deceased family members who had held high senatorial office. And although the masks were hidden behind closed doors for most of the year, they exerted a powerful influence on the living. Each cupboard was carefully labelled with the distinguished offices and exploits of each ancestor. Other reminders of the glorious past lurked throughout the house; portraits, bronze busts and images on shields. The Roman aristocrat found himself under intense pressure to equal or better the exploits of those who had gone before him. Roman senatorial families were in essence a brand, and like all brands they needed constant maintenance.

The top families ferociously competed with one another for the highest office. What made it harder for some, but easier for others, was that talent alone was no guarantor of success. Theoretically, all those elected into the Senate had an equal chance of obtaining a consulship, the apogee of any glittering political career. But even the briefest look at the consular rolls shows that in reality this was not the case. The same family names – Fabius, Cornelius, Metellius and Marcellus – appear again and again, and there is a positive dearth of new names. To speak of a Roman senatorial elite is to ignore the fact that political life was controlled by an *über* class made up of just a few select families. Others might become senators, but it was rare for them to break into the charmed circle of consular families. When individuals from less exalted senatorial families did achieve this, it was usually because they had the support of one of the grand aristocratic houses. Once a consulship had been attained, then a family could dare to hope that more might follow and that eventually they might too join the rarefied ranks of the *nobiles*.

One might think that because senatorial officials were publicly elected by the citizen body of Rome, such a closed shop would be impossible to maintain. Paradoxically, it seems to have made it easier. The great senatorial families had ready access to the contacts, resources and support needed to garner votes in popular elections. This was machine politics at its most fluent. Political life in Rome revolved around an intricate web of reciprocal relationships between social, political and economic unequals. In return for the influence that richer, more powerful individuals might be able to wield on their behalf, less well-heeled Roman citizens would lend their political support. The top senatorial families could claim whole towns, cities and even provinces as their clients. Of course, it was a naive politician who considered patronage a guaranteed source of votes. Lying to politicians about the way we are going to vote is an age-old tradition. The benefits of patronage were considerably qualified on both sides: patrons often maintained their client base with the *possibility* that they might intervene to improve their lives. Clients, aware that they operated in the hope rather than the knowledge that good things might come their way, tended to be promiscuous in their endorsements, often juggling a number of patrons at the same time.

The atmosphere of ambition and competition that pervaded the Roman aristocracy created tensions that could quickly escalate into conflict and potentially ruinous civil war. The first big danger was that, with so few senior political jobs to go around, disaffection would grow among those who failed to get what they wanted. Expectations had to be managed, and they were, for over three centuries. The generally accepted rules of the game were that the high offices that everyone strived for were for a limited duration, usually a year, after which even the most talented or well-born individual was expected to step back into the senatorial ranks. This meant that at least the possibility of attaining high office was open to a wide enough range of individuals to prevent the growth of a strong flank of malcontents. There was another antidote to overweening personal ambition in the form of the moral code by which the Roman senator was meant to conduct himself. This ethos was encapsulated in the virtue of *civilitas*, which went far beyond mere politeness. It was being a good citizen; for a Roman senator, that meant always abiding by the rules of the political game as described in the constitution. Each senator was expected to live up to a rigid set of virtues that discouraged tyrannical impulses and encapsulated the noble ethos: courage, clemency, wisdom, duty, modesty and gravitas.

But as the list of Rome's conquests grew, the pressures on this delicately poised status quo began to mount. The tipping point can be traced back to 270 BC when Rome, after defeating the Greek cities in southern Italy, had at last conquered the whole Italian mainland. If Rome wanted to expand now it would have to be into non-Italian territory. The first and most tempting target was the island of Sicily. Geographically it made sense because of its proximity to the Italian peninsula. It made sense economically, too. Sicily was not only agriculturally rich, but its sea-ports were key stopping points on the lucrative trade routes that linked Greece, Italy and North Africa. There was, however, a problem. The western half of the island was under the control of the most powerful city-state in the Mediterranean world at that time. Rome, if it wanted to expand southwards, would have to move up to the big league. It had to take on Carthage.

11

'CARTHAGE MUST BE DESTROYED!'

The city of Carthage, situated on what is now the coast of Tunisia, was a colony founded by Tyre during the halcyon days of the Levant–Spain metal trade of the early eighth century BC. Carthage was never quite just another Phoenician outpost, though: its Phoenician name, *Qart-Hadasht* ('New City'), suggests that it was set up as a colonial settlement and not just a trading station. The site could not have been better chosen, for it stood on the nexus of the two most important trans-Mediterranean trading routes: the east–west route that connected Spain to Tyre, and the north–south route that linked Greece, Italy and North Africa.

The real source of Carthaginian power was its shipping fleet; for hundreds of years, it was the greatest in the Mediterranean. Its flotilla of merchant ships made Carthage the centre of a vast trading network, transporting food, wine, oil, metals, luxury goods and more across the Mediterranean. And if a couple of much later Greek and Roman sources are to be believed, then Carthaginian expeditions also made their way into the Atlantic, travelling as far afield as Cameroon in West Africa and Brittany in northern France.

RIGHT
Bearded head pendants made from sand core glass, Carthage (c. fourth and third centuries BC). These pendants were worn as amulets to protect against evil.

Carthage was quickly to become one of the major mercantile power-houses of the ancient Mediterranean. At first luxury goods were imported from the Levant, Egypt and other areas of the Near East, but by the mid seventh century BC Carthage had become a major manufacturer, with a thriving industrial area outside the city walls producing a very diverse range of products from fine jewellery and blown ostrich eggs to purple dye. Carthage had an unerring ability to re-invent itself, to turn a weakness to an advantage. During its early years, it had been hamstrung by its limited hinterland and was forced to import much of its food, but in the sixth century BC the Carthaginians started to seize the fertile lands of their Libyan neighbours. A host of farmsteads and settlements were built, and Carthage was transformed into an agricultural power-house, producing food and wine not only for domestic consumption but also for export. The Carthaginians even had a mini-agricultural revolution of their own, inventing the *tribulum plostellum Punicum*, or Punic cart, a primitive but effective threshing machine. The Carthaginians' amazingly varied diet included wheat and barley, plenty of vegetables and lentils, fruits like pomegranates, figs, grapes, olives, peaches, plums, melons and apricots, as well as almonds and pistachios. Fish and other seafood, sheep, goats, pigs, chicken and even dogs were also eaten.

In the first decades of the sixth century BC, Tyre fell into decline and Carthage emerged as the Phoenician capital in the central and western Mediterranean and one of the most vibrant and creative city-states of the ancient world. Rome at this time was well off the pace. Curiously, though, Carthage never built up a citizen standing army, relying instead on mercenaries. However, it did possess the most feared war fleet in the Mediterranean. In the fourth century BC, the Carthaginians were the first to develop the quadreme, which was bigger and more powerful than the trireme, the ship that had dominated naval warfare for 200 years. Marine archaeologists examining the remains of several Carthaginian ships lying on the sea bed just off the west coast of Sicily discovered that each piece of the boat was carefully marked with a letter, so that the complex design could be easily and swiftly assembled. The Carthaginians had developed what was, in essence, a flat-pack warship.

Culturally, the Carthaginians were proud of their Phoenician origins. Their language, Punic, was a Phoenician dialect, and the chief deities of the city – Baal Hammon and his consort Tanit – had been imported from Phoenicia. One religious tradition that they had brought from the Levant was the practice of *molk*, which simply meant 'gift' or 'offering'. The word was often used to describe the sacrifice of first-born children to appease the gods when the communities were facing a particularly calamitous situation.

I was working on the archaeological excavation of the Tophet in Carthage, a sanctuary dedicated to Baal and Tanit, when we unearthed around fifty urns containing the burnt remains from the sanctuary. It is an unnerving sight when you first set eyes on the contents of one of these urns – small charred bones, tiny amulets, rings and other pieces of jewellery mixed into the ash. I certainly did not sleep well when the urns were stacked in crates in my bedroom, not helped by the lurid pictures of gruesome mass sacrifices of infants painted by hostile ancient Greek sources. The fullest and most dramatic description comes from the Sicilian historian Diodorus:

There was in their city a bronze statue of Cronus [the Greek name for Baal Hammon], its hands stretched out, palms facing up and sloping towards the ground, so that every child when positioned on it fell down into a yawning fire-filled pit.

Such testimonies, designed to portray the Carthaginians in the poorest possible light, need to be taken with a pinch of salt. There is in fact good evidence that, in times of real crisis, the Carthaginians did occasionally practise child sacrifice, but in the main young animals were used. Recent scientific analysis of the urns suggests that most of the sacrifices were infants or foetuses that had died of natural causes. It appears that the Carthaginians gave up what was most precious to them to appease their gods only in times of extreme turmoil.

This lurid emphasis on child sacrifice obscures the fact that the Carthaginians were rather cosmopolitan, and really not as barbarically different from the Greeks as such descriptions seemed to suggest. On Sicily, Greek, Punic and indigenous communities intermarried and worshipped each other's gods and goddesses, as well as trading and making war and political alliances with one another. Indeed it was often the deep, longstanding relationships that existed between these supposedly bitter rivals that drove the creation of a surprisingly cohesive and interconnected central and western Mediterranean. The Carthaginians were well versed in Greek culture and language. The famous Carthaginian general Hannibal was said to have written several books in Greek. The Carthaginian political system, like Rome a mixture of monarchical, oligarchic and democratic elements, was praised for its balance by no less than Aristotle.

The influence of Carthage over much of North Africa, Malta, Sicily, Sardinia, Ibiza and southern Spain did not translate into what we would recognize as imperial rule. The Carthaginians were interested in controlling trading monopolies and, as long as these were not challenged, others were left pretty much to their own devices. Sicily was the one place where the Carthaginians became heavily involved in political affairs, exactly because its trading interests had come under threat. Sicily had long been ethnically split between Phoenician and indigenous cities in the western half of the island and Greek city-states in the east. From the fifth century BC, Carthage had had regularly to intervene militarily to defend their allies, particularly against the ambitions of Syracuse, the most powerful Greek city on Sicily. Carthage's interest was once again primarily economic. The old Phoenician ports on the western coast of the island were essential staging posts for the lucrative trade routes which Carthage had long controlled.

Given the scale and economic importance of Carthage's investment in Sicily, it is hardly surprising that the Carthaginians would not welcome any Roman intervention. In fact, Rome and Carthage were long-term allies. The first treaty between them had been signed as far back as 509 BC, but at that point the Carthaginians were the senior partners, and Rome was in awe of them. More recently they had a common enemy to bring them together – Pyrrhus. But as the Romans took hold of the Italian peninsula, mutual suspicion grew until war between the two superpowers became inevitable, and the battleground was set to be Sicily.

The flashpoint was the Sicilian town of Messene and the much larger city of Syracuse. Some years previously, Messene had been seized by a band of roving Italian mercenaries called the Mamertines. After being hired to protect the city, the Mamertines had slaughtered its menfolk and taken their wives and daughters. Now they were worried that they themselves were going to be the subject of a hostile takeover by the much larger city of Syracuse. Hedging their bets, the Mamertines appealed for help from both Carthage and Rome. Rome sent a force to the island which quickly became involved in a standoff with the nervously defensive Carthaginians. And so, in 264 BC, the great conflict between Rome and Carthage, known as the Punic Wars, began.

It is worth stopping for a while and pondering on quite what these two sides represented and what, therefore, was at stake. The Punic Wars are often presented as a mighty Clash of Civilizations – in the same vein as the conflict between the Greeks and the Persians. But just as we found with the Persian Wars, the reality was a good deal less clear cut. For a start, Carthage, which had existed for over 500 years, was clearly no oriental interloper, despite the best efforts of hostile Greek and Roman writers to portray it as such. Similarly Rome, who had no fleet at all and had not really fought any overseas campaigns, was the newcomer to the central and western Mediterranean. If this was really a struggle between old and new Mediterraneans then it was Carthage that represented the former and Rome the latter. The real differences between the two lay in what each offered to those whom they conquered or controlled. As long as their trading monopolies were respected, then Carthage was generally happy to give their allies considerable political and cultural autonomy. Carthage acted far more like the head of a kind of commonwealth of cities in the central and western Mediterranean. Rome, on the other hand, developed what we now view as the traditional imperialist model of a far more integrated system of political, cultural and economic control while offering attractive incentives to the elites of subjugated states if they participated willingly in this system.

The First Punic War lasted for over twenty years, and for most of that time neither Carthage nor Rome managed to gain the upper hand. On land it was almost exclusively fought in Sicily, a grinding war of attrition with neither side managing to break the stalemate. One of the few pitched battles took place in the city of Agrigentum in 261 BC. It was the first time in the Punic Wars that the Carthaginians used war elephants, but it did not help. The battle was decided in the Romans' favour by their superior infantry. They sacked the city and sold its population, including Greeks, into slavery. It was not the way to win the hearts and minds of the people, but the Senate, buoyed by victory, vowed to drive the Carthaginians out of Sicily and decided to build a fleet.

The deadlock would finally be broken at sea, but astonishingly it was not Carthage that prevailed. At the start of the conflict, the Romans, basically a nation of landlubbers, had no navy to speak of. They turned this round after capturing a Carthaginian ship, which they copied plank for plank, using the convenient 'flat-pack' numbering system. Having the ships was one thing, but knowing how to use them effectively was quite another. The first naval encounter with Carthage was an utter embarrassment. The consul, Gnaeus Cornelius Scipio, aptly nicknamed Asina or 'donkey', charged in with a small flotilla of seventeen ships and seized the harbour on the Lipari Islands. But Asina was quickly penned in by a larger Carthaginian fleet; he duly abandoned his ships and fled ashore. The ships ended up being burnt to cinders and Asina was captured – an ignominious and not entirely unexpected start to Rome's naval history.

The Romans were not going to be put off by this minor setback. They still had more than 130 ships left and they developed an ingenious device to even up the odds against the far superior Carthaginian navy: the *corbus*, or crow. It was a kind of boarding bridge, over a metre wide and twenty metres long. The bridge was levered up by a pulley and then in battle it was released so it fell on the enemy's deck. A heavy pointed spike on the underside of the bridge would pierce the timber of the deck, so that the ships were effectively fixed together, and the Romans marines could use the bridge to board the enemy. The beauty of this system was that it negated the Roman fleet's manifold disadvantages: its lack of manoeuvrability, slowness, and the inexperience of its crews.

The Carthaginians, unaware of this innovation, were understandably confident as they embarked on the first major naval battle of the Punic Wars, which took place off the coast of the city of Mylae, modern-day Milazzo. They were highly skilled in the traditional method of sinking enemy ships – ramming them and holing them beneath the waterline. The Greek historian Polybius described the Carthaginians as 'quite overjoyed and eager, as they despised the inexperience of the Romans'. The complacent Carthaginian fleet stormed in, lost their shape and were sucked into the Roman trap. The Romans used the crow with great effect against the first wave of Carthaginian galleys, among them their flag ship which was forced to flee. It was the most humiliating of defeats. The mighty Carthaginian navy had been annihilated by a bunch of novices.

Despite the success of the crow, both sides still sustained huge losses at sea, through bad weather as well as conflict. One of Rome's most memorable catastrophes took place in 249 BC under the leadership of the incompetent drunk Publius Claudius Pulcher, who became infamous for throwing the sacred chickens used to gauge divine favour overboard when they went off their feed

ABOVE
Punic coins (fourth to third centuries BC) excavated at Eryx, Sicily. The use of typically Carthaginian motifs – the prancing horse, the horses' head, the palm tree and the head of the female goddess – shows the strong influence of Carthage over the western part of the island in this period.

– a sign that battle should be avoided – with the tart comment that perhaps they were thirsty instead. Pulcher went on to preside over one of Rome's greatest ever naval disasters. In the end, though, Rome prevailed simply because its conquest of Italy provided it with a greater reservoir of men and resources. If a fleet was lost, they built and manned another one. Carthage, despite its seeming superiority at the start of the war, was by the mid 240s succumbing to economic exhaustion, a fact demonstrated by the poor quality of the coinage it was minting to pay its mercenary troops, which contained debased silver and was often underweight. The problem was that Sicily had been an important source of revenue for the Carthaginian exchequer, and the war cut off those funds. Rome's growing confidence at sea had also severely affected trade in other parts of Carthage's far-reaching commercial empire.

In 241 BC, Carthage had to surrender because it simply could not afford to keep the conflict going. As well as relinquishing its overseas possessions and being forced to pay an enormous indemnity to Rome, Carthage, the greatest sea power of the ancient world, also suffered the indignity of losing its fleet. The Romans, who twenty years previously did not know one end of a trireme from the other, started to call the Mediterranean *Mare Nostrum*, 'Our Sea'.

Carthage, however, was not finished: its best remaining general, Hamilcar Barca, was sent to southern Spain to revive Carthage's shattered fortunes by capturing the bounteous silver mines of that region. In a depressing sign of how far the sea power had fallen, Hamilcar and his troops had to walk most of the way. After subduing the areas where the richest mines were located, Hamilcar completely reorganized the mining process, and the operations soon became hugely profitable. The colossal scale of both Punic and Roman mining can be judged by the 6,600,000 tonnes of mainly silver slag found at Rio Tinto that

can be dated to that period. Using Spanish silver, Carthage paid off the last instalment of its vast war reparations by 228 BC.

Hamilcar stayed on in Spain. The Barcid clan, initially commanded by Hamilcar, followed by his son-in-law Hasdrubal, and finally led by his own son Hannibal, built up a powerful protectorate in southern Spain, harnessing the plentiful silver supply to develop a huge army of 50,000 infantry, 6,000 cavalry and 200 elephants. One gets a sense of how impressive this comeback was from the fine coins that the Barcids minted for their army; they were heavy with silver of exceptional purity. With the Carthaginians rebuilding at such a rate, it was only a matter of time before they clashed with Rome again. A concerned Rome sent ambassadors to Spain and then on to Carthage with ultimatums. Hannibal was not willing to listen and a second war between Carthage and Rome broke out in 218 BC.

The Second Punic War was a very different conflict from the first. For a start, the Carthaginians had no navy to speak of, so it was fought almost entirely on land. Secondly, most of the fighting took place in Italy. In 218 Hannibal stunned the Romans by marching his army, including a troop of elephants, from his base in southern Spain to Italy. It was an epic journey, requiring them to cross both the Pyrenees and the Alps, a feat that had never been completed before.

In Italy, Hannibal won a series of astounding victories over the increasingly disoriented and disheartened Romans. This run of success culminated in the crushing defeat of the Roman legions at Cannae in south-east Italy, in 216. Carefully studying the Roman battle line, Hannibal had noticed that the infantry in the centre were packed so closely together that they would find it difficult to manoeuvre. So he set in place a highly unorthodox but tactically brilliant formation. In the centre he stood some of his lighter infantry companies in a shallow-stepped line, and at each end of the line he placed his elite, heavily armoured foot soldiers, thus leaving a deliberately weakened centre. He then placed his cavalry on the left and right wings.

When battle started, the Roman infantry quickly drove forward into the weakened centre, surging into the vacuum at the middle of the Carthaginian formation. At the same time, the elite Carthaginian troops on the wings stood firm. This meant that as the Romans pushed forward, the Carthaginian battle line became crescent shaped. The trap was now sprung and the Romans were surrounded on all three sides. Matters got worse when the Carthaginian cavalry, after defeating their Roman counterparts, attacked the infantry from the rear. There was now no escape, and bloody slaughter ensued. Cannae was Rome's greatest ever military disaster. It is estimated that 70,000 Roman soldiers were killed and another 10,000 captured. Twenty-nine senior Roman commanders and eighty senators, as well as Paullus, a Roman consul, lost their lives.

With the Roman armies annihilated, it looked as if the city of Rome was at Hannibal's mercy. But in one of history's great puzzles, the Carthaginian general let his exhausted army rest, giving the Romans time to regroup. This inactivity seems to have bewildered even Hannibal's own subordinates, one of whom was said to have commented: 'The gods have not given all their gifts to one man. You know how to win victory, Hannibal, but you do not know how to use it.' In fact, by not going for the jugular, Hannibal was merely following the rules of warfare of his day. The main objective was not to annihilate the enemy but to force them to the negotiating table. After Cannae, Hannibal probably thought that he had achieved that. Despite later dramatic stories about Hannibal, as a child, swearing an oath of everlasting hatred for Rome, he was really quite pragmatic: he wanted to relegate Rome to nothing more than a central Italian power, with the Italian cities liberated and Sardinia and Punic Sicily reclaimed for Carthage. But if Hannibal thought the war was over, he had badly miscalculated. As we have seen before, Rome had no reverse gear. And for Rome, the Italian peninsula was not merely a piece of conquered territory that could be traded or bartered. It would have been a brave politician in Rome who suggested that they compromise with their enemies or retreat from the hard-won Italian dominions. The senators that Hannibal faced had been raised on stories of their forebears' obstinate refusal to negotiate with the enemy, even in the most desperate of circumstances.

So Rome somehow raised new troops and war continued. Recognizing the folly of challenging such a brilliant general in the open field, the hard-nosed Romans avoided direct confrontation and took to stalking and harrying the Carthaginian army as it crisscrossed Italy. At the same time Roman forces were sent to Spain and ultimately North Africa to put pressure on Carthage. It worked: an increasingly beleaguered Hannibal was recalled to Carthage in 203 to defend his homeland. But even the presence of their greatest commander could not save Carthage; he was soundly defeated by a younger but equally talented Roman general, Scipio Africanus, at the battle of Zama in 201. The Carthaginians could do little but sue for peace once again.

After such a long and damaging conflict, the peace terms were harsh: a war indemnity of 10,000 talents (26,000 kilogrammes) of silver to be paid over fifty years, nearly ten times the amount demanded by Rome at the end of the First Punic War. Carthage was also forbidden from waging any war without the permission of Rome; in other words, it was reduced to little more than a Roman client state. Carthage was then left to its own devices for the next thirty years as

R. Guadalquivir
Baecula
Gades
(Cadiz)
Mala

Rome dominions, allies

Carthage dominions, alli

Hannibal's campaigns

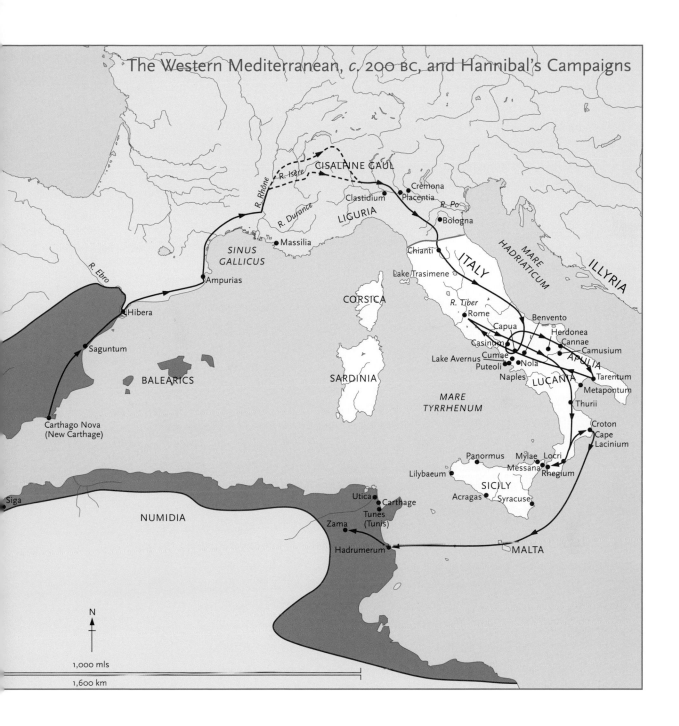

The Western Mediterranean, c. 200 BC, and Hannibal's Campaigns

R. Rhône
R. Isère
R. Durance
CISALPINE GAUL
Clastidium
Cremona
Placentia
R. Po
Bologna
LIGURIA
Massilia
SINUS GALLICUS
Chianti
ITALY
MARE HADRIATICUM
ILLYRIA
R. Ebro
Ampurias
Lake Trasimene
CORSICA
R. Tiber
Rome
Benvento
Herdonea
Cannae
Camusium
Hibera
Capua
Casinum
Cumae
Lake Avernus
Puteoli
Nola
Naples
APULIA
LUCANIA
Tarentum
Metapontum
Saguntum
BALEARICS
SARDINIA
MARE TYRRHENUM
Thurii
Croton
Cape Lacinium
Carthago Nova
(New Carthage)
Panormus
Mylae
Locri
Messana
Rhegium
Lilybaeum
SICILY
Acragas
Syracuse
Siga
NUMIDIA
Utica
Carthage
Tunes
(Tunis)
Zama
Hadrumerum
MALTA

N

1,000 mls
1,600 km

Rome busied itself with a series of victories against the Hellenistic kings to the east. But then, in one of the most extraordinary acts of delayed retribution in the whole of history, in the 150s BC Carthage found itself under renewed Roman pressure – despite the fact that it offered no threat at all to Roman supremacy.

There are various reasons for the recommencement of Roman hostilities towards Carthage. Firstly, the wars against the Hellenistic kingdoms had left the Roman exchequer seriously depleted, and Carthage, although not the power it had once been, was again a very wealthy city. Secondly, there was a residual element of fear and a desire for revenge. The older generation of Roman senators still remembered the terrible shadow that Hannibal had cast over Italy and looked on Carthage's rehabilitation with grave suspicion. The greatest proponent of action against Carthage was the senator Cato the Elder. After visiting Carthage as part of an embassy, Cato took to finishing every speech with the unequivocal statement *'delenda est Carthago!'* – 'Carthage must be destroyed!' The usually rather austere Cato even started to engage in uncharacteristic theatrics. During one speech he pulled ripe figs out from his toga, telling his audience that they had come from Carthage, just a three-day sail away. In fact, the figs were probably from Cato's own estate, but the point was made: Carthage was prosperous again and a danger to Rome.

Carthage had indeed staged an extraordinary economic recovery, paying off its huge indemnity a number of years early. The Carthaginians were clearly aware that some in Rome were calling for their destruction: they built an ingenious circular harbour and ship sheds with room for an extra 170 warships. The countdown to Carthage's final destruction started with a series of unreasonable demands and provocations on the part of the Romans, culminating in the outrageous command that the Carthaginians leave their city and found a new settlement at least fifteen kilometres from the sea. Rejecting these terms, the whole population of Carthage feverishly prepared for war. All public spaces, including temples, were turned into workshops, with men and women working shifts. Each day 100 shields, 300 swords, 1,000 ballistic missiles and 500 darts and spears were produced, and the women cut off their long hair for use as catapult string.

The Roman siege of Carthage lasted three years before the city finally fell to Scipio Aemilianus, the adopted grandson of Scipio Africanus, in 146 BC. The slaughter was immense as the legionaries fought their way up the Byrsa Hill, the administrative and religious centre of Carthage. Scipio employed special cleaning teams to drag the corpses from the streets so that his troops could advance unimpeded. Many of the buildings were set alight to flush out defenders, and in some places it is still possible to see the scorch marks from the blistering

RIGHT
Highly speculative picture of the storming of the Byrsa, Carthage.

heat on the ruined walls. Eventually, 50,000 citizens surrendered and were sold as slaves; the remainder were killed. After the city had fallen, fire burnt much of the centre, while Scipio ordered that its walls and ramparts be demolished. Once he had collected what he needed, the city was turned over to his troops to be thoroughly looted. As a final last statement, Scipio placed a curse on anyone who dared build on the site of the ruined city.

Remarkably, Carthage was not the only venerable city to be destroyed by the Romans in 146 BC. In the same year a Roman army captured, looted and destroyed much of the Greek city of Corinth, following a rebellion. The parallel fate of Corinth gives the lie to Roman claims that it was their particular fear of Carthage that had led to the extraordinarily brutal and unwarranted treatment of the city. What happened in Corinth also strongly suggests that there was more to the destruction of Carthage than simple aggression. The sacking of two of the richest port-cities in the ancient Mediterranean was, for one thing, a hugely profitable business. Both cities were comprehensively stripped of their wealth, and their works of art were shipped back to Rome. Slave auctions and the seizure of a large swathe of Carthaginian territory, which became public land owned by the Roman state, brought a massive infusion of both public and private wealth into Roman coffers. The egregious destruction of two ancient and powerful cities sent a clear message: dissent from Rome would not be tolerated, and past glories counted for nothing in this new world. The ruins of Carthage and Corinth stood as bloody memorials to the cost of resistance to Rome, and as apocalyptic symbols of Rome's coming of age as a new world power.

III

EMPIRE AND THE END OF THE REPUBLIC

The senatorial families who had dominated Rome for centuries continued as if conquering much of the Mediterranean world had changed nothing. They were wrong; it had changed everything. Rome was now a world city, where careers could be launched, dreams fulfilled and fortunes made. Rome became the cultural epicentre of the ancient world. Greek philosophers, musicians and cooks all flocked to the city and their presence helped forge a cultural awakening.

Rome's attitudes to its Greek subjects would always be rather conflicted. The Romans certainly recognized that they owed much to Greece: on the advice of the

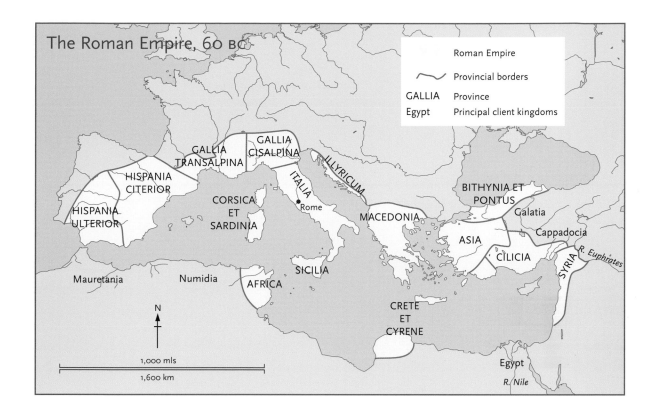

The Roman Empire, 60 BC

Legend:
Roman Empire
Provincial borders
GALLIA — Province
Egypt — Principal client kingdoms

GALLIA CISALPINA
GALLIA TRANSALPINA
HISPANIA CITERIOR
HISPANIA ULTERIOR
CORSICA ET SARDINIA
ITALIA
Rome
ILLYRICUM
BITHYNIA ET PONTUS
Galatia
Cappadocia
ASIA
MACEDONIA
CILICIA
SYRIA
R. Euphrates
Mauretania
Numidia
AFRICA
SICILIA
CRETE ET CYRENE
Egypt
R. Nile

N

1,000 mls
1,600 km

oracle of Delphi they had even erected statues of the wisest and bravest Greeks in their forum. As their exposure to the Greek world increased, Romans recognized the superiority of Greek culture, taking in its art, architecture, literature, philosophy and much else besides. But there was also much about the Greeks that they disapproved of. The Greeks were frivolous, they talked too much, were too clever by half and were decadent: Greek male citizens had sexual relations with one another (Roman males were supposed only to do so with slaves or inferior non-Romans); Greeks exercised and competed naked. Even their much vaunted intellectual prowess could sometimes be too much for more conservative Romans. In 155 BC, Athens sent some of their leading philosophers to Rome. One of them, the sceptic Carneades, pleaded one day for justice in politics and, on the next day, for injustice. The no-nonsense Cato the Elder was so disgusted by this morally ambivalent sophistry that he wanted the Athenians thrown out of Rome before they corrupted its youth.

Rome's acquisition of an empire created more serious problems than pederasty and intellectual gymnastics. Huge wealth, earned in a series of military victories across the second century BC, largely found its way into senatorial pockets. The senators were keen to invest their new riches in prime agricultural

land, much of which was still in the hands of small peasant farmers. In turn, many of these smallholdings were heavily in debt because their men had been called up to serve in the Roman armies, often for many years. A land grab ensued, in which Italian smallholders were kicked off and their farms became part of the huge estates owned by extremely rich senators. The evicted peasant farmers went to swell the ranks of the dispossessed urban poor in Rome. They could not stay and work as agricultural labourers because there was already a glut of cheap slaves, prisoners of war captured in the campaigns against Carthage and the Hellenistic kings.

Most senators turned a blind eye to this social upheaval and the discontent it caused. But occasionally some of their number decided to do something about it, most famously two brothers, Tiberius and Gaius Gracchus, the idealistic offspring of one of the best-connected senatorial families in Rome. Their grandfather was Hannibal's vanquisher, Scipio Africanus. Their sister was married to Scipio Aemilianus, the destroyer of Carthage, and their father had been a successful politician and general, attaining the consulship twice. Their mother, Cornelia, was feted for her cultured demeanour and devotion to her sons; she even turned down an offer of marriage from Ptolemy, king of Egypt, so that she could concentrate on bringing up her boys, on whose education she spared no expense.

The Gracchi had wealth, influence, talent and glamour. But neither Tiberius nor Gaius had any intention of following the safe and predictable political career that would have undoubtedly culminated in an important military or provincial command and the consulship. They wanted to change the world rather than conquer it, and this made them extremely unpopular with the aristocracy that they came from. The issue that they took up – land reform – was particularly inflammatory. What made the Gracchi most dangerous of all was that they were willing to bend the rules to get what they wanted.

In the late 130s BC, and then again in the late 120s, the Gracchi directly challenged the political status quo. Their scheme was a good one: the redistribution of the huge bank of public land that the Roman state had accumulated during its conquest of Italy and the central Mediterranean region, and the setting up of subsidized corn rations in Rome. But these proposals put them on a direct collision course with their fellow senators, many of whom had appropriated much of this public land for themselves. The methods used by the Gracchi to get their reforms passed as law also cemented the opposition of many in the Senate. To circumvent the Senate, which would never pass their legislation, the Gracchi exploited a constitutional loophole. They got themselves elected as Popular Tribunes, the position created in the fifth century BC to protect the

ΑΧΙΛΛΕΥΣ ΠΡΟΣΥΜ
ΧΑΙΡΕ ΚΑΙΚΑΤ
ΧΘΟΝΕΣ

ABOVE
Roman-era funerary monument
from Lilybaeum, Sicily. Although
the inscription is in Greek, the
language of the deceased, an
older Punic influence in what
had once been a Punic city can
be seen in the portrayal of raised
hands in the act of blessing.

OVERLEAF
Tomb of the Scipios, Via Appia.

interests of the Plebeians in the Senate. These tribunes had extensive powers, the most important of which were the right to pass legislation through the Popular Assembly and to veto senatorial legislation. After the Gracchi's land reforms were rejected in the Senate, they went straight to the Popular Assembly; this earned them the undying enmity of the rattled Senate. When they realized that they could not stop the Gracchi by legitimate means, the senators took the law into their hands. In 133 BC, Tiberius was battered to death on Capitol Hill by senators armed with clubs and planks. In 122 Gaius and 3,000 of his supporters were killed, with swords this time. The corpses of both brothers ended up in the Tiber.

The Gracchi left a very destructive legacy, a product more of the obduracy of their opponents than anything they did themselves. They had shown that it was possible to thwart the authority of the Senate. Any smart young politician now knew that the quickest way to get on was to become a tribune and proclaim the message of popular empowerment. The Popular Assembly also woke up to the enormous power that it wielded. The Senate would never again have the prestige and authority that for centuries it had enjoyed. After 400 years of relative

calm, a political dispute had ended in violence; it was the curtain-raiser for the blood-stained finale of the last decades of the Roman Republic.

In plumping for narrow self-interest over much-needed reform, the Senate stored up more problems for the future. Rome was awash with disgruntled military veterans. Italy would be beset with slave uprisings that highlighted Rome's over-reliance on servile labour and the problem of what to do about army recruitment. Roman legionaries had to be property owners yet debt and the senatorial land grab had seriously depleted the pool of potential landowning recruits. The Senate soon discovered that if they could not resolve these problems, then others would.

Within twenty years, the Roman general Gaius Marius had dispensed with the property qualifications for soldiers and started recruiting from the landless poor declaring: 'I'm sorry, the noise of battle prevented me from hearing the law.' As there was no state provision for paying soldiers, this was the responsibility of the generals, usually through the division of the spoils of war. The troops owed their livelihoods, and their loyalty, to the men who led them rather than to the state. For the rest of its existence, the Roman Republic was beleaguered by what can only be described as private armies. In defeating the Gracchi, the Roman Senate had merely built the foundations for the rise of a new breed of military hard man.

Marius himself was a case in point. He was consul an unprecedented and unconstitutional seven times, and was willing on at least one occasion to send his veterans into the Forum to crack the heads of his political opponents. Lucius Cornelius Sulla, once Marius' lieutenant and then his nemesis, went even further. When his own political position and military commands were threatened by the machinations of his enemies, Sulla twice marched his army on Rome. On both occasions he got what he wanted. In 82 BC, after several weeks of seemingly indiscriminate murder which followed his second seizure of Rome, he formalized this political violence into what became known as the proscriptions. Lists were posted up in the Forum carrying the names of the proscribed – enemies of the state, according to Sulla. These unfortunates could be struck down with impunity, and they even carried a bounty on their heads. The penalty was also borne by the family of the accused, as their estate was immediately turned over to the treasury and their children and grandchildren were barred from standing for public office and the Senate.

A reign of terror developed, with the accused being escorted from their homes by ex-slaves freed by Sulla to carry out his dirty work. The victims would never be seen alive again, although later the decapitated heads of some would appear on spikes in the Forum. Even more sinister was the fact that each of the freed slaves bore the name Lucius Cornelius, after the man who had freed them. It was as if Rome was swarming with thousands of murderous, vengeful Sullas. The killing spree gained more momentum as Sulla's henchmen started to settle scores or make some money: many names ended up on the proscription lists that had no link with Sulla's enemies at all. In the first wave of assassinations, it was said that over 1,500 people were murdered, with the number eventually reaching around 9,000.

There was a practical element to Sulla's proscriptions: Sulla needed a huge amount of cash and land to pay off the veterans from his army, which numbered around 120,000. The property confiscated from the proscribed, combined with wholesale land grabs throughout Italy, helped meet this need. The Senate was utterly cowed and gave him political *carte blanche*: Sulla was offered the position of dictator, a position that reflected the untrammelled personal power that he now wielded.

Extraordinarily, with Rome at his feet, Sulla set about reconstructing the authority and dignity of the body that he had done so much to undermine. In a series of reforms he bolstered the legislative powers of the Senate and stripped the Popular Assembly and the Tribunate of the powers that they had accrued at the expense of the Senate. Under the Sullan reforms the Senate would once again be the undisputed sovereign body of the Roman Republic. Sulla also legislated against anyone doing what he had done: generals were now banned from leaving their provinces or waging war without the permission of the Senate. In 79 BC, his work done, Sulla abruptly gave up the dictatorship and retired into a private life infamous for its debauchery. Perhaps unsurprisingly he died the next year. His epitaph recorded that no friend ever surpassed him in kindness and no enemy in malice.

Sulla failed to resolve the political crisis that was destroying the Republic. His attempt to strengthen the Senate through fear and murder merely revealed the extent to which political violence had infected the state. A new generation of ambitious men had grown up under the patronage of Sulla, and despite their erstwhile mentor's restitution of senatorial authority, these men saw no reason why they should not further their careers in the way that Sulla had. The biggest winner of this constitutional land grab was Gnaeus Pompey. Sulla had partly resorted to brutal tactics because, although from an old noble family, he was not well connected and he had no money. Pompey, by comparison, had both wealth and good connections. His father had been an important general as well as holding the consulship and the family estates were vast; when he joined Sulla's cause, the 23-year-old Pompey had turned up with three legions raised on these ancestral lands. Pompey did not use violence because he feared that he might

not reach the summit of political power via the senatorial career ladder; that was, after all, his due. It was the time that it took to get to the consulship that frustrated Pompey. Consular rank was never going to be enough to sate Pompey's ambition. His aim was to be universally recognized as the greatest man in Rome. To achieve this end, Pompey had most of the measures that Sulla had put into place to safeguard the dignity and authority of the Senate repealed.

Pompey greatly aided his cause by ensuring that the formidable powers of the Tribunate, taken away by Sulla, were restored. By making sure that a series of loyal supporters were elected to the newly bolstered Tribunate, Pompey effectively hijacked the Roman Republic. Any bills in the Senate that might be harmful to his interests were vetoed, and at the same time legislation favourable to him but unpalatable to the Senate was simply passed through the Popular Assembly. By the middle decades of the first century BC, the great offices of the Roman Republic had become little more than tools for the tyranny that they were supposed to protect against. The people were easily bought off with vague promises of cheap corn and land reform. The age of bread and circuses had arrived.

Pompey was soon loaded with offices, military commands and grand triumphs. During his campaigns against King Mithridates in what is now northern Turkey, from 67 to 63 BC, he annexed large tracts of territory into the Roman Empire without permission. He made peace deals without consulting the Senate. He behaved in Asia Minor and Syria as if he were a Hellenistic monarch, minting coins with his image on them, naming cities after himself, and even being worshipped as a god. He could now count on the loyalty of whole kingdoms as well as the hundreds of thousands of troops who fought under him. On his triumphant return to Rome in 62 BC, Pompey, now sporting the nickname Magnus, 'the Great', with no hint of playfulness, was able to make a one-off payment of 480 million sesterces to the Roman treasury. His hugely successful reorganization of the East increased annual revenue from these regions from 200 to 340 million sesterces. Pompey stood as a living embodiment of how the huge material and territorial gains that Rome had made in the previous century had fundamentally destabilized the delicate political balance of the Roman Republic.

In the Senate, the Optimates, a traditionalist political group led by Cato the Younger (grandson of the Elder), tried to resist Pompey, but without success. When the Senate refused to ratify his eastern settlement or provide land for his veterans, Pompey simply went straight to the Popular Assembly, where it was quickly passed. Nothing underlined the impotence of the Senate more than when it tried to flex its flaccid muscles. Further humiliation for the Senate and another nail in the coffin of the Roman Republic was soon to come. Pompey joined forces with two political rivals, Marcus Crassus and Julius Caesar (who was Pompey's father-in-law). Both Crassus and Caesar had suffered from having their political wings clipped by the conservative elements of the Senate. These three ambitious men, known as the Triumvirate, formed a secret alliance to work together to protect their interests. Caesar would get his consulship, Pompey his eastern settlement and land for his veterans, and Crassus his tax rebate for his businessmen clients who were the main source of his political support. They would achieve this with the help of a huge network of supporters and veterans, colossal wealth, and a team of tame tribunes prepared to do their bidding.

Caesar was easily elected consul in 59 BC. When the Triumvirate's legislation was blocked in the Senate, it was swiftly sent through the Popular Assembly and passed. The Optimates then tried to stymie Caesar by posting him to the forests and byways of Italy. Caesar reacted by getting the Popular Assembly to grant him command over Gaul in the west and Illyricum to the east: two hotspots where war and therefore booty – an absolute necessity for the impecunious Caesar – were a certainty.

In 53 BC, the Triumvirate became two when Crassus was killed by the Parthians (whose empire in the Near East posed a threat to Rome's eastern territory) at the disastrous battle of Carrhae. Jealous of Caesar's enormous military success in Gaul, Pompey became increasingly receptive to the overtures of the Optimates, who now worked hard to push Pompey into finally breaking with Caesar. Eventually they forced the issue by bringing Caesar's Gallic command to a premature end. When Pompey did nothing to help his supposed ally, Caesar must have known that their alliance was over.

Civil war became inevitable in 50 BC, when Senators demanded that Caesar return to Rome and give up his army; they were led by Pompey, who had joined the Optimate cause. Caesar could either unconditionally surrender and face the full wrath of his enemies or take up arms against Pompey and the Optimates. He chose the latter and crossed the Rubicon river into northern Italy with his army. Rome now embarked on the bloodiest and most costly civil war in its history.

If this was a battle for the soul of the Roman Republic, then it had become increasingly difficult to identify who its defenders were or even exactly what they were defending. By 50 BC, the Optimates, the self-styled guardians of traditional senatorial politics, looked like a desperate rump trading on long-gone glories, unable to answer to the needs of the governing superpower of their time. As Cicero observed, the problem with Cato the Younger was that he thought he was living in Plato's Republic rather than the political cesspit of Rome. Their

The main entrance of the
Temple of Horus, Edfu, Egypt.
Built on the west bank of the
Nile by the Ptolemys between
237 and 57 BC, the temple
was dedicated to the Egyptian
falcon-deity Horus and his
Greek counterpart, Apollo.
The temple is one of the best
examples of the Ptolemys' skilful
manipulation of traditional
Egyptian religion to cement their
rule over Egypt, and it was still
being worked on until only two
decades before the Romans
ended Egypt's independence.

weakness and irrelevance had been cruelly exposed by their need to form an alliance with Pompey, supposedly a prime example of what they were fighting against. Pompey stood for nothing apart from his own greatness. The only constant feature in his mercurial political career had been limitless personal ambition.

If Pompey was the epitome of the narcissistic individualism engendered by the rewards of Rome's huge empire, then Julius Caesar was hardly an innocent party. Throughout the Triumvirate he had hijacked the constitutional bodies of the Roman Republic for his own personal gain. It is telling that when Caesar came to justify his decision to cross the Rubicon he made no mention of the Republic or freedom but instead declared that his personal dignity was dearer to him than his own life. The age of the individual had truly emerged.

The civil war itself was relatively short-lived. Pompey and the Optimates immediately clashed over military tactics. Caesar, who was answerable to no one, moved quickly and decisively, forcing Pompey to retreat to Greece. Caesar tried to negotiate a settlement, but Pompey was evasive. Having defeated Pompeian forces in Spain, Caesar moved on to Greece in 48 BC, where he decisively smashed Pompey's army at the battle of Pharsalus. Seeing the bodies of his opponents strewn over the battlefield, Caesar said that 'they would have had it thus': nobody ever wanted to take responsibility for civil war.

Pompey escaped to Egypt, but as he landed he was murdered on the orders of the young pharaoh's advisors, who hoped to ingratiate themselves with Caesar. Pompey, the man who had celebrated his military triumphs by marching a portrait of himself made from pearls through the streets of Rome, ended up a headless corpse on an Egyptian beach. Caesar wept when he was presented with his severed head.

Although the civil war rumbled on, with Pompey's sons and the remaining hardline Optimates leading the resistance, it was an increasingly hopeless cause. Caesar moved to Africa and then on to Spain, picking off the remnants of the Pompeian cause. At the North African port of Utica, Cato the Younger – self-righteous to the end – preferred suicide to surrender. With his opponents dead or in disarray, Caesar was the undisputed master of Rome. He now had to decide what form that mastery should take. His strategy would be very different from that of Sulla, the last man to have occupied such a position of political supremacy. Under Caesar, there were no proscriptions or illegal land grabs. Former enemies were treated with impressive compassion. Cicero, for instance, who had sided with Pompey and the Optimates, was allowed to return to Italy after a sympathetic audience with Caesar.

Under Caesar, poverty was alleviated by debt reform, and new colonies were planned for the landless. Road building and drainage projects were introduced to provide employment and improve the infrastructure of Italy. Economic reforms such as the reintroduction of harbour dues and the issue of new gold coinage were enacted to revive an economy shattered by war and mismanagement. It was not just Italy that benefited from Caesar's energetic management. In the provinces, unfair taxation systems were overhauled and large numbers of provincials were granted Roman citizenship. Many loyal followers were elevated to an enlarged Senate.

Julius Caesar's reforms showed that fair and decent government was easier to achieve under the rule of one man. The previous hundred years of political strife proved that Rome's constitution had not evolved to meet the needs of a city-state that was now a world empire. Rome the superpower required constancy and far-sighted planning from its rulers, not short-term political fixes by politicians who knew that their term of office would end within a year. The

RIGHT
Temple of Mars Ultor (the Avenger), Rome. Built by Augustus in his new forum, in fulfillment of a vow he had made before the battle of Philippi in 42 BC to avenge the assassination of his adopted father Julius Caesar. His position as Caesar's heir was one of the main bulwarks on which Octavian/Augustus built his legitimacy and authority.

internal competition within the senatorial elite that had provided much of the dynamism for Rome's dramatic expansion had metamorphosed into bloody internecine conflict over the spoils of victory.

The greatest problem that Caesar faced, and one that he never had time to resolve, was how to position himself in a Republican power structure where there was no constitutional precedent for one man possessing so much personal power. Initially he attempted to deal with it by holding the dictatorship, as Sulla had done, but that was no long-term solution. Caesar ruled Rome as an autocrat despite his efforts to mask it by showing due deference to the political institutions of the Republic – he held successive consulships, but the idea of Caesar as just another senator was clearly preposterous.

For some, it was simple: if Caesar was monarch in all but name then why not become the eighth king of Rome? In 44 BC, a diadem (the crown) was mysteriously put on Caesar's statue, and bystanders at a festival hailed him as 'Rex', to which he had replied that he was not Rex but Caesar, a play on the fact that Rex was also a Roman family name. Caesar was wise enough to know how dangerous it would be for him if he was thought to be making a play for the kingship, a despised institution against which the whole edifice of the Roman Republic had been constructed. The diadem was quickly taken down and anyone who spoke of him as king was threatened with prosecution. These damaging rumours about Caesar's monarchical ambitions led to his very public refusal of a diadem offered to him at the Lupercalia, a festival held annually to purify the city and to honour the she-wolf who had suckled the abandoned twins, Romulus and Remus. There was no better stage for publicly rejecting his supposed regal aspirations.

Caesar, it seems, did not have a master plan; he simply threw up a series of quick fixes while groping around for a more permanent solution. The man who appeared to have an answer for everything did not know what to do about himself. There were others, though, who had already made a decision. For many of the old senatorial elite who had survived the civil war, the loss of power that had been their due for centuries was too heavy a price to pay for the peace that Caesar offered. They noticed the signs of his lack of respect for the Senate and the other political bodies of the Republic, such as his failure to stand up to greet a senatorial delegation sent to tell him of a series of honours that had been awarded to him. They disliked the personal oath to protect his life that they had been obliged to swear. In fact, they disliked it so much that they decided to break it.

On the ides (the 15th) of March, a group of senators murdered Julius Caesar. When he recognized one of his assassins, Marcus Brutus, an Optimate whom he had pardoned and subsequently admitted into his inner circle, he was said to have cried out *'Et tu, Brute'*, 'Even you, Brutus', words of injured betrayal that have rattled down through the centuries. Caesar was said to have fallen, dying, at the foot of a statue of Pompey.

After a shocked hiatus, the plotters were driven out of Rome, and then Italy, by an enraged urban mob. Despite claims of striking a blow for liberty, the conspirators carried very little support outside their narrow clique of friends. In their high-minded zeal, Brutus and his comrades had forgotten that Caesar's success had been a direct result of the Senate's failure to act responsibly, decisively or generously towards its citizens; but its citizens had not.

As it happened, Caesar had nominated an heir, and on first appearances he did not look good. Marcus Octavius, his nephew and adopted son, was a callow, sickly 18-year-old with no experience of the deadly circus of late Republican politics. Cicero commented that although Octavian had potential, he should be 'praised, honoured, and removed'. But Cicero would eventually come to regret his dismissive words: Octavian soon showed a ruthless political acumen far beyond his tender years. Quickly raising two legions, he cannily offered his services to the Senate, which was anxious to curb the ambitions of Mark Antony, Caesar's ablest lieutenant and Octavian's main rival. Once Antony had been contained, Octavian marched his army to Rome, where he demanded the consulship despite the fact that he was only 20 years old. True to form, the Senate meekly complied. But those, like Cicero, who thought that Octavian could be palmed off with exalted office and senatorial recognition, were proved almost immediately wrong. In November 43 BC, Octavian made a private compact with Mark Antony and another Caesarian stalwart, Marcus Lepidus, which carved up between them not only the political offices of the Roman Republic, but also its entire empire.

The Second Triumvirate was even more naked in its contempt for the Republic than its infamous predecessor. The constitution and normal political procedure were simply suspended. In its place the triumvirs appointed all the magistrates – many for years in advance. At the same time they instigated a brutal purge of their enemies that put the blood soaked proscriptions of the First Triumvirate in the shade. The heads of the condemned were brought to the triumvirs for proof before rewards were paid; slaves who dispatched their masters were rewarded with both money and their freedom; even those who showed pity on fugitives and gave them shelter were put to death. The triumvirs' clear-sighted but chilling justification for all this was that they had learned from the fate of Julius Caesar, who died at the hands of those he had forgiven; the triumvirs preferred to anticipate their enemies. Cicero, who had unwisely insulted Mark Antony in a series of brilliant speeches, paid a heavy price for

OVERLEAF
Really very speculative painting of the battle of Actium, by Lorenzo Castro. The decisive battle of the conflict between Mark Antony and Octavian took place on 2 September 31 BC. Despite Mark Antony having the more powerful fleet, made up of quinqueremes, vast galley ships with huge rams, Octavian's lighter ships were quickly able to outmanoeuvre Antony's lumbering giants, which were undermanned due to a severe outbreak of malaria.

his vitriolic eloquence. Hunted down and murdered, his severed head was later mocked and abused by Mark Antony's vengeful wife.

The triumvirs next turned their attention to Caesar's murderers, who were comprehensively defeated at Philippi in Macedonia in 42 BC. The victors rewarded themselves with huge provincial commands: Gaul and the East for Mark Antony; Africa for Lepidus. Superficially it looked like Octavian was the loser in this carve-up: he only received Italy, which was still impoverished and divided after years of civil war, and Spain and Sardinia, where there was no chance of attaining military glory or funds. Octavian, however, had other ideas. He understood that the political, religious and cultural significance of Rome made it a far greater asset than all the vast resources of the provinces that Antony had at his disposal. After securing the loyalty of military veterans by successfully settling them on Italian land, Octavian moved against the hapless Lepidus, always the lightweight in the Triumvirate. So then there were two.

As Octavian's hand was getting stronger, Mark Antony's was weakening. His reputation as soldier and statesman was diminished by a disastrous military reverse at the hands of the Parthians and his scandalous public dalliance with the Egyptian queen, Cleopatra. Octavian launched a propaganda campaign against Antony that portrayed him as a dissolute drunk in the thrall of a decadent oriental woman. Then Octavian pulled off a master stroke: he successfully contrived to get the whole of Italy to swear a personal oath of allegiance to him against the oriental queen and, by association, Mark Antony.

War was now inevitable, and in September 31 BC the two sides confronted each other at Actium in Greece. Despite superior numbers, Antony's forces were routed. Octavian was now the undisputed master of the Roman Empire. His position was certainly more secure than that of his adoptive father, Caesar, after defeating Pompey at Pharsalus. There were fewer enemies to forgive or execute, for the simple reason that most of them had been killed. A generation of new men, loyal to Octavian, could be brought into the senatorial aristocracy.

Octavian now faced the problem of what to do about the Republican constitution, which looked ridiculously out of step with the political realities of the day. Kingship might have been beyond the pale, but it was clear that most Romans were willing to accept curbs on their political liberty for the chance of a better life free from the ravages of civil war. The answer that Octavian came up with was a name and image change to Augustus, the saviour of the nation, and the introduction of an autocracy that was always carefully camouflaged by a façade of political continuity and tradition.

In the 130s BC, Polybius had seen the rise of Rome as evidence of a cyclical model of history: societies evolve from monarchy to oligarchy to democracy to mob rule and then back to monarchy. He assumed that he was seeing Rome in its oligarchic phase. If he had still been alive in 31 BC to see the city under the thrall of its first emperor, Polybius might very well have changed his mind: under Augustus, Rome had a new stability and a glittering imperial future, but it appeared that the Roman political express had sped from oligarchy to mob rule and then back to monarchy without making its scheduled democratic stop.

6

EMPIRE

RESTORING ROME: VIRTUE REGAINED, FREEDOM LOST

At its height in the second century AD, the Roman Empire extended for 5 million square kilometres, from Hadrian's Wall in the north of England to the banks of the Euphrates in Syria. Its population is estimated to have been around 60 million. Rome was also an empire with a mission; this was not simple slash-and-burn, conquest and annexation. Or, at least, something else came after the slash-and-burn: there was a blueprint for government which was, at its heart, all about the export of civilization. Rome's imperial mission statement was first articulated by the poet Vergil in the *Aeneid*, in about 20 BC:

> Romans do not forget that to rule the world
> Is your great art: Imposing peace in settled manner
> Sparing the vanquished, and smiting the proud.

Vergil was writing at the start of the imperial experiment, when Augustus was skilfully passing himself off as the First Citizen of a revived 'Republic', so we can forgive him for sounding an idealistic note – the empire as 'tough love' for an unruly world.

One hundred years and a dozen or so emperors later – some of them mad, bad and extremely dangerous to know – the historian Tacitus explained how the tribes of Britain were persuaded to exchange their freedom for a kind of stealth slavery, but his description was really aimed at his fellow senators. Tacitus was after all a self-hating senator, a man who had risen to the top under one of the worst of the tyrannical emperors, the ghastly Domitian, who reigned from AD 81 to 96. Rome's aristocracy always bemoaned its lack of freedom, while in its colonies citizens embraced the Roman way of life. Their inscriptions and buildings showed just what a successful political franchising exercise the Roman Empire really was. Tacitus described this merely as subjugation masquerading as civilization:

PREVIOUS PAGE
Frescoes in the Church of St Anthony, Monastery of St Anthony, Red Sea Mountains, Egypt.

LEFT
Cameo of Augustus.

Gradually, they were lured by those luxuries that lead to degeneracy: colonnades, baths and elegant dinners. They called it 'civilization', whilst in reality it was part of their servitude.

The Roman Empire promoted a model of political, legal, cultural and religious inclusivity that had never been seen before in the ancient world. Subject populations were offered the chance to 'become Roman' without having to forsake their own local identities. Yet, however generous this offer might appear, it was still an offer that could not be turned down. Refusal to play the Roman game usually ended in enslavement, destruction and death. Although the cost was heavy, it was a price which some groups within the empire were willing to pay.

It is a trade-off that divides us to this day: the acceptance of globalized cosmopolitanism at the cost of local identity and freedom. The story of the Roman Empire illuminates many of the major themes of the ancient world – the eternal tension between order and liberty, between rulers and the ruled, and between the secular and the spiritual. But the Empire also marks the junction box between Ancient and Modern, connecting back to the first cities of Mesopotamia and forwards to our own world of nation states, where questions about globalization, freedom and security, and the individual and the state are still unresolved.

Augustus, as the last man standing in 31 BC at the end of a brutal civil war, went on to establish the model for Rome's imperial government: it was based on a combination of personal power, military clout and careful nods to constitutional traditions. With this new imperial government, the Mediterranean ancient world experienced a period of peace and stability that was to last nearly 200 years (albeit with a flurry of chaos and civil war in Rome in AD 69, and ongoing warfare and skirmishes on the periphery of the Empire). Augustus was careful to list all his achievements for posterity, in the *Res Gestae Divi Augusti*, 'the things done by the Divine Augustus', written – or at least dictated – by the great man himself. The original inscription was intended for a pair of bronze pillars outside Augustus' mausoleum. These have not survived, but Augustus always had his eye on his legacy, and he ordered copies of the text to be reproduced on monuments and temples throughout the Roman Empire. One of the best-preserved examples can be found in the Turkish capital, Ankara. It begins, at the top, with: *'Annos undeviginti natus ...'*, 'at the age of nineteen ...', and it ends with *'Cum scripsi haec ...'*, 'at the time of writing this I was in my 76th year.' In between is a catalogue of half-truths, evasions and omissions about how he performed his personal metamorphosis from

Octavian the teenage psychopath, who, according to one story, was capable of blinding a man with his own hands, into Augustus *pater patriae*, 'father of the country'. Perhaps even more remarkable is the political metamorphosis this inscription disguises: the transformation of a king-hating Republic into the rock-solid Empire governed by a King of Kings. Augustus' inscription is more than the curriculum vitae of Rome's first emperor; it is also the obituary of the Roman Republic.

For most of the list, what you see is essentially a long and rather pedantic inventory of offices held, honours received, victories won, alliances forged, public works undertaken – everything except for favourite hobbies and pastimes. What is striking, though, is the way Augustus constantly reminds us of his political self-denial: he tells how he did not accept the dictatorship when offered it by the people and the Senate, and he did not accept the consulship when it was offered on a yearly basis, or for life; and he is clear that he did not accept the coronation crown. But of course not accepting does not prevent you from taking. And that is precisely what Augustus did.

If you read through the inscription carefully, you find in paragraph 34 the absolute essence of the myth of 'the king who wasn't'. Here it says that, in Augustus' sixth and seventh consulships (27 and 28 BC), 'when I had extinguished the flames of civil war [meaning, killed off all my rivals], I transferred the Republic from my own control to the will of the Senate and the Roman people. For this service on my part I was given the title of Augustus by decree of the Senate.' The meaning of the name Augustus is the 'set apart' or 'sanctified' one. This was a new title, with religious rather than political meaning, and it was an entirely shrewd choice. Much better than the name he is said to have considered taking, Romulus: someone must have pointed out that the legendary founder of Rome had been murdered when it was suspected that he was setting himself up as king. So Augustus it was. 'After that time,' Augustus goes on, 'I took precedence of all in rank, but of power I possessed no more than those who were my colleagues in any magistracy.' So there you are: proof in chiselled stone that the 'set-apart Caesar' was no more powerful than the Roman senator on the bench next to him. And woe betide anyone who disagreed.

So how should we read the *Res Gestae* and the man behind them? A fitting memorial to the man who restored the Roman Republic, or a sly, cynical set of half-truths and outright distortions, the self-justificatory musings of an autocrat coming to the end of his days, determined to be the master of his own legacy? The answer lies somewhere in between. For Tacitus, looking back on Roman history in his increasingly embittered old age, the rise of Augustus had nothing to do with the restoration of the Roman Republic. Instead it signalled

the permanent removal of ancient freedoms, rights and privileges. But we should be wary of accepting Tacitus' testimony at face value. He and other members of the senatorial elite might have hankered after the old days, before their *libertas* – basically their freedom to rule – was curtailed by the rise of autocracy. But what of the freedom from disastrous civil war that Augustus delivered and maintained for the millions of inhabitants of Rome, Italy and the Empire? To the vast majority of Romans and the generations that came after them, Augustus was a revered hero who had delivered them from the turmoil and horror that had enveloped the late Republic. Today, the word 'republic' is an exclusively political term, but for the Romans it had a much broader meaning that took in the moral, religious and even physical fabric of the state. To many Romans, Augustus' moral reforms, public building works and countless temple restorations meant that his claims to have at least partially resurrected the Republic were entirely credible. Certainly, the restoration of precious peace to the Roman Empire was a powerful weapon in the Augustan propaganda armoury.

ABOVE
Pollice Verso ('Thumbs Down'), by Jean-Léon Gérôme (1872). In fact, from the surviving ancient evidence, it is unclear whether the thumb was turned up, turned down, held horizontally or concealed, or whether it indicated that the vanquished gladiator should die or be spared.

Yet equally there can be no doubt that the rise of Augustus signalled the end of a Roman Empire ruled by the Senate. In 31 BC, having won the civil war, Octavian/Augustus would and could not give up the power that he had amassed. If he was to avoid the fate of Julius Caesar, Augustus needed to develop a subtler and less ad hoc strategy for masking his power: he did this by superficially working within the constitution of the Republic, while at the same time making sure that he controlled its offices and processes from afar. He was to be known as the Princeps, the first citizen of Rome, and this form of imperial government is known as the Principate. In fact, the instrument through which Augustus controlled the Roman state had no constitutional legitimacy at all. Roman writers as well as Augustus himself simply called it *auctoritas*, his personal authority.

From 27 BC onwards, as he became more confident of the strength of his power, Augustus could retreat from all the constitutional offices that the Senate tried to shower on him. He did not need them: Augustus exercised his will by suggestion and advice. Senior senatorial offices continued to be elected by public vote, but at election time Augustus produced lists of 'preferred' candidates and it was a brave man who stood without the imperial nod. Legislation was still passed through the Senate, although it tended to be of a more mundane variety, such as infrastructural improvements. Despite the charade of Augustus leaving the Senate house during debates, senators were far too wary to really speak their minds. By AD 14 popular elections fizzled out, and Tiberius, Augustus' successor from AD 14 to 37, complained that senators were now useless because they were 'born to servitude'. The Senate remained high on prestige but low on power. Augustus ruled Rome by proxy, while boasting that he was just another senator. *Primus inter pares* – first among equals; it was the principle followed for centuries by the emperors that came after Augustus.

Clearly any autocrat who ruled solely through his charisma and personal authority was taking a terrible risk; someone else could come along and claim the same mantle, on exactly the same grounds. Augustus protected himself by keeping firm control of the army, keeping twenty-five legions under arms – some 125,000 men – even in peacetime. He also created the Praetorian Guard, an elite corps charged with protecting the emperor and his family. Stationed in barracks in and around Rome, the Praetorian Guard steadily grew in power until, under Tiberius, the Prefect of the Guard, Sejanus, became the most influential person in the Roman Empire. Augustus also guaranteed loyalty by setting up a new military treasury, which paid all the troops; and in case anyone forgot it, the coins had Augustus' portrait on them. Behind the façade of senatorial collegiality lay the brutal fact that this was a regime backed up by the most powerful army that the ancient world had ever seen.

Then there was the growth of semi-official institutions that matched Augustus' own omnipotent but semi-official status. To camouflage the radical nature of what he was doing, Augustus turned to the time-honoured language of the Roman private household: like all the most enduring revolutionaries, he knew the importance of tradition. This can be seen in his preferred title, *Pater Patriae* – Father of the Country; a seemingly benign paternalistic detail until one realizes that the Roman father had the power of life and death over his children. It can also be seen in the growth of the imperial *domus*, the Latin word for private house. Augustus' house was on the Palatine Hill, and almost egregiously unassuming. But this was only half the story: the *domus* itself was just one part of a much larger complex. All rich and important senators in Rome had a large staff made up of managerial, secretarial and domestic workers, both slave and free. Augustus' wider household, however, was on a previously unimagined scale. It was in all but name a royal court, the nerve centre of the administration that governed this huge Empire. The imperial household became like Buckingham Palace, Whitehall and St Paul's cathedral all wrapped into one.

Under later emperors the imperial household expanded even more, and the senior secretariat that worked there – usually ex-slaves who had been freed by the emperor – wielded huge power, far more than the high-born senators who still competed for the consulship. What appeared to be rather lowly positions were in fact vastly powerful, because they brought with them proximity to the centre of power. A spectacular example of this was Helicon, the chief *Cubicularius* (servant of the bedchamber) to the deranged Caligula (emperor from AD 37 to 41). Helicon was so powerful because, as a contemporary pointed out, 'he played ball with Gaius [Caligula], bathed with him, had meals with him and was with him when he went to bed'. Another of Caligula's freedmen, a Greek named Protogenes, had the job of preparing the lists of the people that his unhinged imperial master wanted to execute. Such was Protogenes' power that one senator was lynched by his colleagues because Protogenes had exchanged angry words with him.

In the same way that the imperial *domus* maintained the elaborate fiction of the imperial family living as just another private household, so the emperor aped the duties and routines of the wealthy, well-connected private citizen. Like any well-to-do Roman senator the emperor would accept the visits of his *amici*, friends, in the morning. According to the rules of the Roman Republican patronage system, these *amici* were not social equals but inferiors who attached themselves to a great man hoping for his support. Clearly, the *amici* of the Roman emperor had a lot to gain from their position. But being a friend to the emperor also brought with it certain pressures. Despite the pretensions of equality, there was no avoiding the fact that your imperial friend had the power of life or death over you. The emperor Claudius (who reigned AD 41–54) insisted on turning up for dinner uninvited at senators' houses. This must have been a rather stressful affair, with the emperor sitting at one end of the table surrounded by soldiers bristling with weapons. The Greek Stoic philosopher Epictetus (AD 55–135) draws a perfect portrait of the fraught vulnerability of an imperial *amicus*:

If not invited then he is upset , and if he is invited then he eats like a slave at his master's table, in continual vigilance that he does not say or do anything foolhardy. And what is it that he is spooked by? … As befits so influential a man, a friend of Caesar no less, he is petrified of losing his head.

Epictetus advised the harassed and cowed *amicus* that there was only one way of maintaining one's dignity in such circumstances: philosophical indifference. This was easier said than done: during the bloody purges of the Senate initiated by the emperor Nero (AD 54–68), some Stoic senators decided to exercise the only freedom they retained by taking their own lives, often in horribly elaborate ways.

Wise emperors, though, knew that they abused senators at their peril. All the most tyrannical emperors – Caligula, Nero and Domitian – came to a bad end when senators could no longer tolerate their misrule. *Civilitas*, that Republican virtue denoting how a great man treated his peers, was still very much applicable to Rome's first citizen, even though his 'peers' were now very much his inferiors. Senators also encouraged their imperial masters to behave civilly by subtly pointing out the possible repercussions of not doing so. In a speech in front of Trajan, the statesman and writer, Pliny the Younger (who lived from AD 61 to *c.* 112), made a pointed comparison with the terrible years of one of his recent predecessors, Domitian (AD 81–96). Pliny pointed out how different his and other senators' visits to the imperial palace were now that Trajan was on the throne:

So we assemble no longer dragging our heels, pallid and in dread as if frightened for our very lives, but contented, without a care in the world, turning up when it suits us … Moreover, when we've paid our respects, there is no headlong rush out of the audience chamber leaving it empty – we hang around as if it is our own house.

The point that Pliny was tactfully trying to get across was that emperors, despite the huge power they wielded, still needed true friends from the senatorial

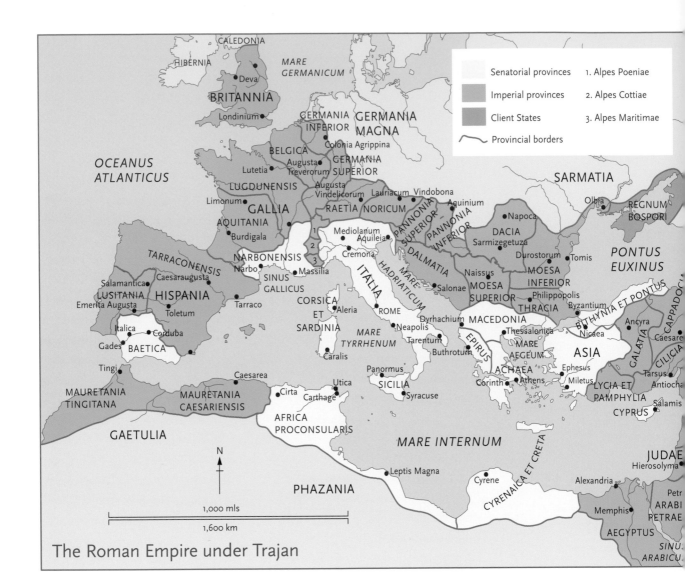

The Roman Empire under Trajan

class. Domitian the tyrant had been surrounded by cowed yes-men. The implicit suggestion in Pliny's speech was that Domitian's violent end and his lack of true senatorial friends were not unrelated.

Despite the end of popular elections during the reign of Tiberius, emperors had to be careful to show sufficient *civilitas* and generosity to their more humble subjects if they wanted to avoid serious unrest. When it came to the Plebeian class, emperors used bread and circuses to buy support; the phrase *panem et circenses* came from the satirist Juvenal, in his description of the way that the plebs' political support was bought with entertainment and a full stomach. Emperors were never really interested in Rome's absolute

IBERIA

ARMENIA
Artaxata
Trapezus

ASSYRIA

REGNUM PARTHICUM

Edessa
Nisibis

MESOPOTAMIA
Palmyra
SYRIA
Babylon
Ctesiphon

ARABIA
MAGNA

underclass, but the 'respectable' poor were important; their support could be critical and they provided troops for the army. Imperial largesse towards the Plebeian class often took the form of free corn and, occasionally, money. Much of the corn was brought from Egypt, while olive oil for sustenance and lighting was imported in huge quantities from southern Spain. The amphorae in which the oil had been transported were discarded after being emptied, and what is now known as Monte Testaccio, located on the right bank of the Tiber river, is an amphorae mountain 35 metres high, made up of over 50 million pottery fragments.

Then there were the games, the vastly expensive public entertainment usually involving gladiatorial combat, chariot racing, beast fights and drama, often lasting for days. It was the duty of every emperor to put on the games, and the trick was to participate without cheapening the dignity of the imperial office. Augustus, true to form, got it completely right. Many of his less feted successors did not: the high-minded Tiberius considered it so vulgar that he rarely bothered to attend, and Domitian turned up but spent most of the time ignoring the action and talking to a dwarf companion. Others were too enthusiastic. Creepily, Claudius liked to watch the expressions on the faces of dying gladiators, while Nero and Commodus took matters even further by actually joining in: Nero as a musician and Commodus as a gladiator. Neither brought glory to the imperial station. Vespasian, who succeeded the hated Nero, bolstered his popularity at a critical time by initiating the building of the Colosseum, a vast elliptical amphitheatre capable of holding around 50,000 spectators. He built it on the site of Nero's despised Golden House, a huge private mansion that had encroached on many public areas of Rome. It was a public relations triumph.

Within Rome itself, the autocracy created a system that ranged between extravagant and bloodthirsty folly and pragmatic nobility and restraint; the immense power of the emperor held in check by the possible treachery of the Senate or the fury of the people. Given how conspicuously so many emperors failed to fulfil even the more basic requirements of leadership (functional levels of sanity and/or intelligence), it seems extraordinary that the Empire lasted as long as it did: but somehow the crazy carousel kept going, held together by the tense balance of relations between emperor, senators and ordinary citizens.

11
THE BUILDING BLOCKS OF EMPIRE

Given that Rome was such a mercurial and violent city, it could be argued that the Romans who most benefitted from the Empire were those who lived furthest from the centre of power. And for all the peccadilloes of its emperors in Rome, the Empire functioned with ruthless efficiency. It achieved this with a skeletal state civil service: throughout the whole Empire there were only about 50,000 officials. It was, in fact, this very 'hands-off' approach to the daily business of colonial rule that allowed the Empire to endure. Across the whole Empire, the same aspirations, the same laws and the same daily routine applied. The Empire's longevity depended on people great and small, Roman and non-Roman, buying into a special brand of civilization defined by an ideal for urban living. Every town worth its salt had a forum; a theatre; a market place; temples; communal latrines and public baths.

A good example is the town of Dougga, in the north of modern-day Tunisia. Dougga has some of the world's best-preserved Roman ruins and gives a real insight into the workings of the Empire. What is most striking is that this town on the edge of empire had buildings and monuments that would not look out of place in Rome. And unlike in Rome, the citizens of Dougga made it work: they self-consciously set out to be part of a huge empire of towns and cities labelled as Roman.

The Roman town was built around an existing Numidian settlement (Numidia being the ancient Berber kingdom in modern Algeria and Tunisia) on a rocky, sloping site, so it does not have the classical grid plan of other cities. Dougga is more of a mish-mash, but still unmistakably Roman. When Roman settlers first moved in, in the first century BC, they lived alongside the native population as two distinct communities with different rights and different laws. The Romans were citizens, while the locals were mere subjects. But over time the communities became more integrated and began to intermarry. Under Emperor Marcus Aurelius (who reigned from AD 161 to 180), Roman law was introduced, and the town's magistrates became Roman citizens. In 205, Emperor Septimius Severus, who was born at Leptis Magna in Libya, made Dougga a *municipium*, which is the second highest class of Roman city. It effectively made the two communities one.

Life in provincial towns like Dougga was for its citizens a shared, communal experience: a goldfish bowl where everybody knew everybody else's business.

People spent little of their time behind closed doors in their own private worlds. Instead, they would be out and about, discussing local politics in the Forum, catching a comedy at the theatre, worshipping at one of the twenty-odd temples or washing in the communal baths. The bath house is one of Rome's great gifts to civilization. The Greeks of course had baths, but they were not on the same scale nor as sophisticated as the Romans'. The baths were naturally central to health and to cleanliness, but they were also places to gossip, discuss business deals and to move along the circulation of urban life.

As in Rome itself, putting on entertainment for the masses was an important vote-winner, and Dougga's theatre is one of the most impressive to survive from the ancient world. Built in AD 168, it was paid for by a local grandee, Publius Marcius Quadratus. The theatre was an exercise in self-aggrandizement: it could seat 3,500 spectators – overkill for a town of just 5,000. Public image meant everything, and the theatre was the ideal place for Quadratus and his associates to preen themselves in public and show their fellow citizens how munificent they were. The plays were unlikely to have been of the high-brow variety. There might have been the odd adaptation by Plautus or Seneca of a Greek tragedy, but in general these provincial Romans seem to have preferred comedies or pantomime.

One motivation for Quadratus to make such a grand statement with his theatre was sibling one-upmanship: his brother, Lucius Marcius Simplex Regillianus, had just built Dougga's imposing Capitol Temple next to the political heart of the town, the Forum. His name is still emblazoned over the doorway to the inner chamber. The temple is dedicated to the protectors of Rome: Jupiter, Juno and Minerva. The pediment depicts Emperor Antoninus Pius being carried to godhood by an eagle. The temple shows that although there were political points to be won by looking after the locals it was just as important to ingratiate yourself with the imperial overlords in Rome.

One of the temples at Dougga is the Temple of Caracalla's Victory in Germany. It was built at the huge cost of 100,000 sesterces. Now, Caracalla was a monster, even by the standards of Roman emperors. The son of Emperor Septimius Severus, he seized power in AD 211 after having his brother, Geta, assassinated in another tale of Roman happy families. But Caracalla's main contribution to Roman history was the granting of Roman citizenship in 212 to all free men within the Empire's now precisely defined borders.

Citizenship had always been highly sought after by Rome's newly subjugated populations. Only citizens could hold positions in the administration of many of the new cities and towns set up by the Romans, and only citizens enjoyed privileges in private law and the right to compose a legally binding will. If non-citizens were found guilty of offences, the punishments they faced were much harsher than those meted out to citizens: in AD 17, for example, when the Senate took action against astrologers in Rome, citizens were exiled while non-citizens were put to death. The story of St Paul further illustrates the useful privileges that came with Roman citizenship. Paul managed to avoid summary justice at the hands of local imperial officials by proclaiming that he was a Roman citizen and using the right of appeal to the emperor himself.

What is extraordinary, bearing in mind the considerable privileges that Roman citizenship conveyed, is the extent to which the authorities were willing to incorporate those whom they had conquered within the Roman citizenship. Citizenship was given to individuals, families and whole communities as a reward for services to Rome. There was something deeply, characteristically pragmatic in Rome's utter lack of preciousness towards citizenship. The eventual universalizing of citizenship by Caracalla was unquestionably financially motivated. Caracalla needed to boost his tax revenue to pay the troops; each citizen became an income-generating unit. In the process, 'plebs', the term that originally designated the lower orders of Rome, became the universal term for the masses throughout the empire. It was as if Rome had cloned itself all over its lands, with every provincial city a Rome in miniature.

A vital part of this process of replication was the Imperial Cult, which gave the emperor a divine right to rule. Indeed, since Augustus the Roman system of governance – the Principate – was based on it. All over the Empire, in towns like Dougga, emperors were worshipped as gods and had temples dedicated to them. The Cult was particularly prevalent in the east; sensible emperors were charier of making more wild and hubristic claims to divinity in the uppity political atmosphere of Rome itself, but in the provinces it was a way of giving the emperor a role in the lives of their citizens. When they paid their respects it was as if they had a one-to-one relationship with him. It exploited the idea of the ruler as the protector of the little people and often disingenuously set the emperor up against the officials who represented him locally. The Cult was a kind of hologram, projecting the emperor into the countless towns and cities of his realm. It created an invaluable link between a figurehead who might have seemed distant at best – peripheral at worst – and the millions of subjects who were never likely to catch a glimpse of him. When it came to religion the Empire was like a sponge, absorbing foreign gods as readily as it gobbled up foreign territory. The Romans were 'big tent' polytheists: all were welcome to bring in their personal, traditional gods, as long as they were also prepared to devote a pinch of incense to the Imperial Cult.

One of the most striking examples of the flexibility that stood at the heart

Temple of Jupiter, Baalbek, Lebanon. Located in the fertile Bekaa valley, Baalbek was known as Heliopolis during the Roman period and was home to one of the most extensive religious sanctuaries in the empire. The major Roman gods worshipped here – Jupiter, Venus, and Bacchus (the god of wine) – were grafted on to the local indigenous deities Baal Hadad, Astarte and a young male god of fertility.

of Roman identity is found in Athens. Some time between AD 114 and 116, the funerary monument of an important Roman dignitary was completed on an imposing hill overlooking the Parthenon, the city which in his retirement he had made his home. The tomb itself was an impressive edifice. Built on a platform, it was a fine two-storey structure, which on a clear day it was possible to see from several kilometres outside the city. The first storey was covered with a magnificent frieze depicting the dead man's inauguration as Roman consul, and a Latin inscription records his distinguished administrative career. On one side of the monument there is another inscription in Greek, recording that this man was also a citizen of Athens and held an honorary archonship, the highest office that the city could confer. There is also a portrait of the deceased's grandfather, Antiochus IV, the last king of Commagne, a small kingdom in eastern Asia Minor. Commagne had been annexed by the emperor Vespasian in AD 72, and Antiochus and his family had been brought to Greece and then to Rome with the honour that befitted their status.

Philopappos, the dead man, was able to present himself as a Roman consul, Athenian archon and member of a Hellenistic royal family, all at the same time. There were other interesting details too. Antiochus, Philopappos' grandfather the Commagnean king, is portrayed in a toga, the dress of a Roman magistrate. Even more extraordinary is the rayed crown that Philopappos seems to be wearing in his consul procession. This denoted divinity, something that by this time could be afforded only to the Roman imperial family. His consular chariot is ornamented with a statue of Heracles, with whom the kings of Commagne had long associated themselves. On his tomb Philopappos demonstrated that even at the high point of his Roman political career he had not lost sight of his local identity and royal ancestry. Philopappos' tomb is a strikingly unique monument in terms of the high-level connections and offices that its well-heeled occupant could boast of, but we should not view Philopappos as a freakish anomaly. Right across the Empire one finds thousands of humbler epitaphs that proudly proclaim both Roman and local identities side by side.

By acculturating and rewarding the opinion-makers and local leaders, Rome forged the ties that made for a durable empire. Rome was successful at integrating the elites of the lands it conquered because it recognized and tolerated local identities and beliefs, while at the same time offering an overarching Roman identity that could run alongside them. The ironic truth about the Roman Empire was that the further you were from the centre the better life could be – you could enjoy the benefits of empire without the heartburn.

Perhaps the best case in point could be found at Palmyra, in central Syria. In the second century AD, Palmyra was on the very edge of the Roman

Empire. In Britain, when talking about the edge of empire we tend to think of Hadrian's famous wall trundling over the rain-soaked hills of Cumbria and Northumberland, manned by homesick soldiers grumbling about their chilblains. But there was no wall at Palmyra, and no chilblains either. Palmyra was known as the 'Queen of the Desert', and it tells a rather different story about what life could be like under the *Pax Romana*. Palmyra was a vital link in the east–west trade route, providing a stopover point between the upper waters of the Euphrates and the Mediterranean coast. For the Palmyreans, the arrival of the Romans simply meant that a whole new market opportunity had opened up: from the workshops and factories of Rome, supplies of manufactured goods; from India and the East, spices and silk. We have met people like this before in our story: the Bronze Age merchants with their mule trains travelling between Assur and Anatolia; the Iron Age Phoenicians with their sturdy ships crisscrossing the Mediterranean. And here they were again in Palmyra: the essential middlemen, stitching together the political map of the ancient world with the thread of trade. And just as the Assyrians had their mules and

BELOW
Hunting scene, Palmyra.

OVERLEAF
Triumphal arch and grand colonnade, Palmyra.

the Phoenicians had their ships, so the Palmyreans had their favoured mode of transport: the camel.

Like all traders, what the Palmyreans needed most was peace and stability, reliable supplies of stock and stable markets so that they could pursue their ultimate objective of getting rich, quick. This was not always easy. To the immediate east of them lay the kingdom of Parthia, a thorn in the side of Rome for centuries. Trajan was the last emperor to tangle with the Parthians. He led his legions into Parthia and beyond to the ancient cities of Mesopotamia, the first 'Western' conqueror to venture that far east since the days of Alexander the Great. But whereas Alexander's victories fuelled an appetite for further adventures, Trajan came to a different conclusion: 'Realizing that the territory was too vast and too distant from Rome to successfully administer it, he turned around and headed back west.' That was AD 117, and if you wanted to date the high-water mark of the Roman Empire this rather world-weary comment of Trajan's would arguably be it.

Under Trajan's successor, Hadrian (reigned from AD 117 to 138), Rome reverted to a policy of peace with its eastern neighbours, the boundaries went up, the Empire was defined, Palmyra became a 'free city', and the good times really began to roll. Some time in the second century AD, and for 150 years afterwards, the Palmyreans achieved the perfect formula for a relationship with Rome. First, they were an important source of goods, providing the spices and silks that Rome wanted. Second, there was no conflict of interest: Palmyra was interested simply in profits, while Rome, like all empires, was groping after an imperial destiny. Just so long as you did not get in the way of the blundering giant, it was fine. Finally, and best of all, the Palmyreans were far enough away from Rome to be left alone to get on with it. And you can see today the virtues of being left alone in the remarkably elaborate family mausoleums which the leading families of Palmyra built for themselves, above and beneath the ground: memorials to their own wealth and status, but also to the benefits of being in the Empire rather than of the Empire.

For all the benefits of Romanization, the Empire certainly had its darker side. Throughout its history there were occasional rebellions against Roman rule, albeit surprisingly few, usually provoked by harsh tax burdens or the arrogance of local officials, Boudicca's uprising in AD 60 or 61 being our most celebrated local rebellion. For those who defied Rome, the punishment was often as harsh as the rewards for cooperation were generous. In AD 66, the Jews revolted, proclaiming Judaea as an independent state. This uprising had been provoked primarily by high taxation and religious tensions, particularly over sacrifices to the emperor Nero being conducted in the temple in Jerusalem. Initially things

ABOVE
Trajan's Kiosk, island of Agilkia,
Egypt. Built as a hypaethral, or
roofless temple, by the Roman
emperor Trajan, this was
originally located on the island
of Philae but moved when the
Aswan High Dam was built in
the 1960s. It is thought to have
been built to shelter the sacred
bark (boat) of the goddess Isis,
who had a temple on Philae.

went well for the rebels; the new state issued its own coinage and easily resisted rather lacklustre Roman attempts to regain control. Rome was at this time in chaos following the forced suicide of Nero and a period of civil war in AD 69, the Year of the Four Emperors (a bout of violence and unrest which eventually resolved itself into the reign of Vespasian). All of that changed in AD 70 with the arrival of Titus, Vespasian's son, in Judaea. Anxious to win an emphatic victory to cement his father's rule, Titus crushed the revolt. Once the city had fallen, much of it was reduced to rubble and the temple itself was completely destroyed. Those who resisted were simply put to the sword. Hundreds of thousands of Jews were killed or sold into slavery.

Rome was tolerant to a point, but if you crossed it the reaction could be one of colossal brutality. Emperor Caracalla, whom we met in Dougga, is a forbidding example of this. When he visited Alexandria, the locals made the mistake of mocking him in a satire. His response, in AD 215, was to slaughter thousands of the city's young men (over 20,000, according to the historian Cassius Dio).

It was particularly important for the Empire to keep North Africa under firm control: it was essential for Rome as a supplier of grain. In the first century AD Tunisia, Algeria and Egypt exported 300,000 tonnes of wheat and barley to Rome every year. Land and agriculture were central to the self-image of the Roman elite, who fancied themselves as the direct descendants of noble warrior farmers like the legendary Cincinnatus, who left his plough to save his country and then returned to his fields. They pined for the imagined simplicities of the rural good life, described so vividly by Augustus' tame poet, Virgil, in the *Georgics*. Cicero piously lauded agriculture as 'the teacher of economy, of industry, and of justice', while Pliny the Younger described in loving detail his country house embedded in the productive acres of its Tuscan farmland, where it was possible to dispense with the toga and get back to what really mattered.

But the rural idyll was something of a fantasy. As Republic morphed into Empire, smallholdings and medium-sized farms in Italy were gobbled up by the *latifundia*, large estates served by slave labour, assembled by the super-rich at the expense of the small farmers. In the provinces, these *latifundia* were of a staggering size. Confiscations of estates under the Emperor Nero revealed that just six senators owned between them half the territory of the province of Africa; they were farms the size of small kingdoms. Like everyone else who came to Egypt, it did not take the Romans long to recognize the near-miraculous blessing of the Nile. For them, the Nile meant one thing above all: food security. As soon as Egypt had been annexed by Augustus he took practical measures to ensure that the wheat and barley that grew here in abundance was diverted to the capital city of his new empire.

To quell discontent, Republican Rome had introduced a free monthly dole of grain for the plebs. In 2 BC Augustus decreed that the number of *plebs frumentaria*, or 'people of the grain', would rise to 200,000, one fifth of the population, a staggering increase. That was where Egypt and the miracle of the Nile came in. Alexandria was one of the busiest ports linking Egypt with its main market in Rome. As Rome's breadbasket, Egypt became one of the Empire's most important provinces. A sense of life under Roman rule can be found at Antinopolis in Egypt, which, some 2,000 years ago, was a thriving Roman city. Archaeologists have excavated the rubbish dumps of Antinopolis, and among the tonnes of broken pottery they made an extraordinary find. In the dust heaps, miraculously preserved by dry desert conditions, were tens of thousands of papyrus fragments containing a wealth of texts in Greek and half a dozen other languages. This abundance of material will allow scholars to reconstruct in minute detail what life was like for the average Roman citizen in the heyday of empire. The richness of the papyri lies in their very ordinariness.

Most of them are the ancient equivalent of those mountains of paper that clog up our lives today: bills, tax returns, personal letters, invitations, certificates, programmes, contracts, to-do lists – the things that seem either too important to throw away or too trivial to be bothered with. Thankfully, the inhabitants of Antinopolis summoned up the necessary energy for regular clear-outs, dumping their papyri by the basket-load on the edge of town. Which is why, today, we probably know more about the everyday workings of their city than we do about Rome itself.

For example, there are papyri from the nearby city of Oxyrhynchus, which include a petition addressing the problem of donkeys being driven too fast through the busy streets. And there is a little note written by two friends, Apion and Epimas, to their schoolmate, Epaphroditos, which contains a rather extraordinary proposition: 'If you let us bugger you and it's OK with you, we shall stop thrashing you.' There is even a helpful little illustration so the poor Epaphroditos knew exactly what was expected of him. Then there is a letter from a landowner, Diogenes, to one of his employees. 'A thousand times I have written to you to cut down the vines at Pahia. But today again I get a letter from you asking what should be done. To which I reply: cut them down, cut them down, cut them down, cut them down, and cut them down! There I say it again and again.'

Among this trivia, archaeologists also found a rather different text:

The kingdom is inside of you and it is outside of you. When you come to know yourselves then you will become known and you will realize that it is you who are the sons of the living God. But if you will not know yourself, you dwell in poverty and it is you who are that poverty.

The words are from the apocryphal Gospel of St Thomas. Three extracts from this Gospel have been found among the bills and the junk mail, and what they show is that alongside their everyday concerns about donkeys and vines, there were people here grappling with profound and unsettling questions about the meaning of life and the fate of their immortal souls. They are questions which the Roman Empire, despite its material wealth, was simply unable to answer.

While the Oxyrhynchus papyri give us the voices of Rome's Egyptian citizens, we can get a glimpse of their faces elsewhere, in the famous Egyptian mummy portraits dating from the first century BC to the third century AD. These eerily naturalistic portraits were painted on to wooden boards, which were then integrated into the cloth of the mummy, allowing the viewer a glimpse of the person buried within. They are among the greatest works of art that have come down to us from the ancient world. They mostly depict ship-owners and soldiers,

Gilded mummy portrait of a
woman, Fayum, *c.* 160–70 AD.
These portraits were
representations of the deceased
that were attached to their
mummified bodies. The artist
has used the expensive and
time-consuming encaustic
technique, in which the wax
creates a complex and rich
texturing. This, coupled with
the subject's fine clothes and
jewellery, suggests that she was
a member of the Romano-
Egyptian elite.

merchants and priests, their wives and their sons and daughters – precisely the class of people that you would expect to do well out of the *Pax Romana*. These are the 'haves' of empire, and their portraits proclaim it, with their chic hair-dos and elaborate accessories. Impeccably Roman in life, these people were unmistakably Egyptian in death, mummified like their ancestors had been for thousands and thousands of years. In these masks, we have yet another example of the Roman genius for producing vigorous hybrids, a kind of multiculturalism with all the political correctness taken out of it.

But it would be a mistake to read only a success story in these vivid faces. The Empire, we know, was good at delivering material success to the local elites who kept things running smoothly. But, as the Oxyrhynchus papyri showed, there is more to life than what you do, what you own, what you wear. And, as we have seen in the disenchantment within Rome, expressed by the likes of Tacitus, outlets for dissent were severely limited under Roman rule. Who knows what discontents, disappointments and unfulfilled aspirations lay behind these apparently serene death masks? All great portraits have a certain ambiguity, a little detail that makes you wonder what were they really thinking or feeling. We do not have any answers for the people whose death masks we are left to contemplate. But we do know somebody who lived in the very heart of their world. Somebody who would have been expected to live the life of a respectable Romano-Egyptian, to have had his body mummified, his portrait made. His name was Anthony, and he rejected the chance of becoming a hyphenated citizen of the Roman Empire. In fact, he dropped out altogether, and headed for the desert, answering the call of that new but increasingly powerful cult: Christianity.

Early in the fourth century AD, Anthony went out into the wilderness to seek divine truth. He chose to settle in a cave high up in the Kolzom Mountains in the Egyptian desert, where he cultivated a garden and weaved mats of rushes. The ascetics who coalesced around him, forming one of the first Christian monasteries, were self-sufficient, growing what they could and bartering goods with Bedouin nomads. St Anthony is the Father of All Monks, and he has become a hero to Christians down the centuries thanks to Athanasius of Alexandria's biography of him, *The Life of St Anthony*. Over 1,500 years of reverence makes it hard to get a sense of the real Anthony, the young man who left behind a privileged existence as a member of the landed gentry for a cave in the desert. But we do know that Christianity was particularly attractive to those who yearned for spiritual rather than material enrichment. For these young men and women, monastic asceticism offered an escape from the Roman straitjacket of private enterprise, public service and family commitment, while at the same time offering them a model for a new life, one of charity, abstinence, poverty and penance.

Christian monasticism became increasingly well organized in the fourth century; it issued written laws and histories, like the *Life of St Anthony*, to spread the word and became particularly strong in the Egyptian desert, which was described as a city of monks. Despite their growing self-sufficiency, the monastic communities were a drain on the Roman Empire's most important resource – the men and women who were its bedrock and, most crucially of all, its tax base. Life at a monastery like St Anthony's would have been the antithesis of the Roman way. The monks did not contribute to the empire and were loyal to their God and their God alone. It is hard to imagine how this small and isolationist cult of gentle, self-effacing ascetics could go on to shake the foundations of the most powerful empire the world had ever seen, with its mighty legions and unimaginable wealth. But, as we shall see in the last section of this book, that is what they were about to do.

Despite its unwieldy size and the large amount of outsourcing of administrative and fiscal duties that went on, it was still possible for an exceptional emperor to stamp his mark on his vast domain. One such man was Diocletian. By the late third century AD, the Roman imperial centre was lurching from one crisis to another. Between 239 and 285 there were a stupefying forty-nine emperors. This instability was the result of a major shift in the balance of power between two of the empire's institutions: the Senate and the army. The frontiers of the empire had come under unprecedented pressure from both barbarian tribes and more established foes. On its eastern borders the rejuvenated Persian Empire overran large swathes of Roman territory, culminating in a disastrous defeat of the Roman army commanded by the emperor Valerian in 253. Valerian was captured and spent the rest of his days in humiliating servitude, being used as a footstool by the Persian king Shapur whenever he mounted his horse.

There was also trouble on the Rhine and Danube frontiers. In the 250s and 260s a confederation of Gothic tribes breached Roman defences and ravaged much of Greece and Asia Minor; even Athens was captured and sacked by one of these barbarian tribes. Others broke into Italy, getting as far as Milan. Another group of Franks swept through Greece before capturing ships and embarking on an orgy of plunder that took them as far as Sicily and Africa. As a result of all this, the importance of the army grew enormously in the third century. Emperors were not only increasingly reliant on their armies, they also spent far more time with them on campaign. With the Empire under attack, emperors had to raise huge amounts of money for military salaries and the one-off gifts that they were expected to pay their troops to mark special occasions. The strain that this

created is evident in how debased the coinage became in the third century AD, with some coins having a silver content of just 5 per cent. These devaluations provided only short-term respite: they caused rampant inflation and the soldiers started to demand payment in supplies, putting yet more strain on already fragile resources. Any emperor who would not or could not pay was simply murdered. The advice given to his sons by the emperor Septimius Severus on his deathbed was: 'Get along with one other, enrich the soldiers and forget everybody else.' One of his sons, Caracalla, heeded his father's second piece of advice even if he ignored the first. After murdering his brother, he addressed the assembled soldiers with the following words: 'I am one of you; only you make my life worth living, it is my ambition to shower you with riches; the treasuries are yours.'

Roman armies began to proclaim their own commanders as emperors, meaning that there were often multiple claimants for the throne. The men elevated by the army were very different from previous emperors: most of these new soldier-emperors were men of humble birth, often from tough frontier

areas such as the Balkans. Now military expertise was the defining feature of imperial office. Above all else, emperors had to be able to inspire soldiers and lead their armies to victories. Diocletian was one of these tough Balkan soldiers. Born into a peasant family in Illyria, he had risen up the ranks of the army through talent and determination. Although his route to the imperial throne was the same one as the other soldier-emperors who had preceded him, Diocletian quickly showed that his ambitions stretched far beyond merely clinging on to power; he aimed to reform the Empire root and branch. As an uneducated military man who had spent his career on the frontiers, he had no sentimental attachment to the traditions of the Principate or the city of Rome. Anxious to avoid the internecine conflict between rival claimants for the throne that had plagued the Roman world for decades, Diocletian came up with a radical solution. He split the Empire into four, dividing it between himself and three of his potential rivals. Although he remained the senior partner of what came to be known as the tetrarchy, each ruler had a seat of government, a civil service and army.

The choice of these tetrarchic capitals also reflected the needs of a changed world. After more than a millennium as the governmental heart of the Empire, Rome was cast aside for more strategically important cities. Trier, Split, Antioch, Milan and Thessalonica would all serve as capitals at various times, depending on the needs of the emperors, until eventually Constantine secured his imperial legacy by building Constantinople on the banks of the Bosphorus.

Diocletian established a huge new central bureaucracy to take over the administrative roles that had previously been fulfilled by the provincial elites. In a clear nod towards their imperial master's martial background this new civil service was organized along military lines, with specific ranks and uniforms. A new census was held so that the imperial exchequer knew exactly what everybody across the Empire was doing.

Diocletian also dispensed with the outmoded conceit of the emperor being nothing more than the first citizen. He was their lord, a distant, forbidding figure whose superiority was clear for all to see. Now all of his subjects, however well born or senior, were expected to prostrate themselves when they came into his presence, after which, if they were favoured, they were allowed to kiss the hem of his purple gown. Imperial iconography from the period makes no concessions to the old image of the citizen-emperor. The statues of the tetrarchs are strangely shorn of their individuality. One is confronted by hard-faced men with flat features, enlivened only by their staring eyes in a state of perpetual vigilance and their insignia of office, a diadem and a purple cloak. Individuality is suppressed in favour of collegiality: the famous statue of the tetrarchs, now part of St Mark's Cathedral, Venice, depicts four grim-faced figures hewn from the same rock, indistinguishable from one another.

The architecture of the palaces that the tetrarchs built for themselves also propagated this image. Diocletian's palace at Split, built for his retirement, was part luxurious pleasure villa and part military camp. Bounded by high walls and forbidding watchtowers, its impression of inaccessibility was very much at odds with Augustus' simple abode on the Palatine. This vast compound contained not only Diocletian's spectacular private apartments but also audience chambers and a domed dining hall, accommodation for his soldiers, servants and bureaucrats, temples, extensive storage magazines and the emperor's mausoleum. In all, the palace complex could have housed up to 10,000 individuals, the population of a small town. This was a structure designed to impress and intimidate rather than to reassure.

In many ways Diocletian's ambitious experiment ended in failure. The tetrarchy needed one dominant figure to hold it together: once Diocletian was gone, his successors soon started killing one another in the hope of not having to share the imperial purple with anyone else. But in other ways, Diocletian's reforms were a resounding success. The top-heavy, centralized, bureaucratic structure that he created survived all the way through to the end of the Byzantine Empire in the late fifteenth century. On a personal level, Diocletian achieved something that very few of his soldier-emperor peers managed. He died after a long and contented retirement, in his bed, in AD 311. It was the same year that Anthony went to Alexandria to become a martyr for the Christian faith.

III
IN THE NAME OF THE CROSS: CHRISTIANIZING THE ROMAN EMPIRE

Christianity might be seen as the revenge of the awkward squad. The Jewish Diaspora that followed destruction of the High Temple of Solomon in Jerusalem in AD 70 carried with it the seeds of the Jewish apocalyptic cult that would become Christianity. These seeds first took root far from Rome. We have seen these places before, in other ages: the cities of Asia Minor, Greece, Macedonia, Phoenicia and Egypt. Christianity had started out as an obscure Jewish sect in Judaea. Despite the fantastic exaggerations and embellishments of later Christian writers, we know very little about early Christianity because nobody, Jewish or Roman, appears to have been terribly interested in it. Nero used Christians as convenient scapegoats for the great fire that burnt down much of Rome in AD 64, probably because he thought that they were so inconsequential no one would mind. In fact, the Roman public did take pity on them: more for the hideousness of their deaths – Christians were used as human torches and dressed in animal skins and torn to pieces by dogs – than any sympathy for or indeed knowledge of their beliefs.

What does seem clear is that Jesus, a charismatic, uneducated Jew from Galilee, gathered a considerable following among his fellow Jews during the reign of the Roman emperor Tiberius (AD 14 to 37). Jesus' activities eventually attracted the attention of the Jewish elite in Jerusalem, who were alarmed by his popularity and lobbied the procurator Pontius Pilate to have him tried and executed by crucifixion as a common criminal in the 30s. The story of Jesus was certainly not a unique one in first-century Judaea. There were other prophetic religious figures from Galilee who attracted considerable followings before falling foul of the Roman authorities or their client kings, the most famous

being John the Baptist. What really made the Christian sect stand out was that Jesus' messianic claims did not die with him. On top of this, Christianity's growing focus on converting gentiles meant that it stopped being just another Jewish sect. Paul of Tarsus was a key figure in this process of broadening the sect's appeal. His upbringing as a member of the Jewish elite and his status as a Roman citizen made him an unusual convert to Christianity, and he started to take the fledgling religious group in a completely new and ambitious direction. Paul began missionary work across Syria, Asia Minor and Greece, and it had a galvanizing effect; by the time of his death in the 60s the sect was still small, although well established in many of the larger cities in these areas. The majority of the members of these new Christian communities were gentiles, mostly artisans. Perhaps because of the hostility they faced, originally from the Jewish elite and later from the Roman authorities, the Christians organized themselves well. They had a clear hierarchy and strong leadership from bishops and priests. Their community had an ethos of charity that made it very attractive to the poorer sections of Roman urban society, who always looked favourably on anyone who fed them and buried their dead.

There were other aspects of Christianity's developing identity that marked it out as different from the many other religions that quite happily co-existed across the Roman Empire. From the beginning, there was a strong sense of a community united by a fixed set of beliefs – incontrovertible truths that had been revealed to the Messiah and a select group of leaders who had come after him. What really put Christianity on a collision course with Rome was its antagonism towards pagan religious practices. It was an inflammatory stance because these practices were the glue that helped hold the Empire together. With their one almighty God, the Christians refuted everybody else's gods and were unwilling to play the Roman game. Take Tertullian, a Christian residing in Carthage during the late second and early third century AD (Carthage had been rebuilt by Julius Caesar in the 40s BC, becoming the major city of Roman Africa and an important centre of early Christianity). Tertullian is generally recognized as the first great Christian writing in Latin, and he urged his co-religionists to stop attending the games and the theatre not only because of the immoral acts that were performed there but also because of their association with pagan divinities and their sacred rites. He commanded that Christian women should wear the veil and avoid gold jewellery, and he praised virginity as the most blessed state for the Christian to live in. For Tertullian, sin lurked around virtually every corner of the Roman city. His opinions, although he was considered a bit of a crazy fanatic by later Christians, were more representative than has often been portrayed. The Romans were tolerant of the views of others when it suited them, while the early Christians made intolerance a way of life; they took pride in their humility and their self-sacrifice.

Persecution quickly followed, although it was usually initiated by local populations rather than the imperial authorities, who were often quite reluctant to get involved. It is clear from Tertullian's writings that the effect of persecution was merely to make Christian attitudes towards the Roman Empire more uncompromising. His sarcastic asides give this sense of embattlement:

If the Tiber rises so high that it floods the city walls, or the Nile falls so low it doesn't flood the fields, if the earth opens up, or the sky does not, if there is famine, if there is plague, instantly the cry rings out, 'The Christians to the lion!' What, all of them? To one lion?

Christians clearly felt that they got the blame for everything. For Tertullian, Rome was the Babylon of the Apocalypse foretold in the Book of Resurrection, drunk on the blood of Christian martyrs; his writings show the extraordinary sense of alienation felt by this well-educated Roman citizen, a lawyer and son of an army officer, towards an empire that had long relied upon individuals just like him. The other great argument that Tertullian provided for firmly rejecting the Imperial Cult came from the New Testament, from Jesus' clever reply to a tricky question on the payment of an imperial poll: 'Render to Caesar what are Caesar's, and what are God's to God.' This was a response that Roman imperial officials would hear a lot in the coming centuries.

In fact, for a long time the Roman imperial authorities were a good deal less keen than the local provincial elites to persecute Christians. When Pliny, in one of his endlessly deferential letters to Trajan, requested guidance on what should be done about the Christians in his province of Bithynia, the emperor counselled that they should not be actively pursued and should be given every opportunity to repent. The Romans struggled to deal with the growing Christian cult because the traditional Roman method of muddling along with other people's gods as long as they respected the Empire just did not wash with these zealots, who were more interested in the afterlife than the here and now.

In AD 203, one of the most horrific massacres of Christian martyrs took place at the amphitheatre in Carthage, one of the largest in the Empire with a capacity of 30,000. Emperor Septimius Severus had launched a persecution of Christians and passed a law banning imperial subjects from becoming Christians. Perpetua, the daughter of a wealthy pagan, had converted to Christianity; this was unusual for somebody of her social standing, and perhaps the sense of class transgression is one of the reasons why this story became so notorious. At the age of just 22 and nursing a young baby, she was arrested with a group of other Christians, including her pregnant servant, Felicitas. Sentenced to die in the amphitheatre, Perpetua resisted intense pressure from her family and the authorities to renounce her faith. During her time in prison Perpetua, like many martyrs, had a number of visions. Some of these proclaimed how her impending martyrdom would help heal not only her own family but also divisions within the wider Christian community, while others made it clear that the real confrontation that she would face in the arena was not with wild beasts but with the devil himself. Meanwhile, Felicitas had grown anxious that the impending birth of her child would bring a halt to her own martyrdom, but the delivery of her baby daughter two days before the games meant that her wish for martyrdom was not thwarted. The child was adopted by a Christian woman, and on the day of the games Perpetua and Felicitas were led naked into the amphitheatre. The crowd protested because Felicitas' lactating breasts were dripping milk, and the women were withdrawn from the arena so that Felicitas could be covered up before being sent out again. After being scourged, the two women were trampled by a wild cow. Grievously injured but still alive, they were then finished off by swordsmen; Perpetua had

to guide the trembling hand of the gladiator so that he was eventually able to cut her throat.

Despite these shocking stories, the numbers of Christians actually martyred remained small until the third century AD, when two efficient and reform-minded emperors, Decius and then Diocletian, became concerned about the spread of a religion that appeared to undermine many of the principles and practices on which the Empire had been built. Both emperors used Christian refusal to sacrifice at the Imperial Cult as a means of rooting out particularly recalcitrant fanatics. Decius issued an edict in 249, ordering a universal sacrifice to the Imperial Cult across the Empire, quickly earning him the reputation among Christians as the agent of the antichrist. Local commissioners were appointed to enforce it and certificates were issued to prove that particular individuals had conducted the sacrifice. Many wealthier Christians used bribery, or paid somebody else to sacrifice on their behalf, in order to acquire one of these certificates. Poorer Christians had a starker choice between death and sacrificing. Thousands lapsed: it was only the real diehards who resisted.

For those determined to resist, martyrdom was not the punishment but the prize. In Christian accounts of martyrdom, there is a striking contrast between the ghastly violence committed on the physical flesh and the exuberant mental state of the martyr. Of course, there is a strong element of revisionist propaganda in such accounts, but even contemporary evidence shows that it was commonly held that martyrdom brought with it a state of spiritual anaesthesia. Some Christians saw themselves as athletes competing in the arena to triumph over Satan, with victory in the form of glorious martyrdom. The Christian Church distributed grisly accounts of martyrdom across the Empire, where they were read out at gatherings of Christians. Rather than destroying the Christian Church, persecution simply made it stronger.

In the so-called Great Persecution launched by Diocletian on 23 February 303, he ordered the destruction of Christian scriptures, liturgical books, and places of worship across the Empire. Christians also lost their legal rights. Christian senators, equestrians and other elite groups were deprived of their ranks and offices, which in itself indicates that by this time Christianity had started making inroads among the imperial aristocracy – in fact, Diocletian's own wife, Prisca, was a Christian. By reviving traditional religious practices, Diocletian wanted to restore the Roman virtue, as Augustus had done three centuries before. Diocletian and the other tetrarchs closely pegged the well-being of the empire to the continued respect for and worship of Rome's traditional pantheon of the gods. It followed on from this that any religion that threatened the empire was treacherous. In the following years, Diocletian and his successors would use different strategies against the Christians, veering into harsher legislation then punctuating it with amnesty, but nothing they did would impede the rise of Christianity.

Then, on 28 October 312, a momentous event in the long history of the Roman Empire occurred. The armies of two warring tetrarchs clashed at the Milvian Bridge in Rome. The battle proved decisive: Constantine was victorious, while his rival, Maxentius, drowned in the Tiber, weighed down by his heavy armour. The battle signalled the beginning of the end for the system of imperial tetrarchy established by Diocletian, and Constantine emerged as the sole ruler of the Roman world. What was really monumental in all this, though, was that Constantine would be responsible for the greatest religious revolution of the ancient world. The battle of Milvian Bridge would be proclaimed as the watershed moment in the previously combative relationship between the Christian Church and the Roman Empire.

Constantine claimed to have been converted to Christianity after he and his soldiers saw the sign of the cross in the sky before their crucial victory. Rather more prosaically, some have suggested that what they saw was a solar halo. But contemporary Christians were confident that it was a sign that God had lent his support to Constantine, the first Roman emperor worthy of having the truth of the Christian universe revealed to him. In 313 an imperial edict of toleration, sponsored by Constantine, at last gave Christians across the empire the freedom to practise their faith and restored previously confiscated property and assets to the Church. With Constantine in control of the whole Empire by the end of protracted civil war in 325, it looked like the Christian Church's extraordinary change in fortune was complete, as the emperor lavished land, funds and influence on it.

In Rome, historically important to Christianity because its first bishop had reputedly been St Peter, a series of magnificent churches was built. Christian bishops were now included in the emperor's inner circle of advisors. Their influence can be detected in the raft of moral and religious reform that Constantine initiated. Clergy were exempted from costly public service, bishops were given judicial privileges. Laws against adultery and promoting marriage were strengthened. At the same time Christianity's intolerance of other religious beliefs and practices began to be felt. Some high-profile pagan temples, long condemned by Christians for immoral practices, were shut down, particularly those associated with the cult of Aphrodite, the goddess of love. Other laws prohibited the practice of magic, divination and some sacrifices.

The big question is why Constantine suddenly embraced Christianity. For the Christians the answer was obvious: the emperor was a true believer. Certainly the idea that the religion's popularity made it politically expedient can be ruled out. By 312, less than 10 per cent of the population of the Roman Empire were Christian, and the majority of those did not hail from classes with any significant political clout. But it is also the case that Constantine was baptized only on his deathbed, which hardly suggests he felt the urgency of a true believer. There is no conclusive evidence pointing to Constantine being either genuinely devout or a cynical manipulator. The question of why Constantine's interest in Christianity was sustained – an astonishing outcome considering that this was a man whose personal religious allegiance had previously flitted between a number of different deities – is perhaps easier to answer. Quite simply, for a man who had demolished the carefully constructed structure of the tetrarchy and replaced it with his own sole rule, Christianity's uncompromisingly monotheistic outlook must have been deeply attractive. This would be the era of one emperor, one god. In an address delivered soon after he had become sole ruler of the entire Roman Empire, Constantine admitted as much when he compared the dangers of polytheism in heaven and on earth.

And surely monarchy far exceeds any other political system and type of government; for that democratic equality of power, which is its total opposite, is in fact nothing more than anarchy and disorder. That is why there is only one God, not two, three or more.

The Christian Church, despite its previously trenchant opposition to worldly empire, was remarkably proficient at adapting to its new exalted circumstances. Church leaders were more than willing to proclaim that Constantine's rule was divinely ordained; it looked like a partnership made, or at least sanctioned, in heaven.

These newly established relations between Christian Church and Roman State would, however, almost immediately come under pressure. It soon became clear that there were limits to Christian influence over Constantine. The emperor was willing to shower riches and resources on the Church, but any measures that might potentially loosen his grip on power were off limits. This was certainly the case with the Imperial Cult, which Constantine still appears to have judged rather useful despite the fact that such pagan rites went against the central tenets of Christianity. In the mid 330s, towards the end of his reign, Constantine granted a request from the citizens of the Italian town of Hispellum to build a temple in honour of himself and the imperial family, with the important proviso that no blood sacrifice should be carried out there. This was a classic Constantinian fudge: finding a way of not seriously alienating anyone, while promoting a cause that maximized his hegemony. The locals got their cult, the

Church their ban on sacrifice. It was a compromise that endured: archaeologists working on late pagan temples and shrines often find smashed eggshells around cult objects, the last polytheists having thus found an ingenious way of serving up a blood-free sacrifice to their gods.

The biggest source of tension between Constantine and the Christians was caused by rows that were going on within the Christian Church. It had not taken long for Constantine to realize that what might appear to be obscure points of theology really mattered to his new allies. What made it worse was that there seemed to be very little agreement among the wider Christian community about what constituted orthodox belief. When a serious dispute arose over whether the Holy Trinity of the Father, Son and Holy Ghost was one body or separate entities with a hierarchy, Constantine, who saw himself as God's representative on earth in both religious and secular affairs, was determined to bring the squabbling to an end by ordering the bishops to find a compromise. He called the Council of Nicaea in 325, where a decision was reached to which virtually all the bishops signed up. But if Constantine thought that this was the end of the doctrinal infighting then he was very much mistaken. It soon turned out that none of the parties were happy with the outcome. Imperial intervention set both a dangerous precedent and significantly upped the ante in Christian doctrinal debates, with disputants eager to use the imperial law book and its often harsh penalties against one another. Equally seriously, those who found themselves on the losing side of imperial legislation came to resent what they viewed as the illegitimate intrusion of the emperor in religious affairs.

After decades of simmering tensions, relations between the Christian Church and the Roman state reached crisis point in the 380s. Ironically it occurred during the reigns of some of the most devoutly Christian emperors, Gratian and Theodosius. The main driving force on the Christian side was a remarkable man, Ambrose, Bishop of Milan. Ambrose had joined the Christian ecclesiastical hierarchy late in life after a successful career as a senator and city governor. An energetic and intelligent man, he was in no way daunted by dealing with emperors; he had, after all, been tutor to one of them. Ambrose firmly believed that the Christian Church, not the Roman emperor, was God's senior representative on earth. Emperors were over-reaching their authority if they intervened in Church affairs without the express permission of its leadership. Even then their remit should be strictly limited to enforcing the decisions of the Church through secular legislation. Such a view was clearly going to bring him into conflict with emperors used to intervening in the affairs of the Christian Church whenever it suited them. The stage for these very public trials of strength between emperor and bishop was the imperial city of Milan.

Round One: Justina, the mother of the young emperor Valentinian II, was an Arian, a follower of the brand of Christianity that had failed to win over the Council of Nicaea but which had survived and at times thrived in the intervening decades. The emperor had requested that Ambrose hand over one of his churches to the Arians. Ambrose refused point blank, so Valentinian called in the troops. Refusing to be intimidated, Ambrose locked himself and his congregation into his church, and an extraordinary standoff ensued. Imperial officials arrived on the scene in an attempt to break the deadlock, but Ambrose stood firm, and went for broke by dramatically upping the ante and pulling out the usual Christian card, with some force:

That which are God's to God, those which are Caesar's to Caesar. The palaces belong to the emperor, the churches to the bishop. Authority is bestowed on you over public, not sacred, buildings.

Clearly unsettled by this stark warning that he risked a breakdown of his relationship, not just with the Church but with God himself, Valentinian blinked first and ordered the withdrawal of the troops. There would be no Arian church in Ambrose's Milan.

Round Two: Valentinian, a mere callow youth with a loose grip on his imperial realm, was never going to be a match for a wily, experienced and determined operator like Ambrose. But Theodosius, who ruled over the eastern half of the Empire, was made of much sterner stuff. A talented and hard-nosed administrator and soldier, he was also famed for his Christian piety. The clash between these two redoubtable men would be the most celebrated of the early Christian history. In 390 Theodosius ordered a massacre in Thessalonica after a rioting mob had lynched his military commander there: 6,000 people were lured to the amphitheatre with the promise of games. When they got there, they were butchered. While undeniably harsh, this was by rights an open and closed case of public order, taken care of with the severity that later Roman emperors customarily used to control unruly subjects. What made this situation different was that Thessalonica was a majority Christian city. Although well out of his jurisdiction, Ambrose felt compelled to respond: he expelled the emperor from the Christian fold. In perhaps the most electric exchange between a Roman emperor and a Christian bishop, Ambrose publically refused to administer the sacraments to Theodosius and even banned him from joining the congregation in his cathedral.

Ambrose was a smart enough player to leave the door open for his imperial master. A permanent schism was in nobody's interests. In a letter to Theodosius, Ambrose gently advised that anger was an illness of the soul which could be healed only by Christian penance. The point was taken. Over the next few months, the citizens of Milan would be treated to the extraordinary spectacle of their emperor, the most powerful and feared man in the Roman world, stripped of the regalia of imperial office and committing acts of public penance. Even when the fully repentant – and grateful – emperor was readmitted, Ambrose made sure that everybody understood that Constantine's model of the emperor as God's vicar was over:

He [Theodosius] tore out his hair and beat his head; his tears wet the ground and he prayed for forgiveness. When it was time for him to bring his offerings to the altar, lamenting all the while he stood up and approached the sacred place, but once again the mighty Ambrose impressed upon him the distinction of places and said: The sanctuary, sir, is only for priests; it is closed to all others; go out and stand where the rest stand; the purple insignia can make emperors but not priests.

The emperor might have been the most powerful man on earth, but in God's house he was just another member of the lay congregation. Ambrose's celebrated victories over the imperial throne would be built on by a new generation of Christian intellectuals anxious to rethink their relationship not only with the Roman state but with the entire earthly world. The most talented of these theologians, indeed the most brilliant mind of the early Christian Church, was baptized by Ambrose's own hands in Milan.

Augustine was born into a moderately prosperous family in the North African town of Thagaste. He took the well-worn path of many generations of talented young provincials before him, a good education in Carthage, the capital of the province, followed by a plum post teaching rhetoric in Milan. Augustine had a youthful flirtation with Manichaeism, a banned religion from Syria. In Milan, though, he fell under the spell of Ambrose, and after baptism he decided to turn his back on his promising public career, return to North Africa and devote himself to the Christian Church. It was a decision that would change his own life and western Christendom for ever.

Inspired by the example of St Anthony, he intended to live quietly at Thagaste, in a small community of fellow Christians, leading a life of poverty, monastic simplicity and contemplation. It was a conscious withdrawal from the world and from the public stage he had once so avidly sought. But it was not to be. A couple of years after his return to Africa, Augustine visited Hippo Regius, a busy port-city with a large Christian community. One of the most intriguing aspects of the early Christian Church was that many of its leading theologians ended up being bishops of real one-horse towns. Hippo Regius was not quite like that, but for somebody like Augustine, who had lived and worked in Carthage and Milan, it was still pretty far-flung. When first asked to become Bishop of Hippo, Augustine was very reluctant. In fact, he was almost kidnapped by the congregation, who saw him as a real catch. Before long, though, Augustine was preaching sermons in the basilica, drawing on all the skills and techniques that had made him such a star turn in Rome and Milan. Every Sunday, the Christians of Hippo stood for two hours and more at a time, spellbound by the words of this superstar orator. When the old bishop died, there was no doubt about who would succeed him. Just ten years after his conversion to Christianity, Augustine was consecrated as Bishop of Hippo.

This was not a comfortable sinecure in a sleepy seaside town: Hippo Regius, like most of North Africa, was in the middle of a religious war between Augustine's Catholics and the Donatists, a rigorous Christian sect who believed that they were the true heirs of the martyrs who had died in North Africa in huge numbers during the persecutions of the third century AD. This war was fought not just with words: there was a real threat of sectarian violence, and Augustine would often complain that he was scared of being lynched when he visited outlying areas of his diocese. Such battles were enough to keep him occupied, but the challenge which made his name was still to come.

In the late summer of 410 shocking news reached Hippo Regius: Rome had fallen to King Alaric and his Visigoth army. Rome had withstood two sieges in recent years, but in August 410 the Visigoths returned for a third time. On the 24th slaves opened the city gates and the German army poured in. Three days of looting followed, and many of Rome's finest buildings were destroyed. The mausoleum of the great Augustus was ransacked, burial urns were overturned and the ashes of emperors were scattered on the streets. In the months that

followed, Hippo filled with refugees from Rome, traumatized by the fall of their city. The question many asked was: why? Why, after eight centuries, had the world's greatest city finally fallen to a barbarian army? Many of the refugees were Christians, but even some of them speculated that the outlawing of pagan rituals by the emperor Theodosius some twenty years before was somehow connected to the appalling events.

For Augustine this suggestion was outrageous, and he swung into action. Taking up his pen, he flung himself into the controversy. He wrote a blistering attack on the myth and mystique of Rome, writing a Christian counter-history of the city, a no-holds-barred 'decline and fall' from the city's virtuous founders to the decadent, selfish, materialistic citizens of his own day. If Rome had fallen, Augustine argued, it was because it deserved to. In his *coup de grâce*, Augustine attacked the very ideals that Rome – and indeed all the great civilizations of the ancient world – aspired to. These 'earthly cities' were doomed to falter and fail because they were the work of corrupt mankind.

It took Augustine thirteen years to complete his masterpiece, *The City of God*. There are few bleaker assessments of the futility of civilization-building. For Augustine, neither purpose nor meaning could be found in the earthly city; only the City of God offered these, and they could only be reached beyond the grave. Until that glorious release, the righteous man should act like a 'pilgrim' in the fallen world of mankind, taking advantage of the peace and security that civilization offered but without ever mistaking it for anything substantial or enduring. The good man was just 'passing through', and the great technological, cultural and political achievements of civilization were mere stepping stones to the greater glory of the City of God.

But behind Augustine's uncompromising words lurked an inconvenient truth: the Roman Empire did still matter, even to its most eloquent detractor. The emphatic victories that had been won over the Donatists and other Christian rivals had been the result not just of the barrage of letters, sermons and treatises that Augustine had written against them but of imperial legislation, which had shut down their churches, banned their priests and fined their congregations. In fact, Augustine and his fellow African bishops had worked hard behind the scenes to make this happen, lobbying imperial officials and also, it was said, greasing a few palms.

It seems impossible that a man as brilliant as Augustine was not aware of the giant paradox that stalked his masterwork. The eloquence and forensic reasoning which he used to such great effect in *The City of God* were not the product of bible study but of an expensive education steeped in the very Classical culture which he sought to denigrate. This was a masterful display of biting the hand that feeds you.

But perhaps the most telling evidence of the continued relevance of the urban-based civilization that had dominated the Near East and the Mediterranean for millennia was the fact that Augustine, when he imagined heaven, imagined it as an earthly city.

CONCLUDING THOUGHTS

In the millennia and a half since the City of God took on the City of Man, other prophets from other faiths have added their voices to the criticism. However, for all its manifest and serial failings, the City of Man has endured. Attempts to impose God's will on earth have proved to be just as fruitless, with theocracies quickly coming to closely resemble the 'godless' regimes that they have replaced. The prosaic business of government can usually be relied upon to bring even the highest-minded religious idealism down to earth.

Such a wide-ranging study as this can only ever sketch out the development of urban civilization across the ancient Near East and Mediterranean world in the broadest possible terms. But the wide-angled, long-distance view does yield some important observations. Many ancient Greek and Roman writers were convinced by the essentially cyclical nature of history. Even the most cursory survey of the history of civilization explains why they had come to this conclusion. Any notion of a continuous line of progress towards a clearly defined goal is undermined by the facts on the ground. Take two from many possible examples. At the end of the Bronze Age many of the facets of urban civilization disappeared completely from areas where they had held sway for centuries or even millennia – only to re-emerge hundreds of years later. In Greece the most radical political experiments in popular political participation and accountability seen until the twentieth century were succeeded by a form of charismatic kingship reminiscent of the 'Big Men' of the Bronze Age Near East and eastern Mediterranean.

Yet lurking behind these seemingly wild oscillations in political systems are a number of constants. The proffered solutions might have been different, but the questions themselves remained the same. Perhaps the most important of these constants is civilization itself. Time and again history shows us that the benefits of cooperation have consistently outweighed the disadvantages and problems that it engenders in the minds of humankind. Another important continuity exists in the key issues that have arisen wherever an urban based civilization has been forged: the need to establish good order across the body politic as a whole versus the desire for individual and group freedoms; elite solidarity versus individual ambition; the maintenance of cultural and political exclusivity versus enfranchisement and the self-conscious export of civilization; the distribution of precious resources and the fruits of collective labour and conquest. All of these conundrums highlight how finding the right balance between two seemingly incompatible instincts lies at the heart of urban civilization.

The most important constant, however, is change itself. What this study of the extraordinary range of solutions offered by ancient societies to the dilemmas posed by civic life shows above all is that no single answer has ever been deemed satisfactory enough to persevere with in the long term. Perhaps civilization itself presents us with a giant paradox. There is no definitive answer because it is our natural instinct to always react against the prevailing status quo.

There is, of course, another certainty. All civilizations come to an end somewhere, somehow. Since Augustine eagerly reported on the fall of Rome, empires, kingdoms, republics and all manner of other regimes have come and gone. Rulers have ruled, been toppled and been replaced. Elaborate schemes for political reform, social justice or national greatness have been tested to destruction. In the darkest days the very idea of civilization has been called into question.

Yet despite all of these calamities, crises and dead-ends, we have returned again and again to the possibilities offered by the City of Man to see if this time we can make it work. The history of our ancestors might suggest that this is the ultimate example of hope triumphing over experience, but we go on hoping all the same. There is no going back now to the comfortable securities of family, kin or tribe. Civilization has transformed us into a species that, for better or worse, chooses to live alongside strangers, and it is for this simple reason more than any other that we continue to search out ways to make that unlikely choice work.

LIST OF ILLUSTRATIONS

Endpapers: Temple of Horus. (Photographer: Chris O'Donnell)

pp. ii–iii. Children playing in the ruins of Siwa. (Photographer: Chris O'Donnell)

vi–vii. The Church of the Holy Sepulchre, Jerusalem. (Photographer: Chris O'Donnell)

1. Giant statues of Thoth, Khmun. (Photographer: Chris O'Donnell)

4. Black basalt lion-hunt stele, National Museum of Iraq, Baghdad. (Photographer: Tim Kirby)

6. The author with bevel-rim bowl, Tell Brak. (Photographer: Tim Kirby)

10–11. Royal Standard of Ur, 'War' (© The Trustees of the British Museum)

13. Naram-Sin sculptural fragment, National Museum of Iraq, Baghdad. (Photographer: Tim Kirby)

14. Victory stele of Naram-Sin, King of Akkad. (Louvre/The Bridgeman Art Library)

18–19. The Nile at Luxor. (Photographer: Chris O'Donnell)

22. Camel with stepped pyramid of Djoser. (Photographer: Chris O'Donnell)

24. Statue of pharaoh Amenhotep III, near Luxor. (Photographer: Chris O'Donnell)

25. Ram-headed sphinxes, Karnak. (Photographer: Tim Kirby)

26–7. Columns in the Great Hypostyle Hall, Karnak. (Photographer: Tim Kirby)

30. The author in the ruins of Kanesh. (Photographer: Chris O'Donnell)

33. Assyrian merchant tablets, Kayseri Museum, Turkey. (Photographer: Tim Kirby)

36. Statue of the official Ebih-il, from the Temple of Ishtar at Mari. (Louvre/Giraudon/ The Bridgeman Art Library)

39. The Royal Palace, Mari. (Photographer: Chris O'Donnell)

40. An archaeologist excavating the Uluburun wreck. (© Institute of Nautical Archaeology)

41. Copper 'oxhide' ingots from the Uluburun wreck, Bodrum Museum of Underwater Archaeology. (Photographer: Tim Kirby)

42. Blue glass ingots from the Uluburun wreck, Bodrum Museum of Underwater Archaeology. (Photographer: Tim Kirby)

44–5. Lion Hunt, stone panel from the Palace of Ashurnasirpal II, Nimrud (© The Trustees of the British Museum)

46. Figurine of the god Baal, Louvre, (© RMN /Franck Raux)

49. 'House of the Ovens', Ugarit. (Photographer: Chris O'Donnell)

52. Lion Gate, Mycenae. (Photographer: Tim Kirby)

53. Mycenae fresco, Mycenae Museum. (Photographer: Tim Kirby)

54. Mycenae snake sculpture, Mycenae Museum. (Photographer: Tim Kirby)

55. Mycenae votive figures, Mycenae Museum. (Photographer: Tim Kirby)

58. Figurines from the Temple of Obelisks,

ACKNOWLEDGEMENTS

A book like this is necessarily a collaborative project. I do not exaggerate when I say that this book would not exist if it were not for the Herculean efforts of Simon Winder, Chloe Campbell, Chris O'Donnell, Tim Dunn, Richard Marston, Richard Duguid, Michael Page and Peter Robinson. I am tremendously grateful for the enormous faith that Janice Hadlow and Martin Davidson have shown in this project over the years. Eamon Hardy was a supportive and cheerful boss, particularly during the tough times. I would also like to thank Patrick Duval, Chris Titus King, Tony Burke, Jon Thomas and Charlotte Chalker for being such great travelling companions and work colleagues as we journeyed around the Mediterranean and Middle East together. Lastly I would like to express my gratitude to Tim Kirby, whose intellectual vision, elegant prose and steely determination transformed a pipe-dream into a television series and a book that I am very proud to be have been part of.

RM

SOURCES OF QUOTATIONS

pp. xiii and xiv: Both texts from 'The Curse of Akkad', 10–39, 176–209, abridged translation based on *The Electronic Text Corpus of Sumerian Literature* (http://etcsl.orinst.ox.ac.uk/)

2: Quotation from *The Epic of Gilgamesh*, 1.18, based on A. George (tr.), *The Babylonian Epic Poem and Other Texts in Akkadian and Sumerian* (London, 1999)

21: Quotation from *The Teaching of King Amenemhat I*, 2–4, based on translation from Digital Egypt for Universities (http://www.digitalegypt.ucl.ac.uk/literature/teachingaisec4.html/)

28: Quotation from Kamose I based on J. Wilson (tr.) and J. Pritchard (ed.), *Ancient Near Eastern Texts Relating to the Old Testament* (Princeton, 1969), p. 232

31–2: Merchant quotes taken from C. Michel, *Correspondance des marchands de Kanish au début du IIe millénaire avant J.-C.* (Paris, 2001)

34: King's letter taken from *Balkan, Letter of King Anum-hirbi of Mama to King Warshama of Kanish. (Türk Tarih Kurumu Yayınlarından VII/31a)* (Ankara, 1957), p. 8

38: Zimri-Lim's letter taken from J. Sasson, J (tr.), 'Texts, Trade and Travellers', in J. Aruz, *Beyond Babylon: Art, Trade and Diplomacy in the Second Millenium BC* (New York, 2000), pp. 95–100

48: Letters quoted from M. Astour (tr.), 'New Evidence on the Last Days of Ugarit', *American Journey of Archaeology* 69.3 (1965), p. 255–8

50: Egyptian account of the Sea People based on J. Wilson (tr.) and J. Pritchard, (ed.), *Ancient Near Eastern Texts Relating to the Old Testament* (Princeton, 1969), p. 262

60: Quotation from Wenamen based on H. Goedicke, *The Report of Wenamun* (Baltimore, 1975), p. 153

65: Lines from *Ezekiel* and other Old Testament quotations taken from H. Wansbrough, *The New Jerusalem Bible: Reader's Edition* (London, 1990)

83: Quotations from the *Iliad*, Book One and Book Twenty-One, taken from H. Hammond (tr.), *Iliad* (Harmondsworth, 1987) Reproduced with the permission of Penguin Books

90: Nietzsche quotation from W. Kaufmann (tr.), *The Portable Nietzsche* (New York, 1976), pp. 32–3

91–2: Author's translation of Hesiod, *Works and Days*, 303–16 abridged, 176–88 abridged, 207–9, and 219–39 abridged

109: Author's translation of Aristotle, *Constitution of Athens*,11.5–12.1

119: Author's translation of Herodotus, *The Histories*, 5.97

131: Author's translation of Thucydides, *History of the Peloponnesian War*, 8.97

135: Author's translation of Aristotle, *Politics*, 7.73

139: Author's translation of Thucydides, *History of the Peloponnesian War*, 3.81.5

141: Author's translation of Xenophon, *Agesilaos*, 11.13

142: Author's translation of Demosthenes, *Third Philippic*, 31

144: Author's translation of Demosthenes, *Against Meidias*, 221, and *Fourth Philippic* 11

150: Author's translation of Arrian, *Anabasis*, 2.14

184: Author's translation of Polybius, *The Histories*, 1.1

197: Author's translation of Diodorus Siculus, *Bibliotheca Historica*, 20.14

233: Author's translation of Vergil, *Aeneid*, 6.851–3

234: Author's translation of Tacitus, *Agricola*, 21.4

239: Author's translation of Epictetus, *Discourse*, 4.2

239: Author's translation of Pliny the Younger, *Panegyric*, 48.1–3

258: Quotations from P. Parsons, *City of the Sharp-Nosed Fish* (London, 2007), pp. 133–4

263: Septimius Severus and Caracalla quotations translated by the author from Cassius Dio, *Roman History*, 77.15 and 77.3

268: Author's translation of Tertullian, *Apology*, 40.2

274: Author's translation of Eusebius, *Oration of Constantine*, 3.6–7

277: Author's translation of Ambrose, *Letter*, 20.19

277–8: Author's translation of Theodoret, *Ecclesiastical History*, 5.17

INDEX

Page numbers in *italics* refer to illustrations in the text.